IMAGES OF THE MEXICAN AMERICAN

IN FICTION AND FILM

IMAGES OF
THE MEXICAN AMERICAN
IN FICTION AND FILM

By Arthur G. Pettit

EDITED WITH AN AFTERWORD BY
Dennis E. Showalter

TEXAS A&M UNIVERSITY PRESS
COLLEGE STATION

Copyright © 1980 by Lynn Pettit
All rights reserved

Library of Congress Cataloging in Publication Data

Pettit, Arthur G.
    Images of the Mexican American in fiction and film.

    Bibliography: p. 246
    Includes index.
    1. American fiction—20th century—History and
criticism. 2. Mexican Americans in literature. 3. Moving-
pictures—United States—History. 4. Mexican Americans
in motion pictures. I. Showalter, Dennis E. II. Title.
PS 374.M48P47   791.43'09'093520368   79-5284
ISBN 0-89096-095-X

Manufactured in the United States of America
First edition

CONTENTS

PREFACE

Art Pettit had been interested in this project long before we became colleagues in the fall of 1969. He saw it as a synthesis of three of his major intellectual pursuits: the history of the Southwest, the Mexican-American experience, and the nature of popular culture. It was, he once told me, something that was fun to work on, but its potential as a scholarly contribution was recognized by Colorado College, which provided several research grants, and by the National Endowment for the Humanities, which awarded him a year's fellowship to complete his study.

I became involved with Art's work because of our common interest in western movies. Art and I spent many an hour discussing plots, characterizations, and interpretations. Our writing styles were sufficiently similar that we were able to criticize each other's work, and early drafts of chapters began passing between us. I found the ideas and the material stimulating enough to encourage me to begin systematic reading on the subject, focusing my own interest in popular culture.

By the fall of 1975 the manuscript had passed through several stages. It was near completion when Art was diagnosed as suffering from cancer. He continued to work as he fought the disease. By April, 1976, when he was too weak to sit at a desk, he asked me if I would act as a copy editor. Our original plan was that I would make editorial and material changes in line with our discussions of each chapter. He would then read what I had done and suggest further revisions until he was satisfied.

Art Pettit never saw any of my work. He grew progressively weaker, dying on June 6, 1976. With the consent of his family, I continued to edit the manuscript. The theme, the scholarship, the interpretations, are Art Pettit's. Mine has been the privilege of bringing, I hope with a minimum of error and distortion, the last work of an outstanding young scholar before the academic community and the reading public.

Art Pettit was an admired colleague and a good friend, a man whose life brightened and enriched the lives of those around him. His epitaph could well be taken from one of the stories he loved—James Manlove Rhodes' "Paso por Aqui." For indeed all who knew Art would agree that "he pass this way, paso por aqui . . . and he mek here good and not weeked." Honor to his memory.

DENNIS E. SHOWALTER

INTRODUCTION

THIS IS A BOOK about the Anglo-American's attitudes toward
the Mexican people in the Southwest, as reflected in the stereotypes of his popular literature and film. It is not a study of the
historical Mexican or of what the Anglo has done to him in
fact, but of the Mexican in the Anglo's literary and cinematic
imagination. It is, in other words, a study of the response of
American popular culture to a different and rival culture.

Published in 1963, Cecil Robinson's *With the Ears of
Strangers: The Mexican in American Literature* employed both
history and fiction as indicators of the Anglo-American's evolv-
ing attitude toward the Mexican and asked what those attitudes might tell us about the Mexican as well as the Anglo.
His *Mexico and the Hispanic Southwest in American Literature* (1977), more of an update than a revision of the earlier
work, incorporates a similar approach. The present study differs from Robinson's in four significant respects. First, it refers
almost exclusively to fictional sources. This enables us to focus
upon the imaginative history of Anglo-Mexican interaction
without constant and frequently confusing references to what
actually happened. The recommendation from *The Man Who
Shot Liberty Valance*, that whenever truth and fiction conflict,
the fiction should be printed, is particularly relevant in this
context. The diaries and personal narratives which play such a
major role in the body of Robinson's work are used here pri-

marily to structure the historical introductions for the book
and its individual sections. Second, this work explores film—a
genre Robinson ignores yet one which, particularly in the
twentieth century, has contributed heavily to the Anglo's
image of the Mexican. Third, this book concentrates primarily,
though not exclusively, on fictional patterns established within
the present boundaries of the United States. By limiting ethnic
images drawn from Mexico proper, those of the Mexican American can be made correspondingly sharper. Finally, my presentation emphasizes works of popular culture.

This emphasis on popular works in turn posed a problem of
selection. Since the publication of *With the Ears of Strangers*,
popular culture has emerged as a separate academic discipline,
with its own journals, degrees, and professors. Yet one seeks in
vain for a generally accepted definition of the subject. Dwight
Macdonald's blunt separation between mass culture and high
culture is now generally regarded as an oversimplification.
Such scholars as John Cawelti and David Madden write of the
need for popular culture to establish its own aesthetics.[1] Popular culture, however, still remains in the stage of description
rather than analysis.

Most of these descriptions manage to agree that popular
culture is by its nature incomplete. It employs general situations and formula plots, conventions and stereotypes, presented
to be filled in by the individual consumer. Popular artists,
moreover, derive all of their livelihood and most of their job
satisfaction from reaching as wide an audience as possible.[2]
We nevertheless remain uncertain just where popular culture
begins and—more importantly—where it ends. Particularly

[1] Cf. Dwight Macdonald, "A Theory of Mass Culture," in *Mass Culture:
The Popular Arts in America,* ed. Bernard Rosenberg and David M. White;
John G. Cawelti, "The Concept of Formula in the Study of Popular Culture,"
Journal of Popular Culture 3 (1969): 381–390; and David Madden, "The
Necessity for an Aesthetics of Popular Culture," *Journal of Popular Culture* 7
(1973): 1–13.
[2] See such standard analyses as Henry Nash Smith, *Virgin Land: The
American West as Symbol and Myth*; Russel B. Nye, *The Unembarrassed
Muse: The Popular Arts in America*; and John G. Cawelti, "Myth, Symbol, and
Formula," *Journal of Popular Culture* 8 (1975): 1–8.

when employing models of formula fiction, it is possible to cite works by major authors using conventional situations only in a very broad sense. In discussing war fiction, for example, E. M. Nathanson's novel *The Dirty Dozen* is obviously a work of popular culture. But is Joseph Heller's *Catch-22*? And where exactly do the novels of James Jones belong? The ethnic focus of this study posed even greater problems of deciding where to draw the line. I chose to concentrate on those works most obviously aimed at a mass audience. When in doubt, I excluded. Such authors as John Steinbeck and Paul Horgan, whose writings occupy at best a middle position in *With the Ears of Strangers*, mark the upper limits of the present work's focus. Even they have been incorporated with some trepidation, and only when a certain book or short story epitomized a point also strongly demonstrated in the lower reaches of popular fiction.

The value of this approach lies in its breaking of ground. Distinguished academicians have presented the ways Anglo-Americans judge themselves in relation to alien cultures—how they have used contrasts to reinforce positive images we entertain of ourselves. Notable examples include Winthrop Jordan's *White over Black* (1968), George Fredrickson's *The Black Image in the White Mind* (1971), and Roy Harvey Pearce's *The Savages of America: A Study of the Indian and the Idea of Civilization* (1965). Richard L. Jackson, *The Black Image in Latin American Literature* (1976), and R. A. Preto-Rodas, *Negritude as a Theme in the Poetry of the Portuguese-Speaking World* (1970), are only two of many scholars who discuss related themes in Spanish- and Portuguese-speaking American societies. This work is concerned with a similar problem: establishing and categorizing popular formulas involving the Mexican in English-language fiction.

Presenting this subject exclusively from the perspective of Anglo culture can generate charges of one-dimensional superficiality, particularly given current climates of Mexican and Chicano militancy. I argue, however, that the approach encourages treatment of the theme from the only viewpoint significant to the vast majority of consumers of this kind of popular culture north of the Rio Grande. Spanish-language fiction and films have a wide audience, particularly in the Southwest, but it is a Mexican/Hispano/Chicano audience. Whatever image of Anglo-Mexican interaction these works might convey is a matter of supreme indifference to a dominant society, relatively few of whose members can read or understand Spanish with fluency. And should such works be translated, that very fact tends to reflect a degree of intellectual quality removing them from the category of popular culture. Few Mexican-made westerns, for example, are dubbed or subtitled for a North American market.

Working with popular material blurs distinctions between the social historian and the literary critic, particularly since the historian-as-critic is often reluctant to explain or define his conceptual framework. C. L. Sonnichsen offers a strong argument that it is pointless to evaluate westerns, and by implication popular fiction generally, on the basis of literary quality. So much of such work falls into a gray area between commercial and serious fiction that it makes more sense for the scholar to "work both sides of the street simultaneously." The point is defensible, but replies to the question of conceptualization by dismissing it. This book is based on an empirical form of the genre approach. Through reading and viewing, I established general models of popular cultural images of the Mexican and attempted to present the elements of a given work in the context of those models. I was not, however, able to follow this pattern with perfect consistency. Some authors and screenwriters—the Steinbecks, the Sam Peckinpahs, the Harvey Fergussons— brought to their work a shaping intelligence, a style and vision rendering genre criticism by itself intellectually incomplete. Such works as *Tortilla Flat* or *The Conquest of Don Pedro* play more of a dual role in American culture than Sonnichsen concedes. They contribute significantly to the formulas which are the subject of this book. They also, however, are frequently incorporated into mainstream literary history. I therefore also applied modified patterns of auteur criticism to those authors whose works presented images of the Mexican reflecting attitudes more complex than market considerations.[3]

It may seem inappropriate to apply to writers a critical approach developed for evaluating screenwriters and directors. On the other hand, the written fiction discussed below frequently resembles film in its emphasis on geographic and historical milieux and its consistent use of formula characters and situations. The mixture of auteur and genre criticism, while awkward in some cases, on balance appeared the best way of balancing the intellectual integrity of a given artist with the essential theme of the present work: how stereotypes are created and maintained.

This methodology led to two related decisions. To analyze critically even half of the books, stories, and films consulted in preparing this study would submerge any generalizations beneath an insupportable burden of detail—a problem enhanced because most of the material involved has limited literary and intellectual significance. On the other hand, because these works do involve stock characters and stock situations, discussion of them cannot be reduced beyond a certain point without unacceptable sacrifices in other areas. The scholarly worth of formula fiction often lies in nuances, in minor twists of plot or quirks of characterization. Much of the genius of formula writing lies in handling conventional situations unconventionally, with just enough of a flair to stimulate the consumer without disturbing him. To ignore this technique is to risk falling into the trap of the digest magazines described in E. B. White's satire which reduced a Hemingway novel to the word bang! As a rule I attempted to construct a narrative framework illustrated by representative examples. And this construction in turn influenced my approach to documentation. In an era of high-cost publishing, no author can hope to present the entire body of his research, even in footnotes. I have therefore provided ex-

[3] C. L. Sonnichsen, *From Hopalong to Hud: Thoughts on Western Fiction*, p. 178. A summary of the critical assumptions most frequently applied to Western films is William T. Pilkington, "Introduction: A Fistful of Westerns," in *Western Movies*, ed. William T. Pilkington and Don Graham, pp. 8–12.

tensive references in the areas where supporting material is likely to be unfamiliar or unavailable, such as the chapters and sections dealing with nineteenth-century dime novels or silent films and early talkies. Where the discussion focuses on recent movies and contemporary paperbacks, I have reduced the footnotes to a minimum. In the interests of brevity I have similarly tried to avoid extensive citation of such background material as histories of the Southwest and discussion of critical debates on the themes and merits of specific novels or films.

The author of social history who uses popular fiction for his primary material runs the risk of writing his own kind of fiction —forming hypotheses and then substantiating them by careful choice of supporting evidence from among literally thousands of available works, most of them likely to be unfamiliar to his readers. My original research was empirical enough to be called promiscuous. I read and evaluated as much fiction and viewed as many films as I could, initially on a deliberately random basis. I have drawn my examples from a comprehensive range of popular literature and film, from such classics as *Viva Zapata!* to pulp westerns and grade B motion pictures. This variety in turn reflects and illustrates the fact that there is, in this field at least, surprisingly little correlation between recognized artistic merit and the use of stereotypes. I have found mindless duplication of stereotypes in the works of talented and serious authors and filmmakers. I have found earnest efforts to modify or debunk stereotyped images in what is otherwise trash. My use of sources, particularly pulp sources, has been comprehensive. It is not, nor could it reasonably be, exhaustive. I cannot state that somewhere in the bowels of a public or university library there do not exist one or several novels, short stories, or screenplays that run counter to my generalizations on a given point. I *am* prepared to state that they are exceptions to overwhelmingly comprehensive rules governing images and caricatures of Spanish-speaking people generated by Anglo-Americans.

When I attempted to structure my findings, one salient point emerged. Aside from the Indian, three major ethnic

xiv

groups exist in American popular fiction: the black, the Jew, and the Mexican. Of the three, the Mexican is most strongly localized. Black characters can and do appear in every kind of fictional setting. While the Jew tends to be characterized as urban, he, too, has a national scope for his activities. The Mexican, on the other hand, is geographically fixed in the Southwest, in Texas and the states carved from the territory ceded in the Treaty of Guadalupe Hidalgo. The Chicano communities of Chicago or Pittsburgh and the migrant workers who follow the crops through the Upper Midwest may have historical and sociological significance, but for the popular writer they are nonexistent. Even the Children's Television Workshop concedes the fact. Its *Sesame Street* includes a Chicano as a regular character. But while the show is set in New York City, Luis's roots are firmly in New Mexico. No one else, whether black, Puerto Rican, Anglo, or New York Jewish, is shown as having such strong ties to his place of birth or ancestral origin. In a week-long sequence first aired in April, 1978, Luis took an assortment of his human and Muppet friends to visit his relatives. Viewers of the five shows witnessed Luis's grandmother milking a cow. They saw how to build a house "Hispano-style" with wood and adobe. They heard Luis render a nostalgic song about the favorite haunts of his childhood. Everything combined to create the impression that Luis really *belongs* in the Southwest. His presence on Sesame Street seems almost accidental.

This localization in turn involves the Mexican in two kinds of formula fiction which are at least as rigid in their conventions as any medieval morality play. The first and most obvious is the western. Frank Gruber divides this genre into seven categories: the ranch story, the cattle empire story, the revenge story, the cavalry-versus-Indians story, the outlaw story, and the law-and-order story. Philip French writes of "Satirical Westerns" and "Sociological Westerns," "Kennedy Westerns" and "Goldwater Westerns." These and other critical organizations are less important for our purposes than the fact that westerns of all varieties require a standard cast of characters to function within a given plot or screenplay. They may behave in unconventional ways, but their outlines are essentially determined by a set of formulaic codes.[4] And since many westerns have a southwestern setting, the Mexican has inevitably found a place in this most rigidly formulaic of American literary genres.

The second type of formula fiction involving Mexicans is less familiar as a separate category. It can best be called conquest fiction, and its essential theme is the defeat, displacement, and/or destruction of one identifiable ethnic group by another. Conquest fiction can be blunt or sophisticated. It can be presented from the viewpoint of victors or vanquished. Its moral statement about the conquest can range from complete acceptance to complete rejection. Leon Uris's novels *Exodus* and *Mila 18*, for example, are both conquest novels written about Jews, yet with entirely different perspectives. Most formula fiction involving the subjugation of the American wilderness or the Native American is also conquest fiction. The theme of moral growth through the overcoming of hostile forces, whether human or natural, is a major element of America's mythic structure.[5] And the Anglo penetration of the Southwest offers a particularly broad scope for creators of conquest fiction with a North American setting. The conquered culture was sufficiently complex, the interaction between victors and vanquished sufficiently tangled, to provide material for generations of plots.

This does not mean that the Mexican has been confined exclusively to these two cultural formulas. He has been fitted into uplift or samaritan fiction, romances, and even detective stories—but virtually always with a southwestern setting. And these limited geographic horizons in turn have structured heav-

---

[4] Frank Gruber, "The Basic Western Novel Plots," *Writer's Year Book*, 1955, pp. 49–53, 160; Philip French, *Westerns*. Cf. also John Cawelti, *The Six-Gun Mystique*, and Will Wright, *Six Guns and Society*.

[5] Of the many studies using this approach, Richard Slotkin, *Regeneration Through Violence: The Mythology of the American Frontier, 1600–1860*, and Francis Jennings, *The Invasion of America: Indians, Colonialism, and the Art of Conquest*, are particularly useful.

ily the roles the Mexican is assigned in American popular culture. Historically, Mexican-American relations have been characterized by conflicts traceable to a wide variety of institutional factors. Overshadowing them all, however, remains another source of tension between the two societies—less tangible than questions of slavery or government, but no less significant. Each people was inclined to exaggerate the differences between them and distort the traits of the other group. The North American descendants of the English who met the Mexican descendants of the Spaniards in the borderlands were predisposed to certain stereotypes of things Spanish and Mexican. The Spanish Mexicans were similarly prejudiced about the Anglo-Americans. The Anglo-American boasted of his Protestant independence, his thrift and industry, his faith in progress and the mechanical arts, his obsession with racial purity. To the Spanish Mexican these qualities appeared as mere combinations of self-righteousness, rootlessness, greed, and churlishness. The Mexican, for his part, prided himself on his Catholicism and hierarchical social order; his veneration of tradition and appreciation of a sedate, measured life; his distrust of technical solutions to life's problems.

To the Anglo, this world view was simply a combination of self-abasement, feudalism, indolence, and immorality. When he set out to bring democracy, progress, and Protestantism to the Hispanic Southwest, he could find a place for the Mexican in what he soon regarded as "his" Southwest only if the Mexican would become, insofar as his limited talents permitted, what the American perceived himself to be: enterprising, steady, and Protestant—in a word, civilized. Yet somehow the Mexican remained something else in the Anglo-American's eye: shiftless, unreliable, and alternately decadent or barbaric. Thus, it seemed to be the American's manifest destiny to conquer and convert this errant race. In the process it was also necessary to destroy a culture the Mexican would not willingly surrender. Operating from such moral absolutes, the Anglo was able to achieve a satisfactory interpretation of his racial and cultural superiority. He could flatter himself that he was not deprecating a race, but standing up for civilization. He could persuade himself, in fact, that he was not guilty of racism in any sense that we understand the term. For if the Mexican could be evaluated only in terms of the civilization to which, by the laws of nature, God, and history alike, he had to give way, then how could the conqueror be blamed for what was destined to happen? The Anglo-American thus came to see the indigenous way of life in what became the American Southwest as inherently and irrevocably inferior and hostile to his own institutions.[6]

The very shabbiness of these images enhances their importance, for they established the standards of fair and foul play that characterized the Anglo's approach to relations between the two societies in the American Southwest. The mid-nineteenth-century notion of America as the embodiment of Protestant virtue and republican government determined his reactions to the alien society he encountered in his push southwestward across the continent. Messianic in his expansiveness, confident that he had rendered obsolete the customs and institutions, the poverty and pestilence, of Europe and its Latin offshoots in the New World, the Anglo-American was confident that his was the system of the future.

Since the days of Henry Nash Smith, popular fiction has generally been considered an accurate gauge of popular attitudes.[7] This partly reflects a common-sense assumption. Popular culture is a consumption culture, essentially designed to

[6] Among scholarly works pertinent to this issue, see particularly Lewis Hanke, *The Spanish Struggle for Justice in the Conquest of America*; Magnus Morner, ed., *Race and Class in Latin America*; Magnus Morner, *Race Mixture in the History of Latin America*; and José de Oñís, *The United States as Seen by Spanish American Writers, 1776–1890*. "The Two Black Legends," by Sonnichsen in *From Hopalong to Hud*, pp. 83–102, is a stimulating introduction to the problem of mutual antagonism between Anglo and Spanish/Mexican cultures.

[7] Smith details some of his research methods and some of their underlying assumptions in "Can 'American Studies' Develop a Method?" *American Quarterly* 9 (1957): 197–208. Among the most open and successful applications of Smith's technique is Leo Marx, *The Machine in the Garden: Technology and the Pastoral Ideal in America*. See also Richard W. Etulain, "Recent Views of the American Literary West," *Journal of Popular Culture* 3 (1969): 144–153.

sell. Therefore it must reflect the feelings and faith of its pur-
chasers. The identification of fiction with attitudes probably
also owes something to the fact that most of the scholars of
popular culture, including many of the discipline's leading
figures, began as students of literature.[8] Concentration on the
content of material as opposed to the attitudes of its consumers
comes naturally to these academicians. Intellectual historians
also frequently tend to assume direct correlations among ideas,
attitudes, and behavior. The existence of popular anti-Semitism
in nineteenth-century Germany, for example, is frequently presented as a prefiguration of Auschwitz.[9]

In the past decade, however, an increasing number of
scholars have denied that literature in general and popular
fiction in particular are accurate, or even very reliable, guides
to public attitudes on any given subject. Entertainment forms
are not incarnations of basic values. People cannot be defined
by analyzing their leisure-time activities, particularly in terms
of an aesthetic irrelevant to everyone but the professor who
developed it. Students of popular culture must concentrate
instead on the impact of that culture. They must study the
effect of formula plots and stereotyped characters on consuming audiences sharing varied networks of sociocultural relationships.[10]

From the social historian's perspective, these critics initially
appear to have a point. The basic fictional stereotypes of Anglo
and Mexican appear at the time and place where the characters and incidents first appear: that is, in works written in the
heat of emotion generated by the Texas Revolution, the war

[8] Cf. Bruce A. Lohof, "Popular Culture: The *Journal* and the State of
the Study," *Journal of Popular Culture* 6 (1972): 453–462; and Alan R.
Havig, "American Historians and the Study of Popular Culture," *Journal of
Popular Culture* 11 (1977): 190, fn. 2.
[9] As in George L. Mosse, *The Crisis of German Ideology: Intellectual
Origins of the Third Reich* (New York: Grosset and Dunlap, 1964). See also
the general discussion by Franklin L. Baumer, "Intellectual History and Its
Problems," *The Journal of Modern History* 21 (1949): 191–203.
[10] Gregory H. Singleton, "Popular Culture or the Culture of the Populace?" *Journal of Popular Culture* 11 (1977): 254–266, is a useful introduction to this issue. See also Herbert J. Gans, *Popular Culture and High Culture:
An Analysis and Evaluation of Taste*.

with Mexico, and the invasion of the far Southwest. Yet for more than a century, few authors have attempted to refute or avoid these images. Part of the explanation is literary. Writers of popular fiction quickly perceive the acceptability of a given series of stereotypes, and they begin to copy each other. Moreover, distance from the subject does not lend detachment. Many of the earliest treatments of the theme were written by men and women who knew their subject first-hand: newspaper reporters on assignment in Mexico or the Southwest, wives who followed their husbands to new careers in the Southwest, Texas Rangers who wrote novels in their spare time. More than half the novelists who wrote about the Texas Revolution either were native-born Texans or made Texas their adopted home. Conversely, more than half the novelists who wrote about the conquests of New Mexico and California were easterners who had no direct knowledge of their subject. And most of the recent treatments of the theme stem from journalists and teachers, screenwriters and amateurs, novelists who use the Southwest primarily as a backdrop for various kinds of fiction. Yet as the following pages demonstrate, these distinctions do not seem to influence the manner in which these writers approach their material.

What will be made clear as this study develops is that the concept of Anglo-Saxon superiority and Mexican inferiority is not only thoroughly established in popular fiction, but also tends to be self-reinforcing. It is sustained by constant repetition of tried and tested positive American projections of themselves juxtaposed to negative projections of the Mexican as opposition. All that is needed is to list certain elements of American character on one side of the fictional ledger, and offset them with traits attributed to the Mexican. As a result the Mexican tends to be defined negatively, in terms of qualities diametrically opposed to an Anglo prototype.

This process reflects little concern for historical accuracy. Most of the fiction written about the conquest of the Hispanic Southwest, for example, reflects a sizable gap between reality and romance, between the actual history of the conquest and its fictional treatment. From diaries and journals, travel histories and newspaper articles, we know that not all Americans who moved south by west were blond giants and golden belles. Some were average-sized or small. Some had dark hair, eyes, and complexion. Some were married before they came West and were thus burdened with husbands, wives, children, and family responsibilities. Not all Americans who entered Mexican territory were successful Yankee merchants, brawny Ohio Valley farmers, or benevolent southern slaveowners. Some were European immigrants recently arrived on America's shores. Some were common laborers and shopkeepers, bank clerks and ribbon clerks, lawyers and land speculators, clergymen and criminals. Some homesteaders failed. Some merchants went bankrupt. Some settlers returned East. Some Protestants became Catholics. And—heresy of heresies—some male Americans who settled in Mexico or the Southwest actually married into the "common" class of Mexican women. Not all American newcomers negotiated contractual arrangements with lovely Castilian dark ladies and thereafter lived lordly lives on spacious "Spanish" haciendas.

Popular fiction dealing with the Anglo conquest of the Southwest is similarly incomplete in its treatment of the Mexican. It portrays few sheepherders or farmers, vaqueros or miners, politicians or storekeepers. It incorporates few traces of the enterprising farmers and ranchers who withstood the marauding Apaches and Comanches for almost two centuries before the arrival of the Americans and built a sturdy society which—in its system of land tenure and irrigation, language and religion, mining codes and cultural customs—long survived the American conquest and exists to the present day.

It is possible, and perhaps legitimate, to argue that fiction written in such a fashion teaches us more about elitist racial fantasies than social realities. It describes more about what Anglo-Americans have wished to believe about themselves than what they actually were like; more about what they wished to happen than what actually happened; more about things as writers believed they should have been than things as they were. Yet to suggest that these enduring stereotypes and inaccuracies reflect a correspondingly static attitude on the part of the primary consuming audience would be more of a political than an intellectual statement. The particular prejudices embodied in formula fiction dealing with Anglo-Mexican relations also reflect a consistent need on the part of writers and readers alike to defend, justify, or apologize for the bigoted manner in which Anglo characters in such fiction behave. And this in turn implies two more intellectually defensible reasons for the consistency of popular culture's treatment of the Mexican.

The first explanation for this pattern is in the general nature of formula fiction. Such fiction depends heavily for its success on conventions generally acceptable to its readers. The detective story, the western, the thriller, the romance—all are so rigidly structured as to be virtually stylized. They offer little room for finely honed degrees of heroism and villainy. Nor is there much scope for radical experimentation with questions of caste and color, right and wrong, or until recently, chastity and promiscuity. Similarly, the issue of historical truth in popular fiction with a historical setting is less important than the use of background information to create an air of plausibility, linking an essentially imaginary world to some sort of reality. Kingsley Amis aptly calls this process the Fleming effect, after the creator of James Bond.[11] In fiction involving Anglo-Mexican interaction and written for an Anglo audience, the Fleming effect generally involves establishing a sharp dichotomy between white and brown. Such a process cannot be dismissed as a mere manifestation of racism. To some extent at least the Mexican is simply another element in the local color of the Southwest. For example, formula fiction usually features some kind of villain to offset and oppose the hero. It is correspondingly logical for English-language formula fiction set in Mexico or the Southwest to feature brown villains to counterpoint the courageous Saxon heroes. Arguably, the equally formulaic

[11] Kingsley Amis, *The James Bond Dossier*, pp. 110 ff.

corridos do the same thing by reversing stereotyped images and pitting the heroic border Mexican against the cowardly *rinches*.[12] And just as surely as formula novels written before the sexual revolution feature forbidden female temptresses to offset virtuous heroines, such novels with a southwestern setting tend to feature loose-principled brown women as counterpoints to the chaste white heroines and tests of the hero's degree of moral commitment.

This cultural and ethnic myopia embodies, however, another element than plot requirements for villains and sex objects. Works of popular culture very rarely demand high degrees of concentration for extended periods. On the other hand, popular culture is pervasive. To avoid exposure to it demands deliberate, consistent effort. And this in turn suggests that both parties in the debate outlined at the beginning of this section have exaggerated their positions. Popular culture may not embody some pseudo-Jungian version of collective unconsciousness. On the other hand, it *is* likely to reflect a minimum acceptable denominator of its consumers' attitudes. A good illustration of this hypothesis is the role of the Jewish issue in attracting support for National Socialism in Germany. What is significant is not that Germans were receptive to Hitler's anti-Semitism, but that they were not sufficiently alienated by it to reject other elements of his appeal. Anti-Semitism by itself did not bring Hitler to power. Neither did it prevent his rise to dictatorship.[13]

Similarly, the images of the Mexican in English-language popular culture may appropriately be described as having a negative effect. They are seen as sufficiently familiar, and sufficiently necessary to the kinds of fiction where they most often appear, westerns and conquest stories, that they do not en-

[12] See particularly Américo Paredes' two works *"With His Pistol in His Hand"* and *A Texas-Mexican Cancionero*, esp. pp. 19 ff. in the latter.
[13] Perceptive English-language discussions of this issue include Karl Schleunes, *The Twisted Road to Auschwitz* (Urbana: University of Illinois Press, 1970), esp. pp. 59–61; and William S. Allen, *The Nazi Seizure of Power: The Experience of A Single German Town* (Chicago: Quadrangle, 1965).

courage the consumer to reject them in disgust or dismiss them as obsolete. The images are part of formulas—formulas frequently involving settings geographically and temporally remote enough to discourage guilt formation. Their impact on positive behavior may remain debatable, but it is safe to say that they have done nothing to discourage, discredit, or prevent institutional and attitudinal racism. For this reason an emphasis on popular fiction can assist in developing an understanding of the roots and the pervasiveness of Anglo attitudes towards the Spanish-speaking cultures with which they have been in closest contact. The ultimate value of the works discussed herein may differ from that intended by some of the authors. These works can, however, contribute to an important lesson in race attitudes.

My approach to this subject raises a final issue requiring extended explanation of the use of racial terms and epithets. I have tried to follow one basic precept: to accept what the races in a given time and place called themselves and each other. Such words as *Spaniard, Spanish-American, Chicano, Tejano, Nuevo Mexicano,* and *Californio* are used with as much care as possible out of respect for Spanish-speaking people's self-definition. On the other hand, *Mexican* has been what most Anglo-Americans have called most Spanish-speaking people most of the time, whether the people so addressed have liked it or not. I have therefore used it in a similarly comprehensive fashion. I have also used it where a more modern term seems inappropriate or insulting. To call, for example, a dime-novel bandido or a California grandee of the 1840's a Chicano is to distort the latter concept out of all meaning. Similarly, *Saxon* is a term especially favored by many of the nineteenth-century authors studied here as an honorific for their own race. *White* is a common twentieth-century equivalent. In the same fidelity to period, place, and prejudice, I have applied the words *American* and *Texan* exclusively to Anglo-Americans, for the simple reason that the Anglos quickly appropriated these terms for themselves. *Anglo* is used as a neutral synonym for North Americans despite a growing tendency among many descendants of non-English European immigrants to dislike the term. As for the consistent use of epithets like *Mex, nigger, brown nigger, halfbreed, greaser,* or, for that matter, *gringo* in a study like this, where attitudes and images are so important, it is unfortunately necessary to use this vicious racial terminology routinely, particularly in the earlier chapters. This use in turn has led to a decision to dispense with ironic quotation marks except in particularly outrageous cases. Otherwise, almost every page would be so pockmarked with them that they would represent an insult to both the author's integrity and the reader's intelligence.

The above list has been described as "cold-bloodedly complete" in its insulting epithets applied to the Chicano but correspondingly inadequate for the Anglo. This reflects two facts. While border Spanish is rich in unflattering euphemisms for *Anglo*, few of them appear in English-language popular fiction because authors of this fiction seem to have assumed—probably correctly—that the overwhelming majority of their readers would not understand them. *Gabacho*, for example, tends to draw blank stares even from Anglo southwesterners not fluent in Spanish. Only *gringo* seems to have the status of a universally recognizable derogatory epithet. The issue is further complicated because in general an ethnic insult as delivered in the Spanish of the Southwest puts most of the emphasis on the insult as opposed to the racial epithet, which tends to be a descriptive adjective rather than a fighting word in itself. *Gringa puta* and *greaser slut* are not exact equivalents. And in the final analysis, description is not synonymous with approval. Here the book must speak for itself.

IMAGES OF THE MEXICAN AMERICAN

IN FICTION AND FILM

CHAPTER ONE

ANTECEDENTS OF THE IMAGES

To COMPREHEND CLEARLY the fictional images and stereo-types that are the core of this study, we must also have in mind an outline of the history of the establishment of the northern part of the Spanish-American empire and the subsequent clash of the two cultures in the American Southwest.[1] The most re-markable fact about the original Spanish colonization of the borderlands is not that the Spaniards achieved so much with so few against so many, but that they did not manage more. With few exceptions, Native American opposition was minimal. Yet at the same time, the Spanish Southwest remained weak economically and politically in 1821, when Mexico became independent and Americans began to stream into the border-lands.

This weakness was partly a factor of geography. Distance and terrain made transportation and commerce difficult. Throughout the period of Spanish sovereignty, no lateral lines of communication crossed the vast regions in the north; all

---

[1] The three classic histories of the borderlands are Hubert Howe Bancroft, *History of Arizona and New Mexico, 1530–1888,* greatly outdated; Adolph A. Bandelier, *A History of the Southwest,* Vol. 1 (of 5 volumes to be published), ed. Ernest J. Burrus, S.J.; and Herbert J. Bolton, *The Spanish Borderlands.* Cf. also John Francis Bannon, *The Spanish Borderlands Frontier, 1513–1821;* Donald J. Lehmer, "The Second Frontier: The Spanish," in *The American West: An Appraisal,* ed. Robert G. Ferris; and Silvio Zavala, "The Frontiers of Hispanic America," in *The Frontier in Perspective,* ed. Walker D. Wyman and Clifton B. Kroeber.

roads led south to Mexico City. The Spaniards found little mineral wealth north of the Rio Grande. Farming depended on scarce water. The need for security encouraged close association. Ironically, as a result the Spaniards were actually more crowded in this land of distances than were their contemporaries in the English settlements to the northeast. They could conquer, but could not expand their conquests.

Spanish institutions also had to be substantially modified to accommodate the natural conditions of the borderlands. The classic triad of soldiers who conquered, priests who converted, and *hacendados* who exploited underwent considerable change in the enormous, largely uninhabited, mostly arid northern provinces. One pattern of Spanish-American life, however, endured: race mixing. Most of the soldiers and settlers who journeyed to the borderlands were themselves mestizos, and they intermarried widely with the Native Americans. Yet the rigid class system so firmly rooted in central Mexico was not correspondingly well established on the frontier. Although distinctions based on race did exist, mixed blood was not the serious handicap that it was in the more settled regions to the south. Mestizo settlers on the frontier were sometimes successful in contesting the political and economic supremacy of the "pure" Spaniards. In the upper Rio Grande Valley of New Mexico, mestizo farmers held positions of considerable political power and economic autonomy. In California, the mestizos were able to obtain land grants and establish a new *ranchero* class which had come to be considered "Spanish" by the nineteenth century. In short, notwithstanding the existence of racial prejudice and discrimination, by the beginning of the nineteenth century the mestizo Texanos, Nuevo Mexicanos, and Californios probably enjoyed relatively greater social and economic mobility than their counterparts to the south.

The substantial regional variations in patterns of Spanish settlement in the borderlands were based in part on geographic conditions, in part on the rumored presence or absence of mineral wealth, and in part on the crown's priorities for frontier defense. The province of Nuevo México, settled first by Franciscan missionaries and a few soldiers and later by ranchers and farmers, grew slowly. By 1821, however, New Mexico was the most populous province on the far northern frontier, numbering perhaps forty thousand people. The neighboring province of Arizona, too remote from New Mexico to participate in the trade with Chihuahua and too far removed from California to prosper from the sea trade that linked the Pacific coast with lower Mexico, was the neglected pauper of the Spanish Southwest. Although a few intrepid Jesuit missionaries penetrated the Arizona-Sonora frontier by the 1690's, Apache hostility hindered missionary expansion and discouraged mining and ranching. For better or for worse, the Spanish and Mexican territory of Arizona never knew the reign of the *ricos* or the "golden days" of the dons that gave the peculiar flavor to the adjacent provinces of New Mexico and California.

The province of Texas, initially colonized as a buffer between the settled areas of colonial New Spain to the south and the threatening Comanches and French to the north and east, also grew slowly. By 1820 fewer than twenty-five hundred persons of European descent lived in Texas. Once Mexico achieved its independence in 1821, the new government felt free to parcel out most of the land lying between the Rio Grande and the Nueces in the form of large grants to favorites of the new regime. Consequently, while the Mexican settlements north of the Nueces—in the area soon to be colonized by the Americans—remained sparse and underdeveloped, the large landowners south of the Nueces developed a patriarchal system of peonage that survived long after Mexico lost Texas to the United States.

Like Texas, the northwestern province of California was initially colonized for defensive reasons, specifically against the Russians and the English to the north. Cut off from Mexico City by fifteen hundred miles of desert roamed by hostile Indians and dependent for settlers and supplies upon occasional ships from Mexico, the colony of California, like New Mexico and Texas, grew largely through natural increase. By 1821 the colonists numbered about three thousand, most of them con-

5

gregated in the coastal towns or near the Franciscan missions. After the revolution, the Mexican Congress passed a secularization act releasing the Indian neophytes from all controls and throwing the mission lands open to settlement. As a result, the adobe churches crumbled and the Indians fled to the hills. Giant *ranchos*, supported by native labor and virtually free of interference from the Mexican government, replaced the mission stations as the dominant California institution.

Thus, by the time the Anglo-Americans began to spill into the borderlands early in the nineteenth century, a distinctive culture with its own regional variations had developed there. Modified by exposure to Native American institutions and tempered by geography and isolation, this borderland society hardly fit the conscious preconceptions of the frontier entertained by the advancing Anglos. These preconceptions involved three national images formulated in the Jeffersonian era which reached the peak of their development in the age of Jackson: the virtuous yeoman, the superiority of republican institutions, and America's divine destiny. The hero of this new mythology was the farmer who ventured forth into the wilderness to absorb nature's strength and virtue. The plow was his weapon, the farm his realm, and the frontier his place. The second image, that of republican government, rested on the assumption that within the ranks of the white race each man was roughly the equal of every other man in opportunity, if not condition. These related concepts of yeoman virtue and republican freedom were reinforced by the idea that Americans were a latter-day chosen people destined by God to undertake good works on earth. Americans could therefore commit themselves to aggressive courses of action because in the final analysis they were not responsible. A higher power was in control.

Although the Deity's design was imprinted on all parts of America, the discovery of His will seemed particularly easy on the American frontier, where a generation of poets, prophets, and politicians saw God's hand and the nation's destiny written in western geography. The widely shared belief that Americans were instruments of a superintending providence expressed a

6

need to believe in the moral righteousness of the historical venture in which America was engaged—pushing westward across the continent. The men who bought, negotiated, and fought their way into the Spanish borderlands early in the nineteenth century were able to rationalize their desires and achievements as enlarging the boundaries of republican freedom and agrarian virtue.

By the 1840's another source of inspiration developed: anti-Catholicism. Between 1840 and 1855 the average annual number of immigrants rose to more than three hundred thousand. Most of the newcomers were Irish and German Roman Catholics who settled in the large port cities along the eastern seaboard. Disturbed by the alien speech, mannerisms, work habits, and religion of the immigrants, and stirred by the wave of revivalism which swept the country in the early forties, an increasing number of Americans became convinced that "popery" was America's chief international enemy, whose new-world center lay in Mexico. Propaganda organs such as the *Democratic Review* declared, for example, that the heavy hand of the Pope reached halfway across the globe to choke the peons of Mexico just as surely as it strangled the peasants of the Old World.

The question of what to do about the threat of Catholicism, foreign and domestic, added an extra moral dimension to the notion of America as the land selected by Providence to be the ark of the covenant of republican freedom and the home of agrarian virtue. America was now also God's *Protestant* country on earth—dedicated to religious as well as economic and political regeneration.[2]

From the beginning, these attitudes manifested themselves

[2] For differing interpretations of the era of manifest destiny and national expansion, see Don E. Fehrenbacher, *The Era of Expansion, 1800–1848*; William H. Goetzmann, *When the Eagle Screamed: The Romantic Horizon in American Diplomacy, 1800–1860*; Frederick Merk, *Manifest Destiny and Mission in American History*; and Albert K. Weinberg, *Manifest Destiny*. Richard Slotkin, *Regeneration Through Violence: The Mythology of the American Frontier, 1600–1860*, stresses the mythic elements of conquest and dominance underlying the developing American self-image—elements plain in the conscious images discussed in the text.

7

most clearly in Texas. Texas was first infiltrated by filibustering expeditions early in the nineteenth century. In 1820, the last year of Spain's New-World empire, the crown decided to admit legally a few American settlers as frontier Indian fighters to protect the more populous settlements to the south. Late in 1821 the new Republic of Mexico, using the same argument of frontier defense, initiated the *empresario* system, which permitted an aspiring colonizer to settle a given number of families on specified unoccupied lands at his own expense. The most successful of these *empresarios* was Stephen Austin, who in 1821 brought in the Original Three Hundred families and settled them on the rich lands between the Brazos and Colorado rivers. During the next decade, some twenty thousand Americans, adventurers, debtors, and ambitious farmers, entered the province. As the Mexican government required, they founded towns, signed loyalty oaths, and became "Roman Apostolic Catholics." As the Mexican government did not require, they set up newspapers, formed political organizations, imported slaves, and virtually took over the country, in the process appropriating the title *Texans* for themselves.

As the number of Anglo-Texans increased, so did their disaffection. In 1829 the Mexican government abolished slavery, thus endangering what many new Texans saw as the necessary foundation for successful economic development in the province. Understandably, the republican Mexican officials were perplexed. The Texans said they wanted to "extend the area of freedom," while at the same time the slave sympathizers among them feared that through Mexico's agency Texas might actually become a land where blacks were free. To the Texans, the "freedom" they desired meant republican self-government, not the abolition of black slavery—a paradox hardly as clear in Mexico City as in Nacogdoches.

In 1830 the Mexican government finally prohibited further immigration from the United States. The outraged Texans drew up a states-rights constitution which Stephen Austin carried personally to Mexico City for ratification. The failure of his mission led to increasingly open support for secession. The

8

rest of the story is familiar to most Americans and rankles in the memory of most Mexicans. Santa Anna, personally leading an army of several thousand across the Rio Grande, laid siege to the fortified mission at the Alamo early in March, 1836. Six weeks later he was defeated by Houston's army at the battle of San Jacinto and signed a treaty acknowledging Texas independence in exchange for his own freedom and safe conduct back to Mexico. The outraged Mexican Senate refused to ratify the document. It has not been and never will be ratified.

Yet no matter how bitter the feelings generated by the clash of arms at the Alamo and San Jacinto, the war itself does not entirely explain the emerging long-term hostility between Texans and Mexicans. For Texans, the Mexicans were not only agents of political, economic, and religious tyranny. They were also lazy, cowardly, and culturally backward. For Mexicans, the Texans were more than the advance agents of political, economic, and religious imperialism. They were also coarse, conniving, rapacious, and overbearing. From the 1820's these kinds of deep-seated political and cultural differences gave way to distrust, distrust to antagonism, and antagonism in turn to open confrontation, creating wounds as yet unhealed.[3]

If the particular circumstances of conflict in New Mexico were different, the outcome was similar. The first Anglo-Americans to enter New Mexico were fur trappers. From the early 1800's, the village of Taos, situated just north of Santa Fe near the beaver streams of the southern Rockies, served as the supply center and rendezvous point for the southwestern portion of the American fur trade. Since Taos was also the seat of a Mexican customs house, and since trapping by foreigners was illegal, the American trapper had to deal with authorities who took a lively interest in his cargo. If the trapper was lucky, he found officials who could be bribed. If he was unlucky, his

---

[3] The most readable introduction to the Texas colonial period is D. M. Vigness, *Revolutionary Decades, 1810–1836*. Probably the best examinations of the cultural conflicts between Texas and Mexico are Samuel H. Lowrie's *Culture and Conflict in Texas* and Eugene C. Barker's *Mexico and Texas, 1821–1835*.

bales were confiscated. If he resisted, he was sometimes taken to Santa Fe and jailed. More often than not, satisfactory arrangements were made and the mountain man was permitted to exchange part of his cache of furs for supplies and to take in the dubious pleasures of Taos before embarking on a new season.[4]

At the peak of the trapping bonanza another profitable economic link emerged: trade. Between 1822, when the Santa Fe Trail was officially opened, and 1843, when Santa Anna closed the customs houses of the Rio Grande, New Mexico became a virtual economic colony of the United States, more dependent for goods on St. Louis to the east than on Chihuahua, six hundred miles and five months to the south. Some American merchants even settled permanently at Taos or Santa Fe, became Roman Catholics and citizens, learned New Mexican customs, and married or lived with New Mexican women.[5] Their opinions about the Nuevo Mexicanos were not always favorable. Indeed, most travelers and traders in this region seemed persuaded that the Mexican people were lazy, filthy, deceitful, cowardly, priest-ridden, and promiscuous. Francis Parkman wrote disdainfully of "squalid," "mean," "miserable," and "swarthy" Mexicans. Lewis Garrard, Santa Fe trader at the ripe age of seventeen, felt that the New Mexicans were "the most contemptibly servile objects to be seen; and with their whining voices, shrugs of the shoulder, and dastardly expression of their villainous countenances, they commend themselves unreservedly to one's contempt." George Brewerton, a

4 Robert Glass Cleland, *This Reckless Breed of Men: The Trappers and Fur Traders of the Southwest*; Carl P. Russell, *Firearms, Traps and Tools of the Mountain Men*; David J. Weber, *The Taos Trappers: The Fur Trade in the Far Southwest, 1540–1846*. David J. Weber, "Spanish Fur Trade from New Mexico, 1540–1821," *The Americas* 24 (October, 1967): 122–136, offers several reasons why the Nuevo Mexicanos did not fully exploit local fur resources.

5 The journals and memoirs about life on the Santa Fe Trail with the widest circulation included L. H. Garrard, *Wah-To-Yah and the Taos Trail*, and Josiah Gregg, *Commerce of the Prairies; or, The Journal of a Santa Fe Trader*. Max L. Moorhead, *New Mexico's Royal Road: Trade and Travel on the Chihuahua Trail*, pp. 193–197, discusses the role of Mexican merchants in the Missouri-Santa Fe trade and the impact of American merchants on New Mexico.

companion of Kit Carson, declared that the "mixed-bloods" of New Mexico possessed "the cunning and deceit of the Indian, the politeness and the spirit of revenge of the Spaniard, and the imaginative temperament and fiery impulses of the Moor." Moreover, they were wholly lacking in "the stability of character and soundness of intellect that give such vast superiority to the Anglo-Saxon race over every other people."[6]

Of all the Spanish territories that the Anglo-Americans encountered in their movement south by west, California was economically the most attractive. As early as the 1820's, demands for leather to supply New England's emerging shoe industry sent clipper ships around the Horn to trade for Spanish California's chief export commodity: hides. These "California bank notes" provided the local stock raisers with their principal source of income, supplied New Englanders with a main source of leather, and exposed Americans to the attractive climate, rich soils, and untapped mineral resources of Mexico's most northern province.[7] And like their counterparts in Texas and New Mexico, early American visitors and settlers in California generally agreed that the native Californians, though pleasant and hospitable, failed to measure up to the land's potential. They also agreed that the province was ripe for conquest—like the rest of Mexico's northern territories.[8]

[6] Francis Parkman, *The Oregon Trail*, pp. 3, 329, 335; George D. Brewerton, *Overland with Kit Carson*, p. 148. In citing contemporary memoirs, I refer to original versions except where later editions are more complete or accompanied by a useful scholarly apparatus.

[7] Hubert Howe Bancroft, *California Pastoral, 1769–1848*; Charles E. Chapman, *A History of California: The Spanish Period*; Edwin Corle, *The Royal Highway (El Camino Real)*; Alberta Johnson Denis, *Spanish Alta California*; Tirey Lafayette Ford, *Dawn and the Dons: The Romance of Monterey*; Cecil Alan Hutchinson, *Frontier Settlements in Mexican California: The Hijar-Padres Colony and Its Origins, 1769–1835*.

[8] Perhaps the best and most representative account of an American's reaction to the Californios during the gold rush is George W. B. Evans' *Mexican Gold Trail: The Journal of a 49er*. John Russell Bartlett, appointed by President Zachary Taylor as commissioner to survey the boundary between the United States and Mexico in 1850, wrote his *Personal Narrative of Explorations and Incidents in Texas, New Mexico, California, Sonora, and Chihuahua*, which presents Mexican society as ripe for American change. A choleric account of Mexican ineptitude can be found in John Wodehouse Audubon (the

While most Americans were persuaded that the Mexican race would never be able to take full advantage of its country's magnificent resources, the next question was whether it was America's duty to tap those resources for themselves. The issue by the early 1840's was not whether the Mexicans were inferior to the North Americans but whether the Mexicans *as* inferiors ought to be left alone or conquered. Southerners, speaking with the "voice of experience" in dealing with another dark-skinned race, were simultaneously loudest in asserting brown inferiority and strongest in affirming the risks of racial pollution. John C. Calhoun, standing firm on the Old Testament conviction of Ham's degeneracy, argued that the true misfortunes of Spanish America involved the fatal error of placing colored races on an equal footing with white men and maintained that the alternative to racial separation was economic stagnation, political chaos, and genetic pollution. On the other hand, seizure of Mexican territory offered attractive bonuses to offset the danger of racial and institutional contamination: potential mineral wealth, potential black slave territory, and potential brown peonage. Jefferson Davis had both slavery and peonage in mind when he called for annexing much of northern Mexico on the grounds that its economic assets outweighed the liabilities of absorbing a few brown people. Still another southerner proposed that the United States should acquire all of Mexico as far south as the twentieth parallel and deport all freed American blacks thither, thus simultaneously tapping lower Mexico's resources and establishing an ethnic boundary line which would separate most whites from blacks and browns alike.[9]

---

younger of John J. Audubon's two sons), *Audubon's Western Journals, 1849–1850. Being the MS Record of a Trip from New York to Texas and an Overland Journey Through Mexico and Arizona to the Gold-Fields of California.* Equally scornful, but more humorous and satirical, was the transplanted Irishman, J. Ross Browne, whose two best volumes dealing with Arizona and California were published in the 1860's: *Adventures in the Apache Country: A Tour Through Arizona and Sonora* . . . , and *Crusoe's Island . . . with Sketches of Adventure in California and Washoe.*

[9] For a good general discussion of this issue, see Paul Horgan, *Great River: The Rio Grande in North American History,* II, esp. 607–608, 778–781, 906.

For many Northern Whigs, on the other hand, the annexation of the Mexican Southwest loomed as an ill-disguised plot on the part of the southern slavocracy to upset the political balance of power established by the Missouri Compromise of 1820 and possibly to add new slave territories to the Union. New Englanders especially were not convinced that movement south by west was in the national interest—or at least in New England's interest. And if the slaveholders of the South saw the creation of new southwestern territories as the only way their "peculiar domestic institution" could survive, westerners saw the opening of new lands as an outlet for the land-hungry free white farmers who were already beginning to spill out of the Ohio and Mississippi Valleys.

To complicate the sectional issue further, the annexationists were divided over how much southwestern territory ought to be taken. Specifically, caution and common sense suggested that to acquire extensive tropical lands and their brown-skinned Catholic population was to risk altering and eroding basic American institutions. A logical compromise, many Americans agreed, was to limit the conquest to those borderland regions which contained fewer natives than the densely populated regions of lower Mexico—not to mention the Caribbean, the Isthmus, and the vast Andean and Amazonian stretches of the South American continent.[10]

Given the various justifications for invasion, the actual war with Mexico seems in retrospect to have been unavoidable—the finishing touch to a quarter-century of national expansion.[11]

[10] Ibid., pp. 779–781.

[11] For representative accounts stressing the ideological clash between the two countries, see Gene M. Brack, "Mexican Opinion, American Racism, and the War of 1846," *Western Historical Quarterly* 1 (April, 1970): 161–174; Seymour Connor, "Attitudes and Opinions about the Mexican War, 1846–1970," *Journal of the West* 11 (April, 1972): 361–366; Angel Del Río, *The Clash and Attraction of Two Cultures: The Hispanic and Anglo-Saxon Worlds in America*; Peter T. Harstad and Richard W. Resh, "The Causes of the Mexican War: A Note on Changing Interpretations," *Arizona and the West* 6 (Winter, 1964): 289–302; Ramón Eduardo Ruiz, ed., *The Mexican War: Was it Manifest Destiny?*; and, for a concise, well-balanced examination of United States and Mexican historiography on the causes of the war by a Mexican historian, Josefina Vásquez de Knauth, *Mexicanos y norteamericanos ante la guerra del 47*.

Certainly most Mexican officials thought so in 1845, as they watched the Yankees choose their president on the basis of his promise to annex some 240,000 square miles of what they still considered to be Mexican territory. Shortly after his inauguration, James K. Polk asked Mexico to reconsider the northern limits of her country and offered twenty-five million dollars for a boundary incorporating the present states of California, New Mexico, Arizona, Nevada, and Utah. When Mexico turned down the offer, Polk ordered General Zachary Taylor to the mouth of the Rio Grande to defend the river as the rightful boundary between the two countries. Mexican troops, upholding their government's position that the Nueces River was the legitimate boundary, crossed the Rio Grande to contest Taylor's presence there. Polk held brief counsel with his conscience and sent a war memo to Congress declaring that for all his "strong desire to establish peace with Mexico on liberal and honorable terms," Mexico had violated the Texas treaty ratified by the U.S. Congress the year before. Most of Congress agreed that "the cup of forbearance had been exhausted," and that body declared war on Mexico on May 11, 1846.[12] The military course of the war is too well known to require description. But American victory on the battlefield is merely the beginning of a tale, told in full sound and fury, of the interaction of two peoples.[13]

[12] In a diary entry made on May 9, 1846, four days before Congress declared war, Polk wrote that he "stated to the Cabinet that up to this time, as they knew, we had heard of no open act of aggression by the Mexican army, but that the danger was imminent that such acts would be committed. I said that in my opinion we had ample cause of war, and that it was impossible that we could stand in *status quo*, or that I could remain silent much longer; that I thought it was my duty to send a message to Congress very soon and recommend definitive measures." Milo M. Quaife, ed., *The Diary of James K. Polk*, I, 384–386. See also Allan Nevins, ed., *Polk: The Diary of a President, 1845–1849: Covering the Mexican War, the Acquisition of Oregon, and the Conquest of California and the Southwest*, pp. 81–83.

[13] Frederick Merk, *The Monroe Doctrine and American Expansion, 1845–49*; Glenn W. Price, *Origins of the War with Mexico: The Polk-Stockton Intrigue*; and Charles G. Sellers, *James K. Polk, Continentalist: 1843–1864*. The classic anti-Mexican study of the war, now outdated, is Justin H. Smith, *The War with Mexico*. For more recent military accounts, see the bibliography.

Part I
CONQUEST

THE CONQUEST OF THE SOUTHWEST took place on two levels. The first and most obvious involved the overt superimposition of American power and Anglo-Saxon attitudes on the vanquished Mexicans. This is the theme of chapter 2. The length of that chapter reflects the large number of works dealing with the subject in some form. Its significance begins with the fact that most of the early writers dealing with the conquest believed that they were recording fact as well as fiction, history as well as romance. Indeed, many of these works contain cautionary prefaces in which the authors warn that they are "merely" presenting narrative history plain and simple—perhaps changing a few names, places, and dates but remaining essentially true to the facts. The result was that what initially passed as fact in early southwestern diaries, letters, and travel accounts was eventually transposed into fiction; conversely, what passed as fiction or romance became interchangeable with fact to the point that few authors indicated the difference between the two. The outcome was as misleading as it was inevitable. In the minds of most writers—and probably in the minds of most Americans as well—there was, quite simply, no gap between the factual and fictional interpretations of the conquest. The two were one and the same thing. Thus, if few Americans were aware of the existing gap between fact and fiction, then the gap itself could have little or no influence on their cultural perceptions, including their perceptions and feelings about Mexicans.

Historians may demonstrate beyond cavil that the reality and the romance of the conquest were not the same thing. What emerges clearly from conquest fiction, however, is the idea that feelings about Mexicans, far from departing from facts, flow "naturally" from them. Consequently there is no urgent need to feel either a sense of injustice about the conquest or significant moral reservations about the manner in which Mexican territory was taken. That few writers saw anything unconscionable about the conquest means that in fiction, at least, the long-term moral burden of the conflict has proven to be a very light one. Literary agonizing over the trauma of black slavery or the taking of a continent from the Indians in the nineteenth century has not echoed in fictional treatments of the annexation of vast southwestern territories from the Mexicans in the same century.

This relative lack of moral concern over the conquest is especially significant to historians of popular culture who seek to measure and explain the gap between historical accuracy and public opinion. Whatever changing schools of academic opinion may emerge, it is unlikely that there will ever be a "revisionist" school of Anglo popular fiction seeking to reinterpret the conquest of the Hispanic Southwest in a light unfavorable to the winning side. The decades between 1820 and 1850 seem so filled with events suitable for fictional commemoration, so replete with possibilities for character stereotyping, and so apparently harmless in terms of any permanent damage done to the conquered race, that they are likely to remain forever ensconced in the realm of fantasy. And therefore the most that can be said about the moral "lesson" to be learned from fiction dealing with American conquest of the Hispanic Southwest is that the vast majority of writers see no moral lessons in the process.

Where moral judgments about the conquest have been made is in an entirely different sphere—sex. Stereotypes, after all, need not always be negative. From the earliest travel pieces

18

to the most recent fiction, a striking number of American writers have taken pains to exempt attractive Spanish and Mexican women from their disparaging remarks. Josiah Gregg, a merchant-trader between St. Louis and Santa Fe who was usually at a loss to find pleasant things to say about the Spanish Mexicans, was willing to concede that the "finer sort" of New Mexican women possessed "striking traits of beauty." George Kendall, a New Orleans journalist imprisoned by Governor Armijo, jotted excited notes about the "finely turned ankles, well-developed busts, small and classicly [sic] formed hands, dark and lustrous eyes," and "teeth of beautiful shape and dazzling whiteness" possessed by the New Mexican women.[1]

From the beginnings of recorded history, the womenfolk of the vanquished have been considered fair and legitimate spoils of the conqueror. For the nineteenth-century North American, however, it was one thing to admit that a good many Spanish Mexican women were fetching and quite another to permit those feelings of attraction to be carried into amorous action. On the surface, at least, Kendall and other visitors to the Southwest felt that the beauty of the women was "marred" by "provocative posturing" and "Eve-like and scanty garments." Kendall and his countrymen were both excited and repelled by skirts that ended above the knees and blouses that were cut low and bare at the shoulder. And it was but a short step for these male visitors, accustomed to the buttoned, corseted, and unrevealing fashions of eastern America, to conclude that the "semi-nude" fashions of the Southwest fostered "promiscuity." Yet not all Americans expressed the same sense of shock. For example, James Ohio Pattie, a Kentucky trapper who traveled widely through the Southwest, makes plain that when sexual attraction collided with commitment to a higher morality, glands often emerged victorious. Thus he writes that after a New Mexican dance, "it seemed expected of us, that we should each escort a lady home, in whose company we spent the night, and

[1] Josiah Gregg, *Commerce of the Prairies; or, the Journal of a Santa Fe Trader*, pp. 344–345; George Wilkins Kendall, *Narrative of the Texan Santa Fe Expedition*, pp. 393–394, 428–433.

we none of us brought charges of severity against our fair companions."[2]

The problem lay in explaining and justifying such ambivalent attitudes and behavior. As self-consciously civilized and civilizing men, Americans could nevertheless be tempted to escape the routine, responsibility, and sexual controls of Protestant America. But yearning for freedom, they had to reject it. Tempted, Americans could only outface the temptation by denouncing the tempters. Translated into fictional terms, this process forms the theme of chapter 3. Authors of conquest fiction tend to divide all Spanish Mexican women into two categories: a majority of dark-skinned halfbreed harlots and a minority of Castilian dark ladies who are actually no darker than the American heroines, and may or may not be virtuous, depending on the demand of plot. The one similarity between these two types of women is that both are "naturally" sexual. However, their sexuality takes different forms, each based on color. The sexual behavior of the Castilian dark ladies is carefully programmed and controlled. The sexual behavior of the halfbreed women is spontaneous, constant, and entirely lacking in control, if not design. These brown-skinned flirts throw themselves at the invaders in wild abandon, pleading helplessness in the face of the gringo's overpowering effect on their senses. For their part, the Americans, initially attracted to these "swart" beauties, eventually triumph over their base desires and hurl the "whores" away in self-righteous disgust. Perhaps, indeed, the failure to draw moral lessons from the actual, physical conquest of the Southwest has been sublimated into the ambiguous attitude towards southwestern women so characteristic of conquest fiction. Certainly if the Saxons are often permitted to taste the feminine fruit of their triumph, they tend to find the process at best bittersweet.

[2] Timothy Flint, ed., *The Personal Narrative of James O. Pattie of Kentucky*, pp. 190, 264. For summaries of eastern attitudes toward New Mexican women, cf. James M. Lacy, "New Mexican Women in Early American Writings," *New Mexico Historical Review* 34 (January, 1959): 40–42; and Beverly Trulio, "Anglo-American Attitudes toward New Mexican Women," *Journal of the West* 12 (April, 1973): 229–239.

A final word on the internal organization of these chapters seems desirable. To remove all references to women in the chapter dealing with the overt conquest would distort beyond recognition most of the works analyzed. Adventure stories do usually make use of heroines, temptresses, and villainesses. Where women appear in chapter 2, therefore, they are essentially confined to these roles: someone for the hero to marry or desire; someone whom the enemy has or might get; someone before whom males can preen. Chapter 3 deals with explicit treatments of sexual interactions between Saxons and Mexicans. The distinction, admittedly somewhat artificial, seems a necessary sacrifice to clarity. It has been made with the intention of reducing duplication and repetition to a minimum.

CHAPTER TWO

GRINGO VERSUS GREASER
IN CONQUEST FICTION

THE EARLIEST FICTION about the American conquest of the
Southwest was written in the aftermath of the Texas Revolution. Finding little to admire in the dark-skinned "foreigners"
they had recently conquered, these authors filled their pages
with swaggering self-righteousness. In *Mexico versus Texas*
(1838), by Anthony Ganilh, one of the "Saxon" characters explains why it is his country's "divine duty" to carry the conquest
beyond Texas to take in the rest of Mexico and perhaps all of
South America as well: "In point of chastity, the most important and influential qualification of Northern nations, we are
infinitely superior to you—Lust is, with us, hateful and shame-
ful; with you, it is a matter of indifference. *This* is the chief
curse of the South: the leprosy which unnerves both body and
mind. . . . The Southern races must be [morally] renewed, and
the United States are the *officina gentium* for the new Continent" (pp. 205–206).[1] Similarly, in Jeremiah Clemins' *Bernard
Lile: An Historical Romance*, the Texan hero sternly reminds
his readers that if the Texans fail to take all of Mexico to the
Isthmus, "a great work will have to be commenced anew; but
it *will be* commenced, and it *will be* completed!" (pp. 270–
271).

[1] Other Texas novels published later in the century that vary little in their
approach to Mexicans include William Osborn Stoddard, *The Lost Gold of the
Montezumas: A Story of The Alamo*, and Edward Stratemeyer, *For the Liberty
of Texas*.

22

In these early works there is no such thing as a dark-haired, brown-eyed protagonist. Nor is there a French, Irish, or German immigrant-hero among them. The eye that sights down the gun barrels in the Texas war for independence is inevitably grey-blue and "Saxon"; ranged against the sun-bronzed but "naturally" pale Texans is the greaser enemy.

The "Tex-Mex" as a formula scoundrel in these early novels is the victim of three forces beyond his control: the fictional need for villains who offer maximum contrast to the heroes; the actual presence of some difference in skin color between the two ethnic groups; and the unabashed racial bigotry that characterized the United States between the first years of manifest destiny and the outbreak of the Civil War. In an era preoccupied by fear of abolition and "miscegenation" and bombarded with pamphlets and lectures by quack ethnologists, abolitionists, and slaveowners, it is not surprising that a good many authors who chose as a theme the Texas Revolution—many of them native southerners—easily transferred long-established notions about one dark-skinned race to another.[2] A consistent central theme of these early novels is that the "pure" racial stock of the Spanish conquerors has been polluted beyond cleansing by mixing with the native populations, and that this pollution in turn largely explains the chronic cowardice of the Spaniards' "contaminated" offspring, the Mexicans. Samuel A. Hammett, a Yankee businessman who settled for a time in Texas and fought in the revolution, wrote a popular romance, *Piney Woods Tavern; or, Sam Slick in Texas* (1858), which includes a typical description of Mexican cowardice: "Put your Mexican on horseback and he will cavort with the best . . . until some one drops—and then he's off! Plant him behind a safe wall, and he will shoot you a cannon as well as the next man; but never trust him at close quarters, where bayonets and bowie knives are in fashion. He can't stand it and will not . . ." (p. 280). In the verse play *Michael Bonham: or, The Fall of*

---

[2] See, for example, Eric L. McKitrick, ed., *Slavery Defended: The Views of the Old South*; and John L. Thomas, ed., *Slavery Attacked: The Abolitionist Crusade.*

Bexar (1852), by the celebrated South Carolina writer William Gilmore Simms, a defender of the Alamo shouts after the fleeing Mexicans: "They fly before us! They can hold no ground with the old Saxon stock" (p. 29).

This contempt extended beyond the battlefield. With neither guilt, scruple, nor self-consciousness, popular writers on the Mexican War described Catholic tyranny, halfbreed degeneracy, Mexican sexuality, and the unfitness of the mass of "greasers" to run their own country. One of the more outspoken jingoists was A. J. H. Duganne, a founder of the Native American or "Know-Nothing" Party and a prolific author of novels, poems, and patriotic pieces. Duganne wrote two novels set in central Mexico on the eve of and during the Mexican War: *The Peon Prince; or, The Yankee Knight-Errant: A Tale of Modern Mexico* (1861), and *Putnam Pomfret's Ward; or, A Vermonter's Adventures in Mexico on the Breaking Out of the Last War* (1861). The hero in both novels is Putnam ("Je-ru-sa-lem!") Pomfret from "Varmount"—a Yankee of the Yankees, "which means, in every foreign land, some offshoot of that great Anglo-Saxon stock." Putnam does not think highly of "greasers and yaller-jackets," "yaller chaps" and "yaller-skins." Declaring that a "pack o' greasers" is no match for one Green Mountain Boy, he ridicules the Mexicans' inability to talk English, "like Christians," and their lack of technology: "as for 'lectric telegraphs or locomotives, I guess they'd as soon believe in harnessin' chain-lightnin' to their old go-carts."

This swaggering American invincibility contrasts sharply with the other race involved in the conquest. Victims of centuries of political chaos, priestly corruption, and racial miscegenation, the mixed-blood and poverty-stricken people of Mexico are fated—have long been fated—to extinction. The theme is sounded repeatedly: the Spaniards and their "polluted" descendants have committed racial and national self-genocide by mixing voluntarily with inferior dark-skinned races.

Conquest fiction does offer one possible avenue of redemption. At least some Mexicans are allowed to perceive their own inferiority and to try to cope with it by joining the conquering race. Work after work presents inefficient, "over-bred" Spanish noblemen of ancient stock, existing to be overturned by upstart Americans. Yet the dichotomy between bad Spanish aristocrat and good American commoner is riddled with ambiguities. The Texan *hacendado*, the New Mexican *rico*, or the Californian don was alternately admired and loathed. Viewed as superior to the run of his race, he commands a number of pages in southwestern fiction far out of proportion to his small numbers, which constituted less than one fiftieth of the population of New Mexico alone. This irresistible attraction to aristocrats is by no means confined to southwestern fiction. Much popular American literature tries to combine the alleged best traits of both aristocracy and democracy. As Henry Nash Smith has pointed out in *Virgin Land: The American West as Symbol and Myth*, the favorite device to mingle aristocrats and democrats in western fiction is to bring eastern businessmen, dudes, and intellectuals into contact with scouts, backwoodsmen, farmers, and cowboys. A similar process occurs with the Spanish aristocrats of the Southwest. As symbols of leisure and luxury, of decadent European aristocracy in conflict with the republican simplicity of Jeffersonian farmers and Jacksonian shopkeepers, these people had to be punished or converted. Yet they *were* also somehow attractive. If the American democrats who invaded the Southwest were quick to decry the spectacle of feudalistic rank and privilege, they were equally quick, in fiction at least, to marry the landed aristocrats' daughters—a subject treated in more detail in the next chapter. Indeed, one gains the impression from early conquest fiction that the Southwest was almost entirely populated with aristocratic fathers and daughters—with a few worthless sons and a scattering of mestizos, "peons," and Indians here and there. The racial future of the Southwest for these novels involved pairing highborn Spanish women with common but naturally noble American men, thus fusing the two peoples into a new race of high quality.

The losers in this genetic redistribution are the Spanish Mexican males. The final message in conquest fiction is that the only way the male Mexicans can survive the conquest of their country is to accept a permanently inferior position to the conquerors. Associations between male Americans and male Mexicans in the new American order are to be confined to a master-servant basis in the case of the peons and mestizos, or a master-pupil basis in the case of the aristocrats. In the over-simplified world of popular romance this means that the Spanish aristocrats, deserted en masse by the women of their own caste, will eventually be forced to mix with inferior mestizas and even Indian women, and are thus doomed to extinction. If they survive at all, they will survive as a "mongrel half-race."

All conquest fiction does not follow this pattern in exact detail. There are regional differences, which will be described below. Most of the works, however, feature similar formula characters: Saxon heroes, degenerate greasers, and declining dons. Whatever may be the individual vagaries of plot, period, or place, the male Spanish and Mexican characters come in two basic colors: off-white aristocrats and all-brown serfs. Most of them would prefer to join American society if given the invitation or the choice. Indeed, they would prefer to *be* Americans if they could somehow change their chromatic makeup. If they are light enough, they sometimes try to join the favored race, or to give honorable battle to it. If they are too dark to pass, they resort to villainy to vent their frustration and cover their failure. Conquest fiction, in short, takes American superiority completely for granted. The only question is how, given that superiority, the conquerors ought to behave.

Perhaps the most persistent early exploiter of these images in popular fiction was Ned Buntline (Edward Zane Carroll Judson, 1821–1886), adventurer, bigamist, and general confidence man who, before he launched Buffalo Bill in show business in the 1880's, wrote a series of adventure stories in the 1840's and 1850's that pioneered the way for later jingoist novels and dime novels. Buntline filled his pages with arrogant hidalgos, lazy peons, evil bandidos, sexy señoritas, and loose-principled priests, all of whom offer unfavorable contrast to the chaste and enterprising Protestants who came south to conquer and sometimes remained to marry—marry, that is, racially suitable "Castilian" aristocrats. Buntline's favorite device to bring the Jacksonian hero-commoners and the Castilian heroine-aristocrats together is unvarying. An arrogant and generally silly Castilian father goes bankrupt because his quixotic pride keeps him from soiling his hands to save his family or estate. He then concludes that his only hope is to hand his beautiful daughter and heavily mortgaged estate to a handsome Yankee entrepreneur. In the ensuing negotiations, the hidalgo bequeaths to the Yankee the social status associated with his aristocratic name and a large dowry of land. The American brings to the match his brain and brawn, which he uses to rebuild the hidalgo's crumbling estate in short order.[3]

Even a casual reader of romances will detect similarities between Buntline's aristocrat-commoner unions and the prince-peasant matches that fill the pages of popular literature from the *Child Ballads* to Barbara Cartland. The dispossessed hidalgo's fate, however, is also intended as a sobering lesson in economics. As traditional custodians of their country's supposed well-being and progress, the hidalgos have behaved so incompetently that they have forfeited their right to remain members of the ruling class. Hence, they must be stripped of power for the good of the country as well as the benefit of the conqueror.[4]

Lower-class Mexican males in Buntline's fiction are either ignored entirely or segregated into two distinctly inferior types:

[3] For representative Ned Buntline stories, see the bibliography. Biographical information is included in Henry Nash Smith, *Virgin Land: The American West as Symbol and Myth*, pp. 103 ff.

[4] A typical example of such a character, Don Ignatio ("Ignorant") Valdez, the hapless aristocrat in Buntline's *Magdalena, the Beautiful Mexican Maid: A Story of Buena Vista*, retains even in poverty four assets: an aristocratic title, "that look of habitual dignity which seems so natural to a Castilian," two lovely daughters, and, most of all, "democratic sympathies" which incline him to support the Americans in their invasion of his country. Like most Buntline hidalgos, however, he assumes that unpaid loans and overdue debts can remain unpaid and overdue forever. At the end of the novel, indigent and homeless, his hacienda burned by a foreclosing bandit, Don Ignatio is forced to seek sanctuary in an American military camp. A *hidalgo* in Buntline's *The Ice-King; or, the Fate of the Lost Steamer* is rescued from bankruptcy by a Yankee businessman before he is foully slain by the villain. Roughly the same fate befalls a ruined hidalgo in Buntline's *The Last Days of Callao.*

peon servants and mestizo bandidos. Of the two, the fawning peons bear startling resemblance to the shuffling Sambos of the era. Their greaser gibberish parrots stage-darky dialect and implies the same bumbling ineptitude and "comical" cowardice. Rolling their eyes skyward, these "coffee-colored" clowns and "brown niggers" take to their heels when faced with danger in a manner indistinguishable from that of any vaudeville "coon."[5] Buntline's mestizo bandidos are, however, substantially different. As "halfbreeds" rather than "Indians" they are a cut above the peons. Indeed, they are dangerous antagonists whose combination of "Spanish" intelligence and "Indian" savagery makes them tougher and more courageous than the decadent hidalgos. Lacking the hidalgos' oppressive sense of honor, the mestizo bandidos have no moral scruples about their ungentlemanly actions. Their lack of a sense of fair play plus their relatively light complexions place them at enough initial advantage to make them reliable nuisances for novels editorially restricted to under one hundred pages. Indeed, it requires considerable patience on the part of the reader and the hero alike to unravel the villainy of such light-skinned rakes as Captain Alvorode in *The B'hoys of New York*, whose evil nature is concealed by a "rather prepossessing appearance," and Colonel Alfrede in *Magdalena, The Beautiful Mexican Maid*, who has a "reputation for gallantry both in the battlefield and ladies' boudoirs." When the American heroes finally "unmask" these poseur gentlemen and expose their wickedness, they either kill them or hurl them back across the color line into "brownness" and disgrace.[6]

Most of Buntline's Mexican women who are not to the hacienda born are graced with voluptuous figures but burdened by loose moral principles. These "Spanish Venuses" are obviously designed to titillate Yankee readers, and titillate they certainly do. Although Buntline himself "married" several

[5] Ned Buntline, *Matanzas; or, a Brother's Revenge*, p. 70. Another cringing "black" peon, Zalupha, appears in *Magdalena*.
[6] Ned Buntline, *The B'hoys of New York: A Sequel to the Mysteries and Miseries of New York*; Buntline, *Magdalena*.

wives simultaneously and wrote some of his most popular work while sitting drunk in a brothel in New York, he was careful to maintain a rigid distinction between his private conduct and his public career as custodian of popular attitudes about race, sex, and color. Conscious of his readers' craving for immoral stimulation followed by moral instruction, he regularly placed his male characters in compromising situations with Mexican women from which they extricate themselves only after a series of close calls which enable Buntline to have it both ways: sex first, sermon afterward. In *The Ice King*, Buntline introduces Doña Elementa, a "handsome, dark-eyed woman, whose brunette cheek, jetty hair, long eyelashes, and delicately voluptuous form, talk of a southern clime for her birthplace [and] an ardent temperament for her heritage," and who is as elemental in her passions as her name implies. She declares to Lord Edward Wimsett, a neurasthenic "Limey" who is traveling with her on a passenger ship bound for some vague destination in the far north, " '. . . if I cannot be your wife, let—let me be—your—mistress!' " Wimsett, who lacks the moral fiber characteristic of his American cousins, hems and haws, but finally summons sufficient courage to inform Elementa that they can only be friends. Elementa promptly puts a match to the powder magazine on the ship and blows the novel's entire cast of characters to kingdom come.[7]

By far the most sensational of Buntline's Mexican characters, however, are a handful of priests who make up in villainy what they lack in number. They personify the fears of a generation of conscious anti-Catholics. Bent less on opposing the American invaders than on seizing control of the Mexican government and subverting the social order of their own country, Buntline's wicked padres traffic in cabalistic secrets, defraud their flocks with counterfeit relics and miracles, and trifle with young virgins in the confessional. In *Matanzas*, Padre Sabano is a dissolute rake who uses the sacrament of confession as a form of blackmail to gain power and wealth over his parish-

[7] Buntline, *The Ice-King*, pp. 34, 88, 93.

ioners while simultaneously luring teenaged damsels into his chambers on pretense of hearing their recitals of penance. When the Castilian heroine, Doña Elisa Lizardo, innocently approaches the padre to confess her sins, Sabano crushes her against his black-frocked bosom and presses his "vile lustful lips to hers." Repulsed by Doña Elisa, the padre captures her betrothed, a French Huguenot named Edouart de Gourges, who is fighting with the Americans, and chains him in a dungeon. Locking Elisa in an adjoining cell, Sabano outlines his plan to rape her while Edouart listens helplessly next door: "I am like the gorged tiger—I can play with my victim for a while till I get hungry; I shall not yet destroy thee, I wish thy young French lover to know that thou art mine." In the nick of time, Edouart escapes and leads his Huguenots against Sabano's "ape-like" "Indian" troops, whom the priest has recruited on threat of exposing their past sins should they refuse to serve him. Although Edouart is murdered by Sabano's "red hoard" (*sic*), causing Elisa to die of a broken heart, the wicked priest is also killed.[8]

Buntline's corrupt priests are the first of a long line of clerical rogues appearing in nineteenth-century fiction set in the American Southwest. The propaganda appeal of "papism and the scarlet lady" was of course not confined to southwestern literature. Anti-Catholicism southwestern style, however, added another regional and ethnic group to the ranks of Irish and Central European Catholics who were thought to be threatening the moral values and institutions of America. While Nathaniel Hawthorne was commenting on priestly corruption and excesses in *The Marble Faun* (1860), Jeremiah Clemens produced *Mustang Grey: A Romance* (1858), with this description of the unseemly advances of a San Antonio priest: "Gradually his manner grew more tender, and at length he clasped me in his arms, and pressed a hot kiss upon my lips. . . . His eyes absolutely glistened with lascivious fire, as they ran over my face and person" (pp. 215–216). Other authors fol-

[8] Buntline, *Matanzas*, pp. 22, 38.

lowed with a formidable cast of corrupt priests who spend more time in abducting and seducing than in saving souls. In *Remember: The Alamo* (1888) by Amelia Barr, a writer of popular romantic novels in the late nineteenth century, a "goblin" priest named Father Ignatius glides about San Antonio during the Texas rebellion with "downcast eyes and folded hands" while plotting theft, rape, and murder. Conniving to seize the house and property of a wealthy Scottish physician and to seduce his daughters, Father Ignatius also daydreams about slitting one American throat per day for the rest of his life and burying his victims in the doctor's house. Not until the doctor returns from fighting in the Texas Revolution does Father Ignatius admit defeat, retreating with hissing curses into the dark sanctuary of his chapel.[9]

The Catholic Church suffers even greater vilification in novels about the conquest of California. Bret Harte, one of the first American writers on the Golden Age of the California dons, was also the first to rail against the Catholic Church in a California setting. His two specialties were greedy priests seizing the lands of gentlemanly dons for Mother Church and fanatic padres forcing conversion of Indians by uniting sword and sceptre. In "Friar Pedro's Ride," a doggerel piece written in 1869, Harte satirized a mission padre who outfits six California regiments with handcuffs, lassos, and missals and escorts them to a small camp of heathen red men. Ordering the soldiers to lasso the savages, he surveys the battle from a hilltop, cheering the troops on with a curious recital of a mock-Latin litany:

> Well thrown, Bautista,—that's another soul!
>   After him Gómez,—try it once again;
> This way, Felipe! there the heathen stole;
>   Bones of St. Francis!—surely that makes *ten*
> *Te deum Laudamus*,—but they're very wild;
>   *Non nobis dominus*,—all right, my child."

[9] Amelia Barr, *Remember: The Alamo*, pp. 118–134.

Not content with looking on passively while tallying the total ("lassoed six and reconverted four"), Father Pedro ropes a young woman himself.[10]

"The Legend of Monte del Diablo" (1873) features a mission padre who sets out—in 1770, a half-century before the arrival of the Americans—to convert savages. Topping a rise and gazing across the plains, the padre sees a devastating threat to his heretofore uncontested supremacy. Looking to the far horizon, he sees a "vision" of future California, a half-century hence, that throws him into a literal fit. In the foreground are the Spanish armies, beating a hasty retreat. Far to the east march the blue-eyed, flaxen-haired Americans—"pushing, bustling, panting, and swaggering" towards California, felling giant trees and rending the bowels of the earth as they tramp onward toward the sea. Searching frantically for some sign of the Holy Church in the American ranks, the padre finds but one medallion hanging from the neck of a trooper—and crosses himself "with holy horror as he perceived it bore the effigy of a bear." The futuristic scenario of his beloved California conquered by John C. Fremont's Bear-Flaggers is too much for the padre, and he passes the remainder of his days in insanity.[11]

The father's nightmare had literary as well as physical reality. From the 1860's through the second decade of the twentieth century, a number of New York publishing houses deluged the newsstands and cigar stores of the nation's cities, towns, and villages with a massive series of cheap fiction designed to entertain America's first mass-educated audience. The most popular and prolific supplier of these stories—they were hardly novels, for they seldom ran to more than thirty

[10] Bret Harte, "Friar Pedro's Ride," originally published in *The Overland Monthly* 2 (April, 1869): 375–376.

[11] Bret Harte, "The Legend of Monte del Diablo," in *Mrs. Skagg's Husbands, and Other Sketches*, pp. 277–298. Though Harte had his imitators, the mass-market serial writers of the nineteenth century left the Catholic clergy almost entirely alone. Priests of any kind rarely appear in the thousands of paperback dime novels which began to appear after the Civil War—perhaps because their authors found a richer source of villains in other Mexican stereotypes.

thousand words—was the publishing house of Beadle and Adams. Many of their hundreds of titles featured pioneering and border conflicts, but their success was predicated on style, not theme. The Beadle appeal rested on stock plots whose uniform packaging guaranteed a standardized and dependable product sounding popular notes of chauvinism, insouciance, and virtue. Bound by tight Victorian codes of morality and by the need to maintain razor-sharp distinctions between heroes and villains, the melodramas published by the house of Beadle were written in conformity with two imperatives of the trade: the hero and the heroine shall be virtuous, and the hero shall not behave violently until the villain has first committed "dirty" violence.[12]

Although the plot lines and moral imperatives were standard, frenzied competition among the house of Beadle and its several rivals gave rise to a constant search for new effects to sustain the high shock value that sparked the initial series. The eventual effect was to make brutality not only bearable but also boring. Killing ever more villains meant exaggerating violence and bloodshed for their own sakes, sometimes to the point of overt sadism. What makes the dime novel genre particularly instructive for our purposes, however, is the fact that many of the writers and editors who produced these novels were men with considerable knowledge of and experience in the Far West: former scouts, Indian fighters, Texas Rangers, land speculators, and frontier hangers-on who, as aging figures from a vanished era, found themselves unemployed.[13] Forced

---

[12] For information on the dime novels, see Ralph Admari, "The House that Beadle Built, 1859–1869," *American Book Collector* 4 (November, 1933): 223–225; W. H. Bishop, "Story-Paper Literature," *Atlantic* 44 (September, 1879): 387; Warren French, "The Cowboy in the Dime Novel," *Texas Studies in English* 30 (1951): 219–234; Charles M. Harvey, "The Dime Novel in American Life," *Atlantic Monthly* 100 (July, 1907): 44; George C. Jenks, "Dime Novel Makers," *Bookman* 22 (October, 1904): 112; Albert Johannsen, *The House of Beadle and Adams and Its Dime and Nickel Novels: The Story of a Vanished Literature*; Edmund Pearson, *Dime Novels; or, Following an Old Trail in Popular Literature*; and Henry Norton Robinson, "Mr. Beadle's Books," *Bookman* 60 (March, 1929): 22.

[13] The two most prolific writers of the Beadle border romances were "Buckskin Sam" Hall and Prentiss Ingraham, both veteran frontiersmen. Major

to conform strictly to the editorial policy laid down by the house of Beadle, under no illusions about what was expected of them, these adventurers turned hack writers ground out stories that bore less and less resemblance to the real West. Qualms of conscience were stifled by economic pressure. If someone did become disgusted enough to resign, he was easily replaced. The gap between their past experiences as frontiersmen and their present duties as writers of fantasy serves to remind us that intimate knowledge of the realities of western life did not prevent rewriting the western experience to suit city tastes any more than Buffalo Bill's actual career as Indian fighter and buffalo hunter precluded staging his Wild West extravaganza in Madison Square Garden before capacity eastern crowds.

The professional duty of dime-novel cowboys is not to herd cattle but to give battle with bad whites, savage redskins, and "yaller-belly" Mexicans. In the several hundred Beadle novels set on or near the Mexican border, the proximity of both "Injuns" and "Mexikins" offered two obvious ethnic villains whose cunning and cowardice could be matched against the cowboy's physical strength, common sense, and moral purity. Both races are so used in the Beadle border series, often in the same story. The Mexican is nevertheless the preferred villain. Perhaps he had the charm of difference: these swarthy rascals were not so liberally scattered throughout the Far West as were the redskins. Moreover, his dark features and "alien" garb offered striking visual contrast to the appearance of the Saxon hero without the shock of complete alienness associated with the Indian.

The Beadle novels feature seven distinct Mexican stereo-

Sam S. Hall, born in Massachusetts, became a Texas Ranger and was a casual acquaintance of Big-Foot Wallace, who figures in several of his stories. After a stint as a Union scout in the Army of the Southwest during the Civil War, Hall was persuaded by Buffalo Bill to join the house of Beadle and Adams. Colonel Prentiss Ingraham, born in Mississippi, served in the Confederacy and fought with the Mexican rebel Benito Juárez against the French in the 1860's and with the Cubans against the Spanish in 1898. Later he joined Buffalo Bill in the West before going to work for Beadle and Adams.

types. A large number of inconsequential loafers and barflies who hunker in the background of the action are contrasted with a handful of good and faithful peon servants. On a higher social level, a scattering of "good" Spanish gentlemen side with the Saxons; a few "bad" Spanish gentlemen fight them. The women include a smattering of halfbreed bandit-Amazons and a large cast of "Castilian" heroines. And all six of these types combined seem outnumbered by the endless hordes of bandidos.

"Good" Mexicans of the "lower sort" are particularly rare. Occasionally a cringing peon servant sets his master's table and tends the "Castilian" heroine. More often, however, these humble household servants either turn out to be "highblooded Spaniards" in disguise or treacherous spies for a local gang of greaser bandidos, especially in Beadle novels set in Texas. In novels set in California and Colorado, on the other hand, a handful of "good" Mexicans appear as "honest" outlaws, gamblers, or devoted servants who help their American masters bring the Mexican villains to justice.[14]

More appealing to dime-novel notions of chivalry are the few all-good "Spanish" gentlemen who side with the Americans against "lowblood" Mexicans. Generally these *caballeros* are found in Texas. Having had the good sense to fight on the winning side in the Texas Revolution and the Mexican War, when "glorious Sam teetotally chawed up the Greasers," these "Spanish" lords of the manor have been rewarded by a subsidiary but secure position in postbellum Texas society. As superior

---

[14] Treacherous household servants in the Texas Beadles appear in Joseph E. Badger, *The Rustler Detective; or, The Bounding Buck from Buffalo Wallow*; Sam S. Hall, *Little Lariat; or, Pecan Pete's Big Rampage*; Sam S. Hall, *The Black Bravo; or, The Tonkaway's Triumph: A Romance of the Frio Ranch*; and Prentiss Ingraham, *The Buckskin Rovers; or, The Prairie Fugitive: A Texas Romance*. Francis Johnson, *The Death Track; or, The Outlaws of the Mountain*, set in San Francisco in 1849, features "Steel-Arm" Pablo, an upright "Outlaw of the Mountains" who does battle with white villains. Honorable Mexican gamblers or household servants who mind their own business and help to corral bad men in Colorado appear in Edward L. Wheeler, *Deadwood Dick in Leadville; or, A Strange Stroke for Liberty: A Wild, Exciting Story of the Leadville Region*; and Edward L. Wheeler, *Little Quick-Shot, the Scarlet Scout; or, The Dead Face of Daggersville*.

members of an inferior race, they hold baronial sway over
thousands of Texas acres and seek to secure their status by
mating their highborn daughters to Anglo heroes. The Texan
commoners, after briefly rejecting the leisured life of the Spanish *hacendados* as undemocratic, agree to take over the vast
holdings of their prospective fathers-in-law and—in a manner
that differs not at all from Ned Buntline's soldier-conquerors—
ultimately settle down to the good life themselves.[15]

These Spanish gentlemen are not particularly interesting
characters. Since their principal function is to hand their haciendas and daughters over to the conquering American heroes,
they rarely appear except in the opening and closing chapters.
More intriguing are the "gentlemen" who look just as well as
their all-good counterparts but who behave almost as badly as
the halfbreed bandidos whom they sometimes lead against the
Americans. These gentlemen bandidos are sometimes effete
gamblers or clerks who lounge about the mining and cattle
towns of the Southwest. They may be well-bred dons of the
range who lead double lives as public-spirited cattlemen and
private leaders of bandit gangs. These handsome, two-faced
figures are invariably apprehended, usually imprisoned after a
proper trial, and executed by a legally sanctioned firing squad.
Moreover, they speak a correct English that enables them to
cover their criminal acts with a veneer of good taste. Indeed,
their diction rivals that of the Saxon heroes. In *The Buckskin
Bowers; or, The Cowboy Pirates of the Rio Grande* (1887), for
example, Captain San Cruz, the gentleman leader of a band
of outlaws called the Cowboy Pirates, is allowed educated diction while his henchman, an Anglo called Tiger Tom, speaks a
vulgar English. When the captain blows a whistle summoning
Tiger Tom to plot a new outrage, the following conversation
takes place:

[15] For a few of the many examples of Spanish *hacendados* who have the
good fortune to marry their wellborn daughters to Texas commoners, see Badger, *Rustler Detective*; Frank Dumont, *Evil Eye, King of Cattle Thieves; or,
The Vultures of the Rio Grande*; Mark Wilton, *Young Kentuck; or, The Red
Lasso*; and indeed most of the dime novels which feature Castilian heroines.

"What's up, cap'n, for I heerd yer blow?"

"I am obliged for your prompt response, Tiger Tom, and it shows that you can be depended upon, for believing me in danger you came to my aid."[16]

More daring and unconventional than either type of gentleman are the Amazonian "tiger-women" of the Beadle novels. Doomed to remain secondary characters because their morals and their complexions alike are shadowed, these dark-hued "halfbreed" women are occasionally figures of considerable sympathy. In *Diamond Dick, the Dandy from Denver* (1882), a New Mexican mixed-blood, Dashing Dolores Martínez, gives birth to a child out of wedlock and must therefore die. The reader is, however, expected to show some compassion for her plight. In *Cool Desmond; or, The Gambler's Big Game: A Romance of the Regions of the Lawless* (1881), a similar fate befalls María Conejos, a halfbreed "who was of a flighty and frivolous disposition," has a passionate love affair with a married man, and meets an inevitable death which is explained as "a happy release" (p. 22). Far more fascinating, however, are the few genuine Mexican Amazons in the Beadle novels— women whose complexions and conduct are alike so tainted that their only recourse is to become outlaws. These dark and sinister beauties differ from their male partners in crime in two important respects. They get their comeuppance from the Saxon heroes because they try to make love, not war. Then, as a concession to their sex, they are permitted to ride off after their capture. A typical example is *The Golden Serpent; or, Tiger Dick's Pledge: A Story of Life in California* (1886). The title character, a "little tarantular of a Greaser" who bears no other name than the Golden Serpent, makes frantic advances to the Saxon hero, Tiger Dick Langley. When Dick rejects her in favor of a pure-blooded American, the Golden Serpent first

---

[16] Prentiss Ingraham, *The Buckskin Bowers; or, The Cowboy Pirates of the Rio Grande: A Story of Texas Adventure and Romance*, p. 8. A similar handsome gentleman-bandido of good family, Elmer Valdos, appears in a dime novel supposedly written by "General" William F. Cody, *Wild Bill, the Wild West Duelist; or, The Girl Mascot of Moonlight Mine: A Romance of the Outlaw Owls of the Rockies*.

considers stabbing Dick with a stiletto she carries in her bosom, then relents and decides to imprison Dick in a cave and starve him to death. Growing impatient with this slow revenge, the Golden Serpent surrounds the cave with her henchmen and, summoning Dick to the entrance, shoots him. However, her aim is not as good as she has consistently claimed it to be, and Dick lives to rejoin his true love and to pardon the Golden Serpent, who rides off—hissing and unrepentant—with her male followers to plot even more foul deeds.

Female bandits like the Golden Serpent and her counterparts may be interesting to the modern reader but were not the type of heroines calculated to appeal to the conventional Beadle audience in the Victorian East. These halfbreed bandidas are therefore rare compared to a more acceptable class of lady: the full-blooded "Spanish" heroine. Beautiful Castilians all, they are variously described as all-white, alabaster-white, lily-white, or olive-white. Such women are clearly not to be confused with dark-skinned mestizas and Indians. Any resemblance is coincidental. Their proper place is at the side of the Saxon heroes, and their looks and loyalty usually find an appropriate reward—unless they are forced to compete with genuinely American heroines.[17]

Even without competition, however, these beauties must work overtime to prove their eligibility for romantic attachments with the "white" race. Volcanic in their emotions—"one moment raging tigresses, the next as loving as cooing doves"[18] —the Beadle Castilians are sometimes totally helpless in the face of danger and sometimes quite capable of taking care of

[17] For example, in Albert W. Aiken, *The Fresh on the Rio Grande; or, The Red Raiders of Rayon: A Story of the Texas Frontier*, p. 3, Isabel Escobedo, a brunette Castilian, "commands admiration," while her blonde sister, Margaret Escobedo, "inspires love." In Badger, *Rustler Detective*, the kidnapped and rescued heroine Nadine Falconer wins the Saxon hero because she is half Texan. Even so, her complexion must be carefully explained: "In the case of a less beautiful woman her skin would have been called sallow; with her, it combined admirably with her full, red lips, her glorious eyes, large and lustrous, full of slumbering fire that needed but a breath to fan into scorching blaze" (p. 23).

[18] Prentiss Ingraham, *Buffalo Bill's Daring Deed; or, The Scourge of the Gold Trail*.

themselves. Indeed, when Anglo heroes are not rescuing Castilian damsels in distress, they in turn are often being rescued by them. Beadle females are forever slipping knives to their lovers, bringing up getaway horses, luring bandido chieftains over cliffs, or otherwise engaging the attention of the enemy long enough for the hero to break the bonds of captivity and reverse the course of the story. Such rescues differ only in detail. The motives and objectives remain the same: to bring hero and heroine before the altar.

Such is the case in Sam Hall's *Little Lone Star; or, The Belle of the Cibolo* (1886), a novel which incorporates most of the stereotypes of the Beadle Mexican into a single plot. Anita de Casas, a physically precocious fourteen-year-old Castilian whose passions and complexion are compared to the red-hot volcanoes of her native Mexico, "burning under a mantle of snow," falls asleep while paddling a canoe through the flower-festooned lagoons on her father's Texas hacienda. Incredibly, Anita remains asleep as the canoe lurches into a swifter stream that will carry her to certain death in the rapids of the Rio Grande. At this point the fair-haired hero, William Waldron, appears on the cliff above, ropes the canoe, and pulls Anita to safety. Although Anita's father, a man of purest Castilian stock, has initial misgivings about wedding his highborn daughter to an American of common ancestry, his doubts are put to rest when Waldron later rescues both Anita and her father from Caldelas the Coyote, a vicious bandido who announces his intention to kill Don José and marry Anita himself. Unable to curb his passions until the wedding vows are exchanged, the drunken Caldelas is on the point of raping Anita (a rare insinuation in the Beadle novels) when he is killed by Waldron. Don José, lifting all restrictions on the match, gives the couple his blessing.

Roughly one-fifth of all Beadle novels feature "halfbreed" bandidos who compete with Indians as the leading ethnic villains in the entire series. In novels set in the Southwest, the percentage is naturally much higher. Whatever their location, however, the greaser villains are burdened with a formidable set of easily identified, ethnic, stereotyped features, traits, and trappings. These include long, greasy hair coiled under huge sombreros, scraggly *mustachios* that offer an unkempt contrast to the fashionably trimmed blond mustaches of the Saxon heroes, tobacco-stained fingers and teeth, and grotesque dialect and curses. Above all, the Beadle bandidos are characterized by complexions shading from pitch black through dark brown to orange, yellow, olive, and gray. Such polychromatic blemishing earns a long list of descriptive adjectives: dusky, dingy, sooty, swarthy, sallow, inky, pitchy, and greasy. These mixed-blood unfortunates are variously called greasers, Mexes, Mexikins, yallers, breeds, mongrels, and niggers—seldom Mexicans. Occasionally they try to pose as "white" men, with predictable results. Generally they cannot even ride, rope, or swear well. The reader often remains at a loss as to what they are trying to say. Therefore, beyond an occasional "Caramba!" or "Carajo!" most of them say very little. Their chief function is to offer overt physical threat to the Saxon hero and implied sexual threat to the Saxon or Castilian heroine. Yet for all their attempts to defile blonde or Castilian maidens by torturing or abusing them as far as the literary constraints of the time will permit, the Beadle bandidos are constantly thwarted in their evil intentions. Beyond baring yellow fangs, swearing (if incoherently), and racing frantically up and down the countryside in pursuit of the elusive hero or heroine, these Mexicans seldom accomplish anything. Far from learning from their past mistakes, they remain dim-witted to the end. When the heroes charitably release them from disastrous encounters to give them a chance to reform, they invariably return for repeat engagements with similar results. This makes them reliable nuisances for as many as twenty or thirty pages, until the Saxons tire of the game and dispatch them peremptorily. Occasionally a bandido is permitted to escape, but only so he can reappear in a sequel.

The Texan Beadle bandidos are by far the most sensational as well as the most numerous, and their Texan enemies are by far the most accomplished "greaser" haters in the entire Beadle series. The general attitude in the Texan branch of the Beadles is well summarized in Hall's *Wild Will, the Mad Ranchero; or, The Terrible Texans* (1880), which opens with an ode to the stalwart sons of the Lone Star Republic who drove "their cruel foes—the painted savage and ruthless, revengeful Mexican . . . from thy green flower-bespangled prairies forever" (p. 1). Texan devices for disposing of these hereditary foes are infinite in variety. In Hall's *Double Dan, the Dastard; or, The Pirates of the Pecos* (1883), a tobacco-spitting, greaser-hating barbarian named Big Foot Wallace leaps from a treetop onto the head of an inattentive sentry and crushes him to death. Climbing another tree, Big Foot repeats the feat, this time landing on the head of a bandido who gives himself away by vicious cursing because of a burn on his lip from the ever-present cornshuck cigarette. With the sentries eliminated, Big Foot crawls unnoticed into the center of the bandit lair, where the villains are "sleeping off the effects of the deep potations they had indulged in." Shoving a sombrero down the throat of a snoring Mexican, the giant-sized mountain man then instructs the younger and more genteel Texan hero Roy Randolph on how to attend to the rest of the slumbering gang: "Keep ther yaller varmints yunder kivered, pard, an' bore 'em ef they makes a jump fer biz. I'll sorter 'sturb ther see-estars . . . without hevin' 'em spit music, ef hit kon be did." It can indeed be done, and Big Foot goes on to capture and hang the entire gang. When congratulated for his feat, the apotheosized Leatherstocking replies: "Hit 'pears ter me thet ye're all makin' a heap o' fuss 'bout wipin' out a few Greasers" (pp. 14–23).

In *The Rough Riders; or, Sharp Eye, the Seminole Scourge: A Tale of the Chaparral* (1883), also by Sam Hall, another salty "Mex"-hater named Old Rocky captures a "dog-gasted greasy, mangy yaller son of a kiote" Mexican and strings him up on suspicion of rustling. Noting that the "greaser's" toes still touch the ground, Rocky wraps the man's feet around his thighs, thus halving his size and making him a suitably "hideous corpse." Later, after capturing and torturing another "mongrel Mex" to the point of confession, Rocky discovers from the near-dead man that he "hanged the wrong Greaser" earlier. Not at all disturbed by this infraction of justice, he declares that two dead "Mexes" are better than one and literally does a waltz-step with the second doomed man, exclaiming: "Le's hev a fandang' 'fore I sen's yer ter kingdom come." After the death-dance, Rocky hangs the Mex, who screams disgracefully as he strangles in the moonlight.

And so it goes through several dozen novels in the Beadle border series. Sometimes the scenes degenerate into sadism, as when a "yellow-skinned greaser" is pinned by the hand to a barroom door with a knife or when several Mexicans at a fandango have their "kiote karkidges" (coyote carcasses) shot full of holes, their ears perforated, and their fingers severed before they are "finally" put to death.[19] Such behavior suggests that although certain proprieties must be rigidly observed by the Beadle heroes—they must not drink, smoke cigarettes, or talk about sex—Saxon codes of fairness may occasionally be suspended, at least when greasers are involved.

The House of Beadle continued to turn out bandidos and *caballeros*, sexy Amazons and lovely Castilians, as long as the market lasted. By the late 1880's, however, the credibility gap was growing larger as serial writers sought ever more sensational devices to lure jaded readers. In Joseph E. Badger's *The Gold-Lace Sport; or, The Texas Samson's Wide Swath* (1897), published in the last year of the four-decade Beadle reign, the protagonist is a crimson-sashed dandy who carries a live rattlesnake coiled in the recesses of his huge hat brim. But even such flamboyant heroes could not keep the Beadle series alive. Its next prominent replacement, emerging in 1905, was the Buffalo Bill Stories. The numerous ghost writers employed by the publishing house of Street and Smith, writing under the common pseudonym of Ned Buntline, made even more use of

[19] Cf. Hall, *The Black Bravo*; Sam S. Hall, *The Serpent of El Paso; or, Frontier Frank, the Scout of the Rio Grande*; Sam S. Hall, *Dandy Dave and His Horse, White Stocking; or, Ducats or Death: A Story of Texan Treachery and Texan Honor*; Sam S. Hall, *Desperate Duke, the Guadaloupe "Galoot"; or, The Angel of the Alamo City*; and Prentiss Ingraham, *Pawnee Bill's Pledge; or, The Cowboy Kidnapper's Doom*.

Mexican characters than had the Beadles. By conservative esti-
mate, fully one-third of the six hundred Buffalo Bills introduce
a Mexican somewhere in their pages.[20] However, in matters
of plot, motivation, and hero-villain relationships, the Buffalo
Bill Stories remain cut from the Beadle cloth. The one notable
difference in the depiction of Mexican characters is that all
Mexicans in the Buffalo Bill series, whether bandidos or dons,
Castilians or Amazons, speak correct English—presumably as
a concession to the genteel standards of the first years of the
twentieth century. In all other respects the Mexican stereotypes remain unchanged. There are still a few good and faithful peon servants who deliver messages and tend the heroines;
still a few good Spanish gentlemen; still a few gentlemen bandidos who dress resplendently (one so much so that he shines
in the moonlight), ride their vast acres by day, and lead bandit
gangs by night.[21]

The Amazon bandida, interestingly, disappears entirely, a
victim of the tightening moral code of the new century. The
same code probably contributed to the fact that unlike their
sisters in the Beadle novels, the Castilian ladies in the Buffalo
Bill series serve almost exclusively as kidnap victims.[22] Their
rescues are made more difficult by the fact that the greaser
bandidos in the Buffalo Bill series, unlike their brothers in
crime in the Beadle novels, often unite with redskins to increase their numerical strength. In *Buffalo Bill on the Staked
Plains*, for example, Buffalo Bill is forced to align himself with

[20] Curiously, at least sixty of the Buffalo Bill stories were published in
Spanish. However, it should be noted that the Barcelona, Spain, publishing
house advertised the Buffalo Bill stories exclusively for children: "Biblioteca
Infantil. Cuentos propios para niños, muy amenos, morales e instructivos."
[21] Cf. *Buffalo Bill and the Affair of Honor; or, Pawnee Bill's Mexican
Comrades; Buffalo Bill among the Cheyenne; or, The Rescue of Paquita;* and
Buffalo Bill and Billy the Kid; or, the Desperadoes of Apacheland.
[22] In *Buffalo Bill among the Cheyenne*, for example, Paquita, a sixteen-
year-old "Castilian" beauty whose father is called the Duke of Cimarron
and whose mother is of French stock, is kidnapped by Cheyenne and held
for ransom until she is rescued by Buffalo Bill. In *Buffalo Bill's Duel; or,
Among the Mexican Miners*, The Buffalo Bill Stories, no. 39 (February 8,
1902), Cody rescues Marcelite Monastery and her quadroon maid and Negro
cook from a gang of bandidos.

the Texas Rangers in order to demolish a coalition of "Yama" Indians from Mexico and a gang of border bandidos. A week later—in the next issue—the Yamas are back again still trying to abduct the Castilian heroine. This time Buffalo Bill slaughters the entire lot.[23]

Fully a decade before the Buffalo Bill series sank on its own demerits in 1912, another had surfaced to outlast all contemporary rivals. From 1902 to 1928, the Wild West Weekly series, penned by anonymous writers under the collective name "An Old Scout" and issued in New York by Frank Tousey Publishers, featured no fewer than 1,294 spectacular escapades of Young Wild West, an "Apollo-like" lad who gallops across the West accompanied by his golden-haired sweetheart, Arietta Murdock, and a large band of followers who are tended by lovers, wives, and Chinese cooks. Young Wild West is a successful capitalist, owner of several ranches and mines. He runs a tightly disciplined, teetotaling organization which has been morally regenerated by its female members. Yet in their attitudes toward greasers, Young Wild West and his Bible-quoting gang are members in good standing of the Buntline-Beadle heritage. Young Wild West himself is a quintessential greaser hater, a man who frequently rides south of the border for no other purpose than to provoke racial hostilities. In *Young Wild West and the Greaser Giant; or, "Mexican Mike's" Mistake* (1919), Wild West deliberately insults the seven-foot Mexican ("Caramba!") Mike. In the course of three pages he downs the hapless giant with a single blow, shoots him twice, forces him

[23] *Buffalo Bill on the Staked Plains; or, Lance, Lasso and Rifle,* The Buffalo Bill Stories, no. 237 (November 25, 1905); and *Buffalo Bill's Border Raid; or, Fighting Redskins and Greasers,* The Buffalo Bill Stories, no. 238 (December 2, 1905). Redskin-bandido alliances abound in the Buffalo Bill series. In *Buffalo Bill's Aztec Runners; or, The Fate of the Gilded Mexican,* The Buffalo Bill Stories, no. 315 (May 25, 1907), Cody aligns himself with the conservative Mexican government to apprehend bandidos who are inciting the Yaqui Indians to revolt. In *Buffalo Bill in Old Mexico; or, The Red Priests of Zataclin,* The Buffalo Bill Stories, no. 325 (August 3, 1907), the Yucatan Indians unite with bandidos to try to sacrifice a white girl. And in *Buffalo Bill's "Totem"; or, The Mystic Symbol of the Yaquis,* The Buffalo Bill Stories, no. 350 (January 5, 1908), bandidos unite with Apaches and Yaquis to capture the Castilian heroine.

to do a street-dance while he shoots off his boot heels, pistol-whips him, shoots a lariat out of his hand, and finally watches him hanged. In *Young Wild West's Scrimmage in Mexico; or, Arietta and the Vaquero Dandy* (1923), the "scrimmage" consists of a barroom brawl with a dozen bandidos, two duels, an abduction, and the near-murder of Arietta at the hands of bandidos before Wild West finally brings the adventure to a close.

In most respects the conquest fiction of the twentieth century offers little more than a restrained coda to that of its predecessor. The Anglo-Saxon's moral and physical superiority over the degenerate Spaniard and the mongrel Mexican remain constant. Color bars remain similarly strong: skin tone is a virtually infallible guide to character and behavior. Only the delivery is more subtle; twentieth-century authors are more self-conscious and defensive in the employment of stereotypes than were the creators of the Beadles and Young Wild West. The audience to which these authors address themselves apparently is perceived as demanding its stereotypes presented with some subtlety. The major innovation in the twentieth-century works is their increased sense of location. The dime novels set their scenes with a few cacti, a desert, and assorted greasers. The modern author usually tries to fix his ethnic images in something more closely resembling a historical setting. For the first time, therefore, conquest fiction can reasonably be considered in terms of the three major areas of the Southwest—Texas, Nuevo México, and California.

The process began with a renewed surge of interest in the Texas Revolution. This was one aspect of a general revival of local-color fiction that followed the enormous success of *Gone With the Wind*, published in 1936. Texas, in particular, offered high drama in a setting combining two regions popular with readers of American romance: the prewar South and the pre-industrial West. Twentieth-century conquest fiction set in Texas closely resembles its nineteenth-century forerunner in both substance and tone. In *North of the Rio Grande*, by Roy Lander Lightfoot, for example, the hero, Tom Todd, attempts to explain what it is about the Mexicans that makes them such an inept foe. Being puny in size, he argues, the Mexicans develop an inferiority complex which makes them puny in both spirit and conduct: "These Mexicans cannot understand that the Anglo-American way of doing things is out in the open and there are no secrets about what they do. . . . These Mexicans are so two-faced that one face is smiling at you while the other is all wrinkled trying to figure out some way to stab you in the back. I don't like that about the Mexicans. . . . It is sort of kissing your hand and kicking you in the pants at the same time."[24]

Other Texan heroes use Mexican cowardice and treachery as points of departure for more ambitious generalizations about the two races and cultures. In *The Road to San Jacinto* (1936) by J. Frank Davis, a young slaveowning Georgian offers an overview of what is bound to happen wherever the two races come together: "The challenge . . . was an Anglo-American challenge to a Latin race and civilization. And it was inevitable that such a challenge should come. . . . Wide as Texas was, there was no room for both these systems to remain. . . . The stream of Anglo-American immigrants . . . had become an ever-widening flood of a breed which could never be assimilated."

The Texans and the Mexicans could not be assimilated for two reasons, both of them having to do with race. The Mexicans are "halfbreeds." They are also opposed to black slavery. At the end of the novel it is left to a woman, a crude pioneer named Mrs. Kempton, to express in unmistakable terms Davis' interpretation of the Texas Revolution. After losing three members of her family in the rebellion, Mrs. Kempton sends her sole surviving son off to war to avenge Santa Anna's antislavery proclamation, telling him to "git ye some Mexicans . . . for Charley and Mary and the baby." "Let him," author Davis admonishes his reader, "who never has had a relative or friend slaughtered in a massacre," dare to condemn the Texans for

[24] Roy Lander Lightfoot, *North of the Rio Grande: A Romance of Texas Pioneer Days*, pp. 92–95, 121–134, 148–155, 197–200.

46

taking revenge on the Alamo by committing similar atrocities at San Jacinto. The author assumes that no Texan who lived through those days can be expected to feel anything but implacable hatred for the Mexican race.[25]

The theme of Texan righteousness and Mexican perversity found still another dimension in the twentieth century. Purely imaginary heroes could hardly bear the moral weight imposed on them by their creators without becoming impossible bores. More and more authors instead began concentrating on five historical actors in the Texas Revolution. All were and remain figures of both history and legend: Stephen Austin, Sam Houston, Jim Bowie, William Travis, and Davy Crockett. Of the five, Houston and Bowie vie for top fictional honors. Crockett remains more Tennessean than Texan. Travis is too much the martinet. Austin, handicapped by a bookish temperament and conciliatory reputation, is often depicted as a kowtowing "submissionist," regarded by the Texan secessionists as little better than the Mexicans. *The Iron Mistress*, for example, a fictional biography of James Bowie by the well-known Western writer Paul Wellman, explains why Austin was admirably suited for peacetime pursuits but poorly equipped for war. His forehead was too high, his mouth too large, his voice too soft, and he used to be a schoolteacher! (p. 372).

Sam Houston is the quintessential Texan of twentieth-century conquest fiction. In the lines of his brow can be traced the troubled course of the Lone Star Republic. From his lips flow Biblical passages about Manifest Destiny and God's Chosen People. Part of his appeal, however, also lies in his fallibility. In *The Lone Star*, by Eugene P. Lyle, Houston is introduced as a sniveling drunkard who has been squatting for months in a remote Cherokee camp, bottle in one hand, *The Iliad* in the other, moping about his bride's rejection of him on their wedding night. Rescued from ruin by Bowie, Houston is transformed overnight from "The Big Drunk" to a "Paleface Viking" who journeys to Texas to free his countrymen from the yoke of Santa Anna. Dee Brown's *Wave High*

[25] J. Frank Davis, *The Road to San Jacinto*, pp. 29–37, 63–82, 313.

the Banner similarly portrays Houston as the frontiersman incarnate, friend of Andrew Jackson and symbol of yeoman, republican America.[26]

James Bowie shares Houston's status as the most eulogized hero of the revolution. When asked by a fellow Texan about the future relations between the Texans and the Mexicans, Bowie explains that the two races are on a collision course because the Mexicans are "completely devoid of reason." Particularly in Wellman's *The Iron Mistress*, Bowie is a paragon of American virtue. Strolling the streets of San Antonio like a blond god, he is showered with compliments by the rich and powerful while the greaser rabble stop dead in their tracks to gawk at the brawny Americano. When the Mexicans march on San Antonio, Bowie declares that since each Texan is worth ten Mexicans, the odds of ninety-two Texans to five hundred Mexicans are actually in their favor.[27]

If twentieth-century conquest fiction makes increasing use of Anglo historical heroes, it also draws a major Mexican stereotype from history: President and Dictator Antonio López de Santa Anna. Moncure Lyne's *From the Alamo to San Jacinto* expands upon the burning of Texan corpses at the Alamo with sadistic thoroughness: "The fire, the cruel, hungry fire, like the Mexicans, knew no mercy. . . . The fumes from the pyre were horrible in the extreme, mingling as they did the smell of burnt wood, charred human flesh, and the buckskin suits of the defenders of the Alamo . . . Santa Anna's. To [Santa Anna] it seemed as incense" (pp. 287–288). In Davis' *Road to San Jacinto* the Napoleon of Mexico pretends to despise black slavery while systematically enslaving the brown peons of his country. In Wellman's *The Iron Mistress* he takes opium and cavorts with a mulatto mistress in his ribbon-bedecked tent on

---

[26] Eugene P. Lyle, *The Lone Star*, pp. 35, 115, 431; Dee Brown, *Wave High the Banner: A Novel Based on the Life of Davy Crockett*, pp. 317–319. Cf. also Davis, *Road to San Jacinto*, p. 116, and Wellman, *Iron Mistress*, p. 314.

[27] Lightfoot, *North of the Rio Grande*, pp. 76–88; Wellman, *Iron Mistress*, pp. 3, 248–265, 366–377. Another fictionalized biography of Bowie that is long on Bowie's heroism and short on the conditions that led to the revolution is Monte Barrett, *Tempered Blade*.

the battlefield. Dee Brown goes so far as to describe Santa Anna as Mexico's Mussolini, the New World equivalent of the Old World dictators who were threatening the western world when *Wave High the Banner* was written.

At this point it is worthwhile to remember that popular fiction remains fiction even when based on historical characters. More than that, it remains conventional fiction; that is, it demands acceptable resolutions to traditional problems of plot and character. In a genre that requires easily identified heroes and villains, there can be no doubt about who is which. Just as surely as there must be a positive Texan stereotype, so there must be a corresponding Mexican negative stereotype. Nevertheless, the fact remains that twentieth-century conquest novels with a Texas setting offer no essential differences between the historical ruler of the Mexican Republic and a Beadle bandido.[28]

In modern fiction treating the American conquest of New Mexico, a long series of Yankee trappers, traders, and merchants replace the Texan filibusterers and revolutionaries as the conquering Saxon heroes. These northerners, however, dislike what they see in New Mexico almost as much as the southerners disliked what they saw in Texas. They serve the same role: advance scouts of a westward-marching, destiny-conscious nation. In *Drum Up the Dawn* by Arthur Carhart, the protagonist, Sergeant William Meek, is more than a courageous hero who contests Spanish authority in New Mexico. He is the publicity agent for America. Captured by Spanish soldiers while on the Pike expedition of 1806, Meek and his men are marched through the upper Rio Grande villages to Santa Fe, commenting freely on Spanish culture as they go. Spaniards are forever

---

[28] Among many other accounts of the Alamo that vary little in their treatments of Santa Anna as brute and the "Texians" as heroic democrats are Birdsall Briscoe, *Spurs from San Isidro: A Novel of the Southwest*; John Earl Brown, *Yesteryears of Texas*; Willis Vernon Cole, *The Star of the Alamo*; Gertrude Crownfield, *Lone Star Rising*; John H. Culp, *The Men of Gonzales*; Clara Driscoll, *In the Shadow of the Alamo*; Leonard London Foreman, *The Road to San Jacinto*; Steve Frazee, *The Alamo*; Foy Gillespie, *The Defenders*; Elmer Staffelbach, *For Texas and Freedom*; and Clarke Venable, *All the Brave Rifles*.

"roosting" their rumps up against whatever means of support happens to be handy, screwing their shoulders into the crumbling adobe walls so it is impossible to tell whether they are holding up the walls or being held up by them. They are so busy doing nothing that their bodies sprout moss on the north side. The principal native occupation is flea scratching, which serves a useful purpose because it enables Spaniards to take exercise without exerting themselves. Even more than by Spanish "laziness" and "filth," however, Sergeant Meek and his men are galled by what they regard as Spanish stupidity and cowardice.

Meek's confrontation with the Spanish governor of New Mexico, Colonel Joaquín del Real Alencastre, is a classic in fictional confrontations between the two peoples. Small-boned and rickety, with a quixotic goatee jutting beneath a beaked nose and covering a weak chin, Alencastre is the prototypical degenerate Spaniard. He dresses elegantly, preens in front of a mirror, and tries to cover his feelings of inferiority by heavy drinking. When Meek is summoned before Alencastre and told to kneel as a token of respect, the American spits out the ultimate insult: "All Spaniards look alike to me." Jailed for his impudence, Meek breaks free and, calling on the besotted governor during the dinner hour, announces himself as "William Epluribus Unum Meek," recently appointed ambassador extraordinary of the United States to New Mexico. Alencastre, too drunk to see through the hoax, apologizes for being temporarily indisposed and sends Meek and his men back to St. Louis freed of all espionage charges.[29]

With the establishment of Mexican independence, the accusations of cowardice and ineptitude made by Meek against the Spaniards are simply transferred by other heroes to the Spaniards' tainted progeny, the Mexicans. In *Eagle in the Sun* (1935), by Hoffman Birney, the hero offers a popular Yankee explanation for Mexican timidity: "Mexicans were proud and patriotic; but they couldn't fight. There was something in their

[29] Arthur Hawthorne Carhart, *Drum Up the Dawn*, pp. 29–49, 63–79, 96–138, 184–197.

characters that made them cut and run rather than face a stub-
born foe whom they might outnumber ten to one. . . . No
Mexican ever seemed able to avoid a punch, particularly one
directed toward his face. They didn't know how to fight with
their fists" (p. 128).

This specific inability is a major theme of Anna Burr's *The
Golden Quicksand* (1936). Secretly harboring feelings of jealousy and fear of the giants from the East, the slack-bodied
New Mexican males of Santa Fe lounge in the shade of the
plaza, wringing their womanly hands in despair each time a
female of their race slaps her thighs and wiggles her buttocks
at the big blond gringos. When these pathetically effete figures try to take revenge, they come off the worse for it. A large
band of perfumed native New Mexicans jumps a single Yankee
at a Taos fandango, whereupon the Yankee's fellow-Americans
form a shoulder-to-shoulder phalanx, toss the greasers through
the air, and slam them up against the wall in a broken heap.

The undisputed fictional symbol of New Mexican cowardice, however, is not a creature of fiction, but Governor Manuel
Armijo. From 1838, when he became governor of the province,
until the arrival of the American armies eight years later,
Armijo was the absolute but uneasy ruler of New Mexico.
Plagued by raiding Comanches, a depleted treasury, and heavy
dependence on the Yankee trading caravans for economic survival, Armijo was viewed by many contemporaries as a talented
but ingenuous man who tried to be all things to all factions
and wound up failing everyone. Recent historians have similarly treated him relatively kindly. In fiction, however, he plays
a role equivalent to that assigned to Santa Anna in the Texas
novels. Ruth Laughlin's *The Wind Leaves No Shadow* features
a barroom showdown between Armijo and a tall Yankee trader
named Fox:

> "Get out of here if you value your life!" Don Manuel shouted
> to Fox. . . . "This place is not large enough for both of us."
> Fox smiled under his broad-brimmed hat and held his glass
> of whiskey in a steady hand. The other hand rested on his hip
> beside his gun. He was known to be a dead shot. He drawled

casually, "I'm enjoying my drink. If this place is not large enough for both of us, I reckon you had better get out" (p. 175).

His bluff called, Armijo turns cringing coward. His bloated body shrinks, his jaw slackens, his eyes bulge out, and his Negroid lips flap incoherently. Just as he is about to be killed, a female gambler places herself between the two men. Faced with a female adversary, Fox drawls, "I'll take on any number of men, but I don't fight women. If he has to hide behind your skirts, ma'am, you win," and stalks out (p. 176). Waiting until the Texan is at a safe distance, Armijo then declares that his patience was almost exhausted and congratulates the woman for sparing the Texan's life.

One novel which attempts a more rounded presentation of Armijo is *The Time of the Gringo* by Elliott Arnold. Arnold's Armijo is cruel, dishonest, vain, and vindictive. He also, however, possesses common sense and solid insight into his country's problems. He is particularly eloquent when discussing one of those problems, the gringo invader: "We are prisoners to the gringos! They own us, our bodies and our souls. The whole year we wait for them, a country, a people, a government holding its breath. . . . We are a joke. We are comical. We are not a nation of men; we are beggars who survive on the garbage of gringos. . . . My poor country is the tail to the American dog."[30]

Armijo's decrying of the New Mexicans' dependence upon the garbage of gringos illustrates the principal theme in most novels about the conquest of New Mexico: the economic infiltration of the province. General Kearny's bloodless invasion of New Mexico has not inspired novelists. Few bother even to discuss military maneuverings and battlefield strategies. More appealing is the influx of Yankee traders who arrived in advance of the U.S. Army and managed their own conquest of a sizable amount of New Mexican real estate by marrying into the resident upper class. The novels that treat this subject are numerous; their plots are virtually identical. Typical is *The*

[30] Elliott Arnold, *The Time of the Gringo*, pp. 7–14, 133–417, 453.

Rose of Santa Fe by Edwin L. Sabin, which matches Richard Andrews of Cincinnati with Señorita Rosa Isidro Gonzales, a pale-hued aristocrat who is contractually bound to an effete blueblood named Don Antonio García y Alarid. The confrontation between Alarid and Andrews, though less violent than many such showdowns in southwestern fiction, is yet another illustration of Yankee courage and efficiency competing with New Mexican cowardice and ineptitude. The two men hunt buffalo. The perfumed and powdered *rico* ropes a bull, with the idea of dragging it to Rosa's feet so she can place her dainty slipper upon the beast's shaggy head before he kills it. Instead, the bull charges him. Alarid flees in disgrace and is rescued from sure death by Dick Andrews, who meanwhile has shot a dozen buffalo without ceremony. Rosa, paying the Yankee trader the ultimate compliment ("Your deeds are greater than your words"), adds that unfortunately she is contracted to marry inside her class and religion. Not easily discouraged, Andrews discovers a lost gold mine near Santa Fe, sets himself up in business, rescues Rosa from hostile Indians, and, having proved his capabilities as a fighter and provider, finally lets it be known that he is actually a practicing Catholic—a fact that he kept to himself until he was certain that Rosa would marry him whether he was a heretic or not. Since Rosa's father had no sons, Andrews also inherits his father-in-law's estate.[31]

The American penetration of New Mexico's social and financial order leaves little room for Mexican men of either the lower or the "higher" sort. They rarely appear in modern conquest fiction set in New Mexico. When they do, they are usually depicted as degenerate, cowardly, and generally inept —inherent racial characteristics that are bound to relegate them to inferior positions in Yankee New Mexico. In *The American* (1934), by Louis Dodge, a Yankee businessman who

[31] Edwin L. Sabin, *The Rose of Santa Fe*, pp. 51–77, 94, 160, 306–307. Other examples of this genre include Harvey Fergusson, *Wolf Song*; Blanche C. Grant, *Dona Lona: A Story of Old Taos and Santa Fe*; Alida Sims Malkus, *Caravans to Santa Fe*; Frank O'Rourke, *The Far Mountains;* and Hallie Hall Violette and Ada Claire Darly, *On The Trail to Santa Fe.*

has married into the Santa Fe aristocracy summarizes what is financially and socially "wrong" with the males of New Mexico:

> You can't speak to them the way we speak to one another, saying what you mean, saving time. You have to back away and approach around a dozen corners and bow and offer a cigarette—when you haven't a minute to lose, and want to talk about business. Pleasure before business—there you have it! . . . Life is to them an everlasting social function, or a sort of minuet. . . . If you shout at one of them it takes him a week to get over it— it's as if you had tarred and feathered him. . . . I can get along with the Mexican women fine; it's only the men that don't suit me.[32]

The major change in the image of the Mexican in twentieth-century conquest fiction develops when we reach California. In contrast to his nineteenth-century image of effeminate indolence, the Californio don, in most modern works set in Spanish or Mexican California, is the shining knight of the sunshine province. That he is maligned and persecuted by the incoming Americans makes him all the more appealing—a southwestern equivalent of the antebellum southern gentleman. Indeed, modern American writers feel so passionately about the dispossessed don that he is sometimes permitted to join the ranks of an elite of western fiction: the wronged outlaw.

This is not entirely a literary invention. Some Californio dons, once their lands were seized by the Americans, did indeed become bandits, launching raids against American ranches, farms, and gold camps in postconquest California.[33] The historical figure lending particular credibility to the stereo-

[32] Louis Dodge, *The American*, pp. 258–262, 277, 279.

[33] Joseph Henry Jackson, *Bad Company: The Story of California's Legendary and Actual Stage-robbers, Bandits, Highwaymen and Outlaws from the Fifties to the Eighties*, pp. xii-xiii, argues that Anglo bandits usually turned to robbery to make a living, while Mexicans had the additional motive of revenge. Leonard Pitt, *The Decline of the Californios: A Social History of the Spanish-Speaking Californians, 1846–1890*, p. 262, estimates that "16 to 20 percent of San Quentin inmates from 1854 to 1865 were Mexicans or Californians," which represented a much higher proportion of Mexican American prisoners than the proportion of Mexican American residents of California.

type is Joaquín Murrieta. That almost nothing is known about Murrieta adds to his fictional potential as a victimized California caballero, a man of "ancient and honorable family" who turns outlaw because of persecution and prejudice.[34] Murrieta's appeal to American readers is also clearly based on his general superiority to the run of his race. He may be a "Mexican" but he looks and acts like a "Spaniard." In Walter Noble Burns's *The Robin Hood of El Dorado* (1932); Dane Coolidge's *Gringo Gold: A Story of Joaquín Murrieta the Bandit* (1939); Samuel Anthony Peeples' *The Dream Ends in Fury* (1949), and a host of paperbacks, including numerous modern ones, the pattern is similar. Born in Sonora of high family and educated in the best schools in Mexico City, the light-skinned Murrieta leaves Mexico because he is "fired with enthusiastic admiration of the American character." Young Joaquín travels to California only to learn that the Americans are not the noble-hearted race he had thought them to be. They make no distinction between pure "Castilians" like himself and the Mexican rabble. They are also cruel and greedy. Beaten and driven from his mining claim after watching his woman ravished before his eyes, Joaquín turns to farming. Beaten again, he tries mining a second time. Driven again from his claim, he is beaten yet a third time. Joaquín's righteous wrath finally leads him to crime. His male companions are dashing California caballeros; the women are lovely "Castilian" camp followers who tend the fires but sleep by themselves. Robin Hoods and Maid Marions all, Joaquín's band of merry men and motherly women steal from the American rich to give to the Californio poor. On the point of retiring peacefully to Mexico, he is brought down by vindictive gringo vigilantes.

The success of the numerous Murrieta novels encouraged other writers to develop the wronged-bandit theme with a totally fictitious protagonist. One of Bret Harte's most popular stories, "The Passing of Enríquez," centers upon a scion of an

---

[34] "Yellow Bird" John Rollin Ridge, *The Life and Adventures of Joaquín Murrieta, The Celebrated California Bandit* (Norman: University of Oklahoma Press, 1955). For a recent biography of Murrieta, see William B. Secrest, *Joaquín: Bloody Bandit of the Mother Lode: The Story of Joaquín Murrieta.*

ancient California "Castilian" family who discovers gold on his estate and hires a group of Yankee technicians and capitalists to develop it. The Americans urge him to cover up the fact that an underground obstruction will make the mining more costly than anticipated. Enríquez replies that there "is not enough gold in your bank, in your San Francisco, in the mines of California, that shall buy a Spanish gentleman." After his disgusted wife rejects him for an engineering professor, he sells out his interest in the mine, retires in poverty to a remote corner of his former three-league estate, and at the end of the story is swallowed up in an earthquake while riding the range with his infant son.[35]

An even more eloquent presentation of the wronged don is Lanier and Sylvia Bartlett's novel *Adios* (1929). Published in five editions in the United States and three in the British Empire and made into a movie, it introduces as its hero Don Francisco Mariano José Delfina, alias El Puma. A dispossessed don with pale skin and blue eyes, El Puma robs the gringo rich to give to the Californio poor and kills only in self-defense. Toward the close of the novel he is mortally wounded by a sheriff, who loves his sister Anita. Refusing to bear a grudge, El Puma conceals his wound, pays a visit to his sister, and gives his blessing to her marriage to the man who has mortally wounded him. Pursued into the mountains by the unrelenting sheriff, El Puma rides to the edge of a cliff, whispers *adios* to his horse, and as the sheriff rides up, the don offers him the animal as a wedding present and leaps into a waterfall that will carry him, by way of the river, to the western sea.

For all their sensationalism and pathos, extreme even in this genre, these and similar works almost invariably present the Californio don sympathetically. He is a figure not only deserving compassion, but embodying a certain kind of competence as well. And these qualities are recognized by his conquerors, at least those of the better sort: ship captains, army

[35] Bret Harte, "The Devotion of Enríquez," *Century Magazine*, November, 1895; and Bret Harte, "The Passing of Enríquez," in *Stories in Light and Shadow*, pp. 244–304.

officers, journalists, men of education and culture. In Peter Kyne's *Tide of Empire*, the Irish-American protagonist describes:

> A wonderful people doomed to oppression and extinction as surely as the Indian. All that these Californians desire from strangers is courtesy and a square deal; dwelling here in pastoral peace, practically without government, dependent upon a code of gallant human conduct, they will be as helpless in the hands of the eager, greedy, empire-building Anglo-Saxon as a sheep in the maw of a tiger. For the wonderful *dolce far niente* spirit that is theirs they will be hated by men who know not how to suck the sweetness from life; for their lack of industry and commerical shrewdness they will be despised as weaklings, regarded as ripe fruit to be plucked and wasted.[Pp. 32–34]

The Californio don, in short, is the one Spanish or Mexican character in popular culture with a southwestern setting who has acquired the status of folk hero—at least in the hearts and minds of the race that destroyed him. Perhaps this process was aided by history. The actual conquest was not entirely bloodless, but there were no Alamos, Goliads, or San Jacintos. Whatever the reason, the Californio grandee remains a symbol of an idyll which its destroyers now commemorate in parades and festivals. He is a fantasy figure which has become an enduring part of our national vision of California as a golden land of prelapsarian innocence and charm. At odd moments probably even the most skeptical of us allow our thoughts to play over the enduring image of the Spanish garden of the Pacific and to concede with mingled pride and regret: "Once it was different out there."

The nostalgic image of the Californio don does not, however, obscure the fact that little change in the treatment of Mexican characters can be discerned in conquest fiction from the 1830's to the 1940's. Whether contemporary tales of the Texas Revolution, dime novels and weekly pulps, or historical romances after the pattern of Margaret Mitchell, such fiction emphasizes color as an ultimate determinant of character. "Good" or "upper-crust" Mexicans are invariably light. Color determines whether Mexican women will be cast-off harlots or first-lead Castilian heroines who might qualify as mates for the Saxon heroes. Color determines whether Mexican men are to be foes or friends. Mexican stereotypes have, of course, their equivalents in other romantic adventure fiction. The gentleman bandit and the Castilian heroine, for example, are products of a color code operating within the white race as well as outside its ranks—witness the novels of James Fenimore Cooper.

Yet crude color stereotyping is not the sole explanation for the role of the Mexican in conquest fiction. This point can best be illustrated by considering in some detail the character of the greaser bandido. He dominates the pages of popular American literature in this ninety-year period, outnumbering all other Mexican characters combined. How much of the treatment of these bandidos was prompted by racism, and how much simply involved the demands of formula fiction? How badly do the brown-skinned bandidos fare when compared to "white" pulp-fiction bandits? How much are they victims of ethnic prejudice and how much of mere plot convention? The answer depends largely on whether we are speaking of stereotyping in terms of action or appearance. The action situations employed in the dime novels—with the puppet-villains stumbling over cliffs, stampeding getaway horses, dozing while on sentry duty, binding the heroine too loosely, or botching the fast draw—are stock devices assigned impartially to all dime-novel bandits, whatever their race or hue. As readers we are placed in the position either of accepting such devices as conventions of the genre or of putting the novel aside altogether. Contrived combinations of malice and incompetence may offend our critical sensibilities, but by themselves they can hardly be called props supporting racism. The feeble plot line that holds together the border dime novels, however shakily, is the same assumption that binds all dime novels. No matter how many times the villains fall prey to the heroes' cleverness or courage, they will seek renewed engagements until they are summarily dispatched at the end of the required dime-novel length.

58

Only when we turn from stereotypical behavior to stereo-typical appearance do we encounter distinctly "greaser" traits and trappings. Some of these—the "half-breed" clothing, the "Tex-Mex" slang, the ubiquitous cornshuck cigarette, the ready use of the blade, the relative difference in skin color—are accurate to a point. Border Mexicans did dress and talk differently both from Anglos and from Mexicans living farther south. They did smoke cornshuck cigarettes. They did prefer knives to fisti-cuffs. The problem, in other words, does not involve creating completely imaginary fictitious stereotypes but of first assign-ing negative values to dress or appearance and then drawing selective conclusions about them. For example, the cigarette-smoking greasers expose uniformly nicotine-stained teeth, while the pipe-puffing Saxons flash pearl-white smiles. This image, however, is a too-general distinguishing mark between hero and villain to be really disturbing. Most white dime-novel ban-dits are also in need of dental attention. More serious is the failure to account for the Mexican preference for knives to guns or fists. No dime-novel writer pauses to instruct us on the fact that border Spanish/Mexican communities historically lacked gunpowder or that close-quarter *mano a mano* knife play was considered by many Mexicans to be more courageous than a long-distance gunfight. Nor do the dime-novel writers discuss other Mexican activities, such as bullfighting and grizzly roping, that can hardly be called acts of cowardice. Such historical and cultural subtleties were beyond the parameters of the dime novel, just as they remain beyond the parameters of the twentieth-century pulp western. What this neglect achieved, however, was massively to reinforce the theme of interracial conflict which already dominated conquest fiction. The overwhelming image of such fiction, whatever its date of composition, is one of deep and abiding hatred of white for brown and brown for white. The hostility cuts both ways and is assumed to be as permanent as the racial barriers be-tween the two peoples. When the Saxon hero in Sam S. Hall's Beadle dime novel *The Merciless Marauders; or, Chaparral Carl's Revenge* (p. 23), throws a dark-skinned villain over a cliff into the Rio Grande, he shouts "Adios, Greaser," a farewell repeated, literally or metaphorically, in countless other novels. And the hapless victim shrieks an epithet as he flies downward that could serve as epigram for the Mexican reaction to the conquest of the Southwest: *"Diablo Americano! Demonio Gringo!"*

CHAPTER THREE

WOMEN OF THE CONQUEST

THE MOST OBVIOUS and least interesting female stereotype in conquest fiction is the halfbreed harlot. Her primary function is a familiar one in formula fiction: to provide as much sexual titillation as current censorship standards will permit. She is inevitably portrayed as the product of a tainted racial heritage, possessing every negative quality—negative, at least, by the standards of Mrs. Grundy. In *Guy Raymond: A Story of the Texas Revolution* by Edward Plummer Alsbury, a halfbreed tart confides to the blond hero that the foundation of Mexican culture rests on seduction followed by contrite confession that opens the way to future infractions. In *The Dark Comes Early* by Pendleton Hogan, a slothful mestiza flirt sarcastically named Pia (meaning "pious") Iturbe is described as "a lithe, dark, attractive vixen" who contains in her voluptuous body "all the characteristics of the women of her race: fire, an adoration of scenes, a love of love."[1] Acceptable for flirtation, sometimes even for bedding, these "dirty halfbreeds" can be no fit subjects for marriage. In *Sun in Their Eyes* by Monte Barrett, for example, the hero Jonathan Kirk is temporarily attracted to Teresa de Lerdo, a lowborn Mediterranean woman who qualifies temporarily as a "Castilian" blueblood only because she *looks* more or less white. Long after we are aware

[1] Edward Plummer Alsbury, *Guy Raymond: A Story of the Texas Revolution*, pp. 15–18, 41–57, 531–533; Pendleton Hogan, *The Dark Comes Early: An American Novel*, pp. 26–27, 113–134.

that she is a self-interested slut and a halfbreed to boot, Jonathan continues to believe that Teresa is both pure-blooded and, even while he beds her, pure-minded. His awakening comes only when she dons a sheer nightgown at mid-day, bares her bosom, and demands that Jonathan make love to her on the spot:

> "Have you lost your mind?" he muttered.
> "Yes, Jontee, yes! What is love but madness?"
> Her lust turned him cold. He had never seen a woman throw away all restraint before and it disgusted him. [P. 266]

Realizing finally that Teresa is a trollop, Jonathan rejoins the loyal southern heroine Cissy Marsten, who has been waiting patiently for him to recover his senses.

Cissy Marsten is typical of the second woman of the conquest: the white virgin, apparently solid from the ankles upward, who patiently rationalizes her husband-to-be's sowing of wild oats on the grounds that he is preserving her own virginity. She is a central character in most conquest fiction, and her hapless rival, the halfbreed harlot, is her necessary counterpart. The harlot fulfills the libidinous needs of the man who will eventually reject her, and she guarantees the chastity of the woman he will eventually marry. Always, however, she is a secondary character. The primary sexual emphasis is on the purity of the white heroine and the corresponding ultimate redemption of the white hero, who is rarely condemned for his transgressions unless he sows oats with white virgins. His return to the embrace and the forgiveness of the white heroine is made possible because the halfbreed harlot is presumed to have been the aggressor. In *The Common Heart*, Paul Horgan offers a common fictional explanation of why the "mixed-blood" women of the Southwest threw themselves at the big blond Americans:

> A heat came on them suddenly . . . when they saw blue eyes, or yellow hair, or pink skin. . . . The soldiers were on the average much bigger than the men of New Mexico. They had laughing humors and in comparison with the dark-skinned New Mexi-

cans, they seemed very open-faced and innocent. They were, in brief, like a lot of huge boys. . . . They were gay without getting drunk, and as conquerors, they were more like guests at a party, charmed with the arrangements, wide-eyed at the social novelties they beheld, and certain that everyone was as nice as could be. [Pp. 41–42]

Repeatedly the theme is sounded: halfbreed flirts may appeal to the American male's baser instincts, but they must be rejected because their religion, their complexions, and their pasts are shadowed. Nevertheless, the overwhelming odds against the dark-hued ladies of the evening do not deter them from frantic efforts to land an American mate. In Ruth Laughlin's *The Wind Leaves No Shadow*, set in Armijo's Santa Fe, the mestiza gambling queen Doña Tules aggressively courts a blond colossus named Jim Matthews, who is spoken for by a New Bedford, Massachusetts, girl named Abigail Bradford. The "pure-blooded" and pure-minded Abigail is everything that the impure, unprincipled, and unwashed Tules is not: a gray-eyed, snow-white Miss Clean who launches fierce attacks on each speck of dust that seeps into her Cape Cod house and provides more long-distance competition than Tules can handle. That we never meet this Yankee woman is testimony to her power. Each time Matthews is tempted by the "half-nude halfbreeds," he is brought up short by memories of Abigail, who would be incensed by the sin, dirt, and "bad blood" of New Mexico. Tules herself, glancing in disgust at her own dark skin, recognizes the dimensions of her disadvantage and in Matthews' best interest sends him back to the ivory-white Abigail.[2] In Elliott Arnold's *The Time of the Gringo*, with a similar setting, the women of New Mexico are similarly drawn to the big blond invaders. Indeed, they are drawn so irresistibly that when the Yankee caravaners come to town, even women of fine family—no common hookers—take to the streets, slithering and sliding, bumping and grinding in a series of demeaning gyrations calculated to ensnare an American passerby—*any* American passerby:

[2] Ruth Laughlin, *The Wind Leaves No Shadow*, pp. 137–151, 290.

The New Mexican woman slapped her groin and wiggled her
buttocks. The American pushed her away. She ran around in
front of him, pleading, posturing, touching him with her hands.
He pushed her away again. . . . A New Mexican male slapped
the American and drew his knife. The American roared with
laughter and . . . lifted him bodily and hurled him through the
air onto a small fire. . . . The American picked up a water jug
and dumped it on the blazing man . . . and then he turned him
around and booted him away. . . . A moment later the woman
accosted another American. He did not refuse her. [Pp. 32–33]

The *chola* halfbreed teaches another moral lesson as well.
Conquest novelists generally tend to regard promiscuity and
Catholicism as virtually synonymous, with the ritual of confession abetting moral laxity. Pia Iturbe, introduced earlier as
typical of the sensuous halfbreed, races to the mission after
each transgression, confesses, repents, and is ready to do the
same thing over again.

Bret Harte also links Catholicism and sin in "What Happened at the Fonda" (1903). The "heroine" Cota Ramierez,
illegitimate offspring of an overnight liaison between a married
woman of "low blood" and a Spanish grandee, is compared to
"a mongrel mare of the extraordinary type known as a 'pinto,'
or 'calico' horse," whose "greenish gray eyes, in which too
much of the white was visible, had . . . a singular similarity of
expression to Cota's own." Cota is regarded by her creator as
little better than an animal in heat, using the confessional box
to relieve her sense of sin. In "A Pupil of Chestnut Ridge"
(1903), Harte made an even more explicit connection between
Catholicism and "half-breed" promiscuity. In the backwoods
community of Chestnut Ridge, California, the New England
schoolmaster, Mr. Brooks, is sought out by a childless couple,
the Hoovers, who have adopted an eleven-year-old Mexican
girl. Eager to redeem the "pre-adolescent" girl, Concha, from
"Papism, the Scarlet Woman, saints, Virgin Marys, visions, and
miracles" by rerouting her into the Free Will Baptist Church
and enlisting her in Mr. Brooks's school, Mrs. Hoover presents
the qualifier:

"But that's one thing more we oughter tell ye. She's—she's a trifle dark complected. . . . She isn't a nigger nor an Injin, ye know, but she's kinder a half-Spanish, half-Mexican Injin, what they call 'mes—mes'—"

"Mestiza," suggested Mr. Brooks; "a half-breed or mongrel."

Though Brooks agrees to take Concha as a pupil, more formidable crises arise when Concha flirts with him during lessons, dances sensually during the noon hour, and finally flees to live out of wedlock with a mestizo suitor. Schoolmaster Brooks is genuinely shocked; but Concha's erstwhile foster parents take the news philosophically: "She wasn't no child, Mr. Brooks," Mrs. Hoover tells him, "she was a grown woman —accordin' to these folks' ways and ages—when she kem here. And that's what bothered me."[3]

If the primary role of the flirtatious halfbreed is to combine sexual titillation with anti-Catholic moralizing, conquest fiction does feature some women who have at least the opportunity to gain the permanent attentions of the American conquerors: the "dark ladies." The dark lady is not confined to southwestern fiction. Well-known examples in mainstream American literature include Hester Prynne, Zenobia, and Miriam in Nathaniel Hawthorne's *The Scarlet Letter*, *The Blithedale Romance*, and *The Marble Faun*, respectively; a number of female characters in James Fenimore Cooper's *Leatherstocking Tales*, the most familiar being Cora of *The Last of the Mohicans*; and, on a somewhat more exotic plane, the Polynesian women in Melville's *Omoo: A Narrative of Adventures in the South Seas* and *Typee: A Romance of the South Seas*.[4]

The dark lady of the Southwest, however, has enough unique qualities to make her *sui generis*. Above all, she exists in two categories. One of the more durable "Spanish" figures

[3] Bret Harte, "What Happened at the Fonda," *From Band Hill to Pine: A Tourist from Injianny*, pp. 193–233; Bret Harte, "A Pupil of Chestnut Ridge," *Trent's Trust: The Crusade of the Excelsior*, IV, 211–230.

[4] For discussions of the roles of light and dark "white" women in classic American Literature, see D. H. Lawrence's *Studies in Classic American Literature* and Henry Nash Smith's analysis of Cooper's heroines in *Virgin Land: The American West as Symbol and Myth*, pp. 62ff.

in modern southwestern literature is the portly and priest-dominated Fat Mama. Once a youthful coquette, vivacious and attractive, this middle-aged doña has grown dumpy in her behavior and dogmatic in her beliefs. Perhaps the most merciless characterization of a ponderous and useless señora occurs in a novel written by another woman: Amelia Barr's *Remember: The Alamo* (1888). Doña María Flores, a handsome, rich, and wellborn daughter of one of San Antonio's first families, is overweight, indolent, and ignorant. Even her husband, a Scottish-American doctor, concludes ruefully that her bulk, appearance, and lack of common sense do not reflect her wealth and pedigree. Civilized enough to hold her own intellectually with the best of her race, Doña María is woefully unable to measure up to her husband. When she enters his well-stocked library, the sight of so many books drives her to distraction, and she falls back on reciting paternosters to compensate for intellectual inferiority. Still handsome in feature, she turns fat and sluggish in middle age from sipping chocolate in bed. When not dozing with "luxurious indolence," Doña María passes the daytime hours smoking endless cornshuck cigarettes, preening before the mirror, and waddling to and from mass. The slightest disruption of this daily routine throws her into fits of rage which lend force to her husband's conclusion that she is, after all, "but a grown-up baby." Doña Salazar of Harvey Fergusson's *Wolf Song* divides her days among sleeping, praying, drinking chocolate, and daydreaming of old-time extramarital affairs with gringos, priests, and "so many others." Doña López y Chávez, the aging matron in *Caravans to Santa Fe*, by Alida Sims Malkus, is another carbon copy: a fat and sad woman anchored with jewelry and caked with white flour who squats in the corner of the *sala*, tapping pudgy feet in rhythm to guitars played for somebody else and dreaming of past adulterous escapades.

The halfbreed harlot of conquest fiction sounds one kind of warning to Anglo protagonists. The decayed doña sounds another, more subtle but no less illuminating: Spanish women do not wear well. The young, lovely, slender heroines who grace the pages of conquest fiction are constantly juxtaposed against the homely and heavy doñas they are fated to become twenty years hence. It therefore behooves aspiring American suitors to look their prospective "Castilian" mothers-in-law over carefully before they decide to marry their daughters. And the young Spanish heroines themselves are warned that they can see the image of their own destinies written in the sagging faces of their mothers, especially if they continue to sip sweet chocolate.[5]

This unmistakable note of warning, missing in other portrayals of the dark lady, indicates the strength of the color barrier in conquest fiction. But while the fruit stays fresh, it can be sufficiently enticing to justify the risks—particularly if it is served American-style. "Castilian" heroines generally require a good deal of acculturation before they are permitted to court the Saxon heroes. A good example of the process is Josefa Urrea in Moncure Lyne's *From the Alamo to San Jacinto*. Descended from "the purest Spanish" stock, Josefa is nevertheless seduced early in the action by a greaser who sneers, "I shall take by force what is denied me by caprice." Fleeing this fellow, Josefa takes shelter in a San Antonio convent, where she is rescued by the southern hero, blond and blue-eyed Charles Dabney of Dabney Plantation, Virginia, who is variously described as a "cavalier scion," a "sculptured god," and an "Apollo Belvedere." Shortly after freeing Josefa from the convent, Dabney launches into a long lecture about the shortcomings of his lady's race. Mexican men are cowardly hypocrites. Mexican women, even high-toned Castilians like Josefa, are intemperate and hyperemotional. Determined to reform his love by curbing her passions, Dabney informs Josefa that "no race loves more tenderly or tenaciously than we Americans; for our love is a compound—having the endurance of the Norseman, the music of the Saxon, and the ardor of the Nor-

[5] Harvey Fergusson, *Wolf Song*, pp. 46–60; Alida Sims Malkus, *Caravans to Santa Fe*, pp. 15–16. Other examples of portly and priest-ridden doñas appear in Arnold, *Time of the Gringo*; G. W. Barrington, *Back from Goliad*; Harvey Fergusson, *Grant of Kingdom*; and Paul I. Wellman, *The Iron Mistress*.

man." He proceeds to tell his prospective wife that she will make an adequate bride under careful supervision.[6]

Such moral lectures are a sufficiently common feature of the conquest novels to suggest the hypothesis that they are meant to symbolize the social and economic transformation of the more salvageable (female) portion of the inferior race. Indeed, the marriages and the Saxon Mission, the matches and the Protestant Message, become one and the same thing in the mind of both the Texan heroes and their creators.

The price which the few chosen Castilian females must pay for admission into the favored race is regarded by Castilians and Saxons alike as indeed a small one: desertion of the males of their race, who give up all too easily—slinking offstage with little protest as their women side with the enemy in overwhelming numbers. In Edward Alsbury's *Guy Raymond*, Beatrice Navarro, daughter of a prominent San Antonio *hidalgo* of the old order, actually lists her qualifications for enlistment in the new American order: she has been educated in the United States, she is whiter than most sunburned Texans, she is wealthy, and she supports the Texan cause. In *Back From Goliad* by G. W. Barrington, the "Castilian" señoritas of San Antonio offer their services to the Texans as cooks, "housemaids," laundresses, and, if the Texans will have them, brides. The historical novels which feature the giants of Texas history and legend—Bowie, Houston, and Crockett—also sometimes feature Castilian dark ladies who invariably initiate the courting process but must fall victims to historical reality in the denouement. In Wellman's *The Iron Mistress*, Ursula Veramendi, the beautiful blonde daughter of the wealthy lieutenant governor of Texas-Coahuila, is permitted to marry James Bowie (a historical fact), but as she herself admits, she is accepted primarily as the final seal on a profitable business relationship.

Dark ladies who facilitate the American takeover of their country are almost as popular in conquest novels set in New Mexico. As was noted in chapter 2, the key theme in the New

---

[6] Moncure Lyne, *From the Alamo to San Jacinto; or, The Grito*, pp. 11–16, 117–118, 154–155, 273–280.

Mexican novels is the premilitary economic infiltration of the province by Yankee traders and merchants who acquire sizable amounts of New Mexican real estate by marrying into the upper class. The function of many New Mexican dark ladies is to hand over the title deeds of the family haciendas to their Yankee suitors. To qualify as loyal aides in the foreign conquest of their country, these beauties must be rich. More importantly, they must look all-white or near-white. The most common color synonyms used to describe the mass of non-dark "dark" ladies in southwestern literature are ivory-white, milk-white, snow-white, chalk-white, satin-white, magnolia-white, and alabaster. Sometimes additional color information is supplied. The heroine in question may be "of the gente fina (better class) . . . the sangre azul—the noble blood" of the Southwest, or she may show "English training" which nicely complements the "clear ivory" of her complexion, or she may be a "pure, Castilian blonde, a rare type in northern Mexico."[7]

The heroine of Malkus' *Caravans to Santa Fe*, Señorita Consuelo Lucero López y Chávez, serves as a composite example of all New Mexican dark ladies of the passive sort. Described as "that most charming of Spanish types, which in profile is straight-nosed, delicately cut, but which in full face appears childish, the nose short, a trifle broad, the eyes large and heavy-lidded, the lips full and petulant," Consuelo is clearly going to waste in the "halfbreed" Southwest. We first meet her where we meet or find most Spanish heroines most of the time: lounging in bed, brooding about her sad fate of marrying a decadent *rico* and becoming the mirror image of her mother, a ponderous and priest-ruled doña who waddles to and from mass and dozes in the *sala*, "her chin lost in the amiable creases which had engulfed the beauty of her youth." Consuelo dreams instead of running off with "one of the rope-haired trappers or the barbaric yanqui caravaners that come over the plains a-trading. *They* are men. What if they do lack *cultivación* and

[7] Edwin L. Sabin, *The Rose of Santa Fe*, pp. 52–53; Robert Ames Bennet, *A Volunteer with Pike: The True Narrative of One Dr. John Robinson and of His Love for the Fair Señorita Vallois*, pp. 15, 38; and Noel M. Loomis, *Short Cut to Red River*, p. 54.

cannot roll their r's. They appeal to me. Yes!" Peering out from her bedroom-prison one day, Consuelo catches a glimpse of a "blonde, hatless Americano, with hair like burnished metal in sun, and a face—a face!" It belongs to tall, blue-eyed Stephen Mercer, a Yankee merchant. Rejecting her family-appointed *rico* suitor, Consuelo marries Stephen. Within a year Mercer has assumed management of the López y Chávez hacienda and formed a business partnership with none other than his wife's rejected suitor, thus managing yet another personal marital and financial conquest of the Southwest long before the coming of the American army.[8]

Thus far it would seem that dark ladies in southwestern fiction are mere pawns in the hands of ambitious ranchers or entrepreneurs—passive parlor fixtures who are fated to play second fiddle to the Saxon heroes and scarcely have minds, much less wills, of their own. Like the California don, however, the California dark lady is a separate case. She has some points in common with the stereotype as a whole. She can be left in the lurch by an Anglo hero. In *A Man o' Wax* by Laura M. Dake, a young Missourian considers marrying a San Diego beauty whose ancestry is half Castilian and half English. A fellow Missourian talks him out of it: "But the blood, Philip,— the blood. Would you mix yours with that of the Latin race?" She is moody and mercurial. Gertrude Atherton's *Californianas* are particularly unstable compounds. In a single instant these emotionally unstable women may embrace and slap, preach and sin, laugh and cry. When betrayed by a lover, they explode with a "May the saints roll you in perdition" or a "May they thrust burning coals into the eyes that lied to me!"[9]

The dark ladies of California possess, however, a key quality distinguishing them from their counterparts elsewhere in the Southwest. They are active and aggressive to the point of masculinity by any but contemporary standards. Gertrude Atherton's "The Ears of Twenty Americans" (1902) introduces

---

[8] Malkus, *Caravans to Santa Fe*, pp. 1–16, 415–416.
[9] Gertrude Atherton, *The Splendid Idle Forties*, pp. 77, 181, 216.

Doña Eustaquia Ortega, ardent hater of all gringos, who excoriates the Americans in a fashion that would have been impossible in a conquest novel set in Texas: "Oh, abomination! Oh, execrable profanation! Mother of God, open thine ocean and suck them down! Smite them with pestilence of they dethrone our Aztec Eagle and flourish their stars and stripes above our fort! O California! That thy sons and thy daughters should live to see thee plucked like a rose by the usurper! . . . O that I were a man! That the women of California were men!"

Admittedly, Doña Eustaquia retracts her promise to exchange all her vast lands for the ears of twenty Americans and instead marries a gracefully graying Yankee sea captain. But her behavior, replicated by many other Californian Castilians, highlights the literary point that these women of blood and breeding do not fall into the arms of the conquering Saxons *until* they have put up at least token resistance—a measure of loyalty and sheer activity not demanded of the women of Texas and New Mexico.[10] Only after they have tried to whip the male weaklings of their race into resistance against the Americans do the ladies of California desert to the enemy. In the process they usually gain a Yankee husband, or sometimes a superior Californio don who shifts to the winning side before it is too late. A classic example of this side-switching occurs in Charlotte Herr's *San Pasqual: A Tale of Old Pasadena* (1924). The heroine, alabaster-hued Señora Refugio Bandini, wife of a Spanish blueblood, does not initially share her husband's pro-American sentiments. When Don Juan Bandini rides to aid General Kearney, Refugio denounces her husband as a traitor to California and joins the native forces opposing the Americans. When her husband is wounded, however, Refugio declares her allegiance to the United States, defending her sudden turnabout on the grounds that her husband is dearer to her than a dozen Californias. As readers, we are urged first to admire Señora Refugio's spunky independence and then to applaud her facile switch to the proper pro-American position.

[10] Ibid., pp. 49–53, 63–69, 79–80.

Refugio Bandini is but one of several heroines who serve the dual purpose of recalling the idyllic life of bygone Spanish California while simultaneously showing the ease with which Californios of the better sort adjusted to American rule.[11] In *Star of the Hills* by Wilder Anthony, the heroine Doña Tara plots to conquer all of California and set herself up as queen of the Independent Republic of Amazonia. In the process of interviewing candidates for the position of king, she meets Richard Osborne, "a good-looking young animal of the true Anglo-Saxon type: blonde, big-framed, blue-eyed, and calm by nature." As first test of Osborne's candidacy, Doña Tara invites him to kiss her. When Osborne refuses, she informs him that he has passed his examination successfully; had he embraced her he would have been impaled on the dagger that dangles under her girdle. As the final test, she orders Osborne to carry her colors to the edge of a cliff overhanging the sea, and give battle to a male competitor. At the last moment Osborne is shoved aside by a slender, effete-looking caballero who declares that he will take the Anglo's place. The newcomer, of course, is Doña Tara in male disguise. After easily defeating Osborne's rival for her hand, Doña Tara informs him that she is no longer interested in becoming queen of California, and the two marry and settle down on her estate.[12]

Given the tendency of fiction writers to eulogize the Californio don as a superior male specimen of his race, there is a certain inconsistency in novels of the same period and place which feature Amazon "Castilians" as superior to their emasculated men. The inconsistency can be explained, if not justified, by the fact that these two rival stereotypes—the manly

[11] For other novels which recall idyllic Spanish California while showing how easily Californios adjusted to the Americans, see Katherine Bernie Hamill, *Flower of Monterey: A Romance of the Californias*; Virginia Myers, *This Land I Hold*, in which the heroine, Magdalena Estrada, initially despises the American invaders but marries one for money and prestige; Scott O'Dell, *Woman of Spain: A Story of Old California*; George W. Ogden, *The Valley of Adventure: A Romance of California Mission Days*; Bertha Sinclair [B. M. Bower], *The Gringos: A Story of Old California Days in 1849*; and Frank Hamilton Spearman, *Carmen of the Ranchos*.

[12] Wilder Anthony, *Star of the Hills*, pp. 43, 55–57, 133, 205.

dons and the pugnacious ladies—rarely appear in the same novel. When the Californio lady does appear, she is far more influential in determining the course of California affairs than her Texan and New Mexican sisters. The contrast among the three regional women is striking. The dark lady of Texas or New Mexico is a submissive Venus who comforts rather than confronts the Anglo hero. The California dark lady actively contests the hero's supremacy. In terms of formula fiction, she is an odd hybrid. Half Diana and half Venus, a veritable tigress on the battlefield, bursting with energy and filled with expletives directed at the unsexed men of her race, she retires at battle's end to recite her rosary or to whisper sweet nothings to a guitar-plucking suitor.[13] Inclined to rant over the reluctance of her menfolk to give battle till death with the Americans, she eventually joins the enemy herself. The California lady is of so many minds and moods, so many masks and costumes, that she frequently leaves the reader at a loss about who she is and what she wants. If her male counterpart has become a figure of nostalgia, the Californiana fails to stand beside him because her lack of identity deprives her of even a symbolic credibility.

A common method of evading the problems of blending passive and active behavior in the dark lady of conquest fiction is to create a character born outside the region and imported to the Southwest for two reasons: to acquire a Saxon mate and to undertake a diplomatic or military assignment demanding that she play an aggressive role. These intelligent and independent women, commonly recruited from the parlors and drawing rooms of Mexico City, Havana, or Madrid, possess one distinct advantage over the native southwestern dark lady.

[13] Examples of such California dark ladies appear in Atherton, *Splendid Idle Forties*; Elizabeth Baker Bohan, *Un Americano: A Story of the Mission Days of California*; Walter Noble Burns, *The Robin Hood of El Dorado*; Dane Coolidge, *Gringo Gold: A Story of Joaquín Murrieta the Bandit*; John Augustine Cull, *The Bride of Mission San José: A Tale of Early California*; Mary Stewart Daggett, *Mariposilla: A Novel*; Bernard McLinville, *Gentleman on Horseback*; Ruth Mitchell, *Old San Francisco*; Kirk Munroe, *Golden Days of '49*; George Ogden, *The Road to Monterey*; and Sidney Herschel Small, *The Splendid Californians*.

They require no further refinement and acculturation before they are permitted to romance the Yankee heroes.

Such a process would be superfluous. These beauties are financially and personally independent. They have French or English accents, foreign educations, Old World titles of nobility, and permanent places of residence in Europe, lower Mexico, or South America. These formidable credentials make the nonsouthwestern dark ladies quite good enough for the Saxon commoners just as they are. These women illustrate the thesis that popular fiction must be essentially "aristocratic" to appeal to "common" readers. They are at least as hardy as their Saxon pioneer sisters without being drudges. Superior in pedigree to commonborn American women, they are also far more spirited than the home-grown southwestern variety of dark lady. Thus they combine the best of two races and cultures. The authors, indeed, frequently imply that if only these women could be persuaded to remain in the Southwest, they would provide superior seed stock for a racially marooned and culture-starved frontier. These foreign-born dark ladies often reach such an advanced state of perfection that the American heroes must actually take the initiative in the courting process. In Robert Bennet's *A Volunteer with Pike: The True Narrative of One Dr. John Robinson and of His Love for the Fair Señorita Vallois* (1909), Dr. Robinson, tall and blond but nevertheless a man of humble origins, is hard put to qualify as suitor to Señorita Alisanda Vallois, a Castilian dark lady whose flaring nostrils and magnolia-hued complexion bespeak pure Spanish ancestry while her learned manner of speech suggests English education. When the two meet at one of President Jefferson's presidential dinners in Washington, where Alisanda's uncle is the Spanish ambassador, Dr. Robinson pays court aggressively but is informed by Alisanda that the name Vallois "crowns the most glorious pages in the history of France" as well as Spain and that one of Alisanda's remote ancestors, Charles de Vallois, executed one of Dr. Robinson's French ancestors, a lowly Huguenot shoemaker. Robinson finally wins the lady by proving that "there are men who are their own ancestors,—men so true and brave and chivalrous that they are kings among their fellows, whatever their birth." The doctor then takes Alisanda in marriage, and the two settle down on a Louisiana plantation.

Another imported Spanish heroine appears in Hoffman Birney's *Eagle in the Sun*. Fair-haired, pale-skinned Señorita Alejandrina Tarrant de la Torre Alta—Sandra High Tower—is the daughter of a wellborn Castilian woman who married a Bostonian Frenchman and settled first in Paris, then in Spain, and finally in Cuba. Sandra High Tower is therefore a genetic and cultural composite of French sexuality, Yankee pragmatism, and Spanish beauty—the entire package set off by a "white Castilian skin that the most savage of tropic suns could tan only to the flushed ivory of a magnolia petal." The family, originally exiled by a Spanish king jealous of its prestige and power, was exiled again to Louisiana when the Mexican rabble unseated its class in 1810. Sandra's mother teaches the girl to ride, shoot, and swear undying hatred for the "pigs of Mexicans" who stole the High Tower's huge tracts of land in Mexico and killed her father at the Alamo. She then journeys to Santa Fe with secret documents authorizing her to deliver a gold shipment into the hands of pro-American forces. In Santa Fe, Sandra stains her skin, dons a black wig, and poses as a prostitute named Rosita, the better to spy on the anti-American New Mexicans. Long after the reader is aware that Sandra and Rosita are the same person, her suitor, Yankee caravaner John Chain, continues to believe that Sandra has mysteriously disappeared and that Rosita is an unaccountably attractive "halfbreed" who keeps trying to lure him into her chamber. Remembering that his Massachusetts relatives would hardly approve of a woman with a complexion "almost as dark as a nigger's," Chain keeps an iron hold on his principles. When it finally dawns on him that "Sandra was Rosita and Rosita was Sandra," the color problem is eliminated and the two leave the Southwest to establish a plantation in the Old World.[14]

One might think that Sandra represents the apogee of the

[14] Hoffman Birney, *Eagle in the Sun*, pp. 2–5, 24–34, 72–73, 104–105, 127–128, 306–312.

dark lady as heroine. Significantly, however, even true Castilians fall short of the highest peak of feminine perfection ascribed to dark ladies in conquest fiction. Even more attractive
than the all-Spanish heroine imported into the Southwest is the
poseur who turns out to be not Spanish at all. Disguised temporarily as a dark lady, this heroine emerges as unmistakably
white: Irish or French, Franco-Irish, sometimes Franco-Spanish
or Irish-Spanish, but always with the emphasis on the northern
elements of her heritage. Whatever her combination of Old
World ancestry, she is just as physically active and sexually
aggressive as the Spanish dark lady, and even more attractive.
In Arthur Carhart's *Drum Up the Dawn*, Doña Liseta Vigil y
Salazar, supposedly a Castilian languishing in Santa Fe in the
early 1800's, is actually a "full-blooded Irish" lass who happened to land in the far fringes of the Spanish Empire because
her father, an Irish revolutionary, was exiled to the New World
by the English government. "Trim as a clipper ship," with red
hair, blue eyes, and a complexion variously described as alabaster, milk-white, and satiny, Doña Liseta is poised, queenly,
and an accomplished flirt, thus offering the fullest possibilities
in the way of sexual charm. She looks "white" yet acts like a
halfbreed harlot—swaying her hips, uncovering her ivory
breasts, bedding the hero in wild frenzy, and giving off an
exotic odor of "barbaric richness" acquired from practicing
New Mexican "promiscuity." This active, arrogant, hot-tempered, and highly sensual woman is by no means alone in
southwestern fiction. In Arnold's *Time of the Gringo*, the supposedly all-"Spanish" heroine, Doña Soledad de Abreu, turns
out to be a Franco-Spanish lady whose superior physical charm
rests in her "Gallic strain . . . born centuries before in Navarre
in the northern-most part of Spain, combining into a subtle
refinement that belonged alone to her." This multitalented
woman watches bullfights with quivering nostrils, out-rides
and out-shoots all rivals, tells obscene jokes, makes love with
loud abandon, and encourages Governor Manuel Armijo to

76

seduce her, then spoils his performance by dubbing him a
capón—a eunuch.[15]

The dark lady of conquest fiction reveals a profound social
and psychological contradiction on the part of her creators.
On the one hand most writers persuaded themselves that wom-
en of truly dark skin—the "halfbreed harlots"—ought to be
avoided and had to be renounced. On the other hand, these
same writers allowed their highly principled Saxon heroes to
experience more or less conscious cravings for mixed-blood
women. The result was the creation of women who are neither
"breeds" nor "Saxons" but who combine halfbreed sexuality
with fair color and European ancestry—the dark lady who is
"dark" in behavior, but never in skin tone.

The process of establishing the stereotypes of the halfbreed
whore and the Castilian dark lady helps reveal the views of
color, sex, and national concepts of morality that authors of
conquest fiction have considered acceptable to their audience.
At the same time that the "degenerate" halfbreeds make the
point about the folly of racial mixture, the pureblooded Saxon
heroes are sorely tempted by these women. Hence they must
be attracted by the very racial mixture which they are compelled to repudiate. And on the other side of the color line, at
the same time that dark ladies must be colored near-white to
conform to conventional codes of morality and complexion,
their touch of brownness, whether inherited or adopted, and
however carefully camouflaged, makes the point that these
magnolia- and olive-hued women are capable of a degree of
sexuality that remained taboo for well-bred "white" heroines.[16]

Conquest fiction embodies more than a simple double
standard. Instead, the reader finds a quadruple color standard
in which two types of women are constantly playing two color-
determined roles apiece, and thus rarely acting as consistently
as either color implies they should act. Although their com-

[15] Arthur Hawthorne Carhart, *Drum Up the Dawn*, pp. 48–55, 216–223,
284–285; Arnold, *Time of the Gringo*, pp. 45–46.
[16] Many of the best discussions of sexual imagery in American race
relations are listed in the bibliography.

plexions remain the same, their behavioral coloring changes constantly in their creator's imagination, and therefore in the reader's as well. Depending on the requirements of plot and the vagaries of a given writer, we may be introduced to a hip-swaying, bosom-flaunting "halfbreed" slut who swills tequila and cavorts half-nude on one page and then reverts to a rosary-counting, repentant "Castilian" on another page. Or we may be treated to a fair-skinned Castilian who sits primly in the parlor in one chapter and then bounces into bed with the hero in the next. Of the two infractions, the halfbreed's posturing as a Castilian is usually intended to be offensive. To permit a brown tart to behave as a prim and proper Castilian virgin was a serious breach of color etiquette that, until recently, had to be amended before the end of the book.[17] Yet it has proved extremely difficult to maintain strict control of the conduct and deportment of women who are so carelessly colored. Even more than the halfbreed whores, the California Castilians and the imported dark ladies of Northern European ancestry are forever slipping across the color line, forever trespassing into forbidden brown sexual territory, forever challenging the "white" codes of propriety they are supposed to uphold. Indeed, it is not too much to say that the headstrong and disobedient dark lady is really two heroines in one. She looks white but she acts so brown that her whiteness is the one thing about her that readers tend to ignore or to forget after the initial introduction. In every characteristic except color—speech and manners, pride and passion, temper and indolence—the near-white dark lady behaves less like the all-white "Saxon" lady she is intended to resemble than the frankly sexual "woman of color" she actually resembles. Betraying her outward appearance by her inner emotions, she joins the mu-

[17] Examples of works in which "halfbreed" whores try to pose as Castilian heroines include: Alsbury, *Guy Raymond*; Anthony, *Star of the Hills*: Arnold, *Time of the Gringo*; several of Atherton's stories in *Splendid Idle Forties*; Barrington, *Back from Goliad*; Birney, *Eagle in the Sun*; Carhart, *Drum Up the Dawn*; Blanche C. Grant, *Dona Lona: A Story of Old Taos and Santa Fe*; several of Bret Harte's short stories; Lyne, *From The Alamo to San Jacinto*; and Wellman, *Iron Mistress*.

latto mistress, the light-red squaw, and the halfbreed temptress as yet another of the curiously shaded "women of color" who generously fill the pages of American literature.

Originally regarded as an attractive and acceptable southwestern alternative to the all-white woman back East, the dark lady of conquest fiction bears testimony to the fact that her creators were trying to have it both ways: to satisfy the prescribed color code while teasing "white" readers with ill-disguised "brown" women of undisguised sexuality. There can be little question about which dark lady is the more appealing character. When obviously intended to be all white, the dark lady is tepid. When occasionally permitted to act all "brown," she is a creature of rare beauty and passion, courage and dignity, vitality and power. Despite the color compromises that crippled her credibility, the very idea of creating a two-toned heroine, capable of running the full range of human passions when permitted to act "brown," was a far more innovative experiment than either the predictably repulsive halfbreed harlot she easily upstaged or the anemic Castilian belle she was intended to be. However incredible her behavior, whatever her shortcomings as a woman without a solid color base, the Castilian or psuedo-Castilian dark lady was an acceptable figure through whom Victorian authors and their modern descendants could indulge in controversial color and sex combinations while simultaneously condemning them. Thus, the dark lady has provided writers and readers alike with titillation *and* conventional morality in a way that was denied the all-American white heroine until recently.

Part II
EXPLOITATION

THE SOUTHWEST, so much in the public eye during the Mexican War, was all but forgotten by most Americans during the last half of the nineteenth and the first quarter of the twentieth centuries. The glory and tragedy of the Civil War, the bitterness of Reconstruction, and the frantic pace of industrial expansion consumed the national energy and attention. Not until the last two decades of the nineteenth century did a rapid increase in the Anglo population of the Southwest combine with increased industrialization and improved transportation to bring changes that far outstripped the transformations effected in the three decades following the Mexican War. In particular, the coming of the railroads in the 1880's marked the beginning of the end of the Mexican-American Southwest. In 1876 the Southern Pacific Railroad connected Los Angeles and San Diego to the eastern United States, bringing the "boom of the 80's" to southern California—an era of heavy Yankee immigration and economic expansion comparable to that the gold rush brought to the northern counties three decades earlier. From a position of numerical superiority in most areas of southern California in the early 1870's, the Californios were reduced to an ethnic minority a dozen years later. As their numbers declined, so did their role in local political, business, and social affairs. Much the same pattern occurred in Texas and Arizona. The coming of the railroad to southern Arizona, connecting the territory to the East, ended the region's long dependence on

Sonoran trade routes and Mexican merchants. And in 1904 a railroad line built through the lower Rio Grande Valley of South Texas linked that region, too, to the rest of the state.

Only in New Mexico, where the Hispano-Americans retained numerical superiority well into the twentieth century, was Saxon rule challenged with any degree of long-term success. Although the Anglo-Americans quickly seized control of the mining and ranching areas in southwestern and southeastern New Mexico, large numbers of Anglos did not settle in the upper Rio Grande Valley until the 1920's and 1930's. Hispano politicos therefore continued to dominate the key elective offices. When New Mexico was admitted to the Union in 1912, the state constitution provided for bilingual sessions for all state business and for the training of bilingual teachers. But even here the Hispano was fighting a rear-guard action.

The process of decline was accelerated by continuous, massive immigration from central and northern Mexico into South Texas, southern Arizona, and southern California. This process, creating in nearly every decade a new generation of unassimilated Mexican Americans, placed the Spanish-speaking inhabitants of the Southwest in a unique category of immigrants. Unlike European newcomers, who generally suffered cultural and economic displacement for little more than a single generation, the incessant waves of arrivals from Mexico meant that Mexican Americans as a group seemed always to be first-generation immigrants, unable simultaneously to absorb new members and enjoy upward mobility in a society that prescribed assimilation first and acceptance—if it came at all—afterward. As early as 1870, some 103,000 Mexican-born persons were living in the United States, and the numbers increased geometrically with each succeeding decade. Between 1900 and 1910 alone nearly a quarter of a million Mexicans migrated to the United States. Some fifty thousand crossed the border annually, drawn by wages double those in Mexico. The 1930 census recorded close to one and one-half million Spanish-speaking people living in the United States, the third largest racial minority in the country. And 80 percent of this population was located in the four southwestern states of California, Arizona, New Mexico, and Texas.

By 1929 the Southwest was producing 40 percent of the nation's supply of fruits and vegetables, most of it without the aid of machines. Laborers from Mexico, immigrants and *braceros*, supplied 65 to 85 percent of the stoop labor used in the production of these crops. The few strikes that took place in the twenties and thirties, especially those in California's Imperial Valley, were ruthlessly suppressed. Moreover, economic practices carried over into political and social discrimination. "White Trade Only" signs appeared in an increasing number of business establishments in towns throughout the Southwest. Segregation in housing, public establishments, and schools ranged from common to universal.

What is important for present purposes is the effect of these developments on cultural images. Two distinct approaches emerge, expressed in two different media. An increasing number of authors chose to deal more or less seriously with the decline of the old order and the rise of the new. Their approach, exemplified in a genre which can be described as the great house novel, is analyzed in chapter 4. The great mass of popular works, however, continued to work with the themes established during the conquest—a tendency arguably encouraged by the continuing influx of unacculturated Mexican nationals who quite literally reinforced negative stereotypes simply by existing. The distinction here, established in chapters 5 and 6, involves media rather than themes. The emergence of the cinema as competitor to, then partial replacement for, pulp fiction, provided visual and auditory reinforcement for contemporary images of the greaser and added a few variations to the theme of Mexican decay and degradation which is the essence of this part.

CHAPTER FOUR

THE DECLINE AND FALL OF THE
HISPANIC GREAT HOUSE

FOR THE WRITERS who turned to the postconquest Southwest for fictional material, history posed severe artistic problems. Treaty provisions, railroad construction, mining opera-
tions, and court litigations hardly provided overtly dramatic
fictional material depicting the collision of two races. As a result, the quest for provocative subject matter led most writers
interested in the postconquest Southwest to search out a single
institution that might symbolize the fall of one race and the
rise of the other. They found what they were looking for in a
simplified presentation of the decline and ruin of the Hispanic
great house, which became a symbol of the decay of the entire
Spanish Mexican order. Historically, the haciendas, or great
houses, of the Southwest had always constituted a minor part
of Spanish Mexican society. Some of them had fallen into decay
even before the Southwest became part of the United States.
The California dons, for example, had suffered an economic
decline some twenty years before the end of Mexican rule—
victims of Mexican dependence upon the Yankee hide and merchandise trade. A number of their counterparts in New Mexico
and Arizona fell on hard times before the Americans took effective possession of the inland Southwest in the 1870's and
1880's—casualties of Apache and Comanche raids, an uncertain
trading and livestock economy which served a limited clientele,
and a precarious patriarchal code which supposedly included

provisions for the protection of peon serfs by patron masters but frequently replaced pride of function with pride of status combining insistence upon special privileges with denial of contractual obligations to peons. The institution of the great house had therefore started to decline significantly from within before it was threatened from without.

This is not to say that a few southwestern lords of the manor did not exercise considerable power over local farmers and villagers, priests and politicos. The key initial point about the Hispanic great house, however, is that its masters were not quite so powerful before the coming of the Americans as several generations of popular novelists made them out to be. Separated from each other by vast distances, the great-house barons rarely banded together for purposes of power or protection. Their authority, moreover, rarely extended beyond their personal preserve, which might be immense in terms of territory but small in terms of numbers of peon subordinates or easily mobilizable wealth.

In spite of their weaknesses, it is also true that some great-house owners retained considerable influence for several decades after the American takeover. The isolation which had been a source of weakness before the American conquest proved to be a source of durability afterwards. American farmers and merchants, miners and ranchers did not settle the inland Southwest in large numbers until after 1865, when federal troops were finally able to offer reliable protection from the Apaches. During the quarter-century between the initial military conquest of the Southwest in 1846 and effective American settlement, the great-house owners in isolated areas of the inland Southwest continued to enjoy many of the privileges and immunities they had enjoyed before the conquest. Speaking strictly in historical terms, therefore, it is safe to conclude that the preconquest domination of the great house was not so complete, nor was its postconquest "fall" so dramatic, as great-house fiction made them out to be.[1]

[1] For historical background, see Alwyn Barr, *Reconstruction to Reform:*

87

This historical matrix was at best marginally relevant to novelists who chose to isolate the great house as the most representative of the alien Spanish Mexican institutions encountered by the conquering Americans. In thus rendering the decline and fall of an institution emblematic of the decline and fall of an entire race, the majority of writers of postconquest fiction categorically ignored or slighted vast numbers of Mexican American citizenry who were viewed—when they were viewed at all—as shadowy, colorless, and unexciting "groups": the "drab" clergy, the "humble" villagers, the "stolid" farmers, the "corrupt" politicos. Most of the Mexican Americans who occupied the lower and middle positions in southwestern society go almost unnoticed in great-house fiction. The internal social and economic weaknesses of the great-house systems also tend to be ignored. Their fates instead reflect their moral shortcomings. As the Americans charge headlong into the Southwest after the Mexican War, the great-house grandees topple by the score, their haciendas bulldozed into rubble by Yankee entrepreneurs who embody the virtues their victims lack and can never develop.

Paradoxically, at the same time that these defenders of democracy and Anglo supremacy felt compelled to destroy or alter radically the great houses of the Southwest, they were also charmed by them. The revelation that a way of life had existed in the recent past within the continental boundaries of the energetic and egalitarian United States that could be described as indolent and elegant, provincial and aristocratic, fascinated

Texas Politics, 1876–1906; Herbert O. Brayer, *William Blackmore: The Spanish-Mexican Land Grants of New Mexico and Colorado, 1863–1878*; William Robert Kenny, "Mexican-American Conflict on the Mining Frontier, 1848–1852," *Journal of the West* 6 (October, 1967): 584–586; Richard Morefield, "The Mexican Adaptation in American California, 1846–1875," pp. 31, 50–52; W. W. Robinson, *Land in California: The Story of Mission Lands, Ranchos, Squatters, Mining Claims, Railroad Grants, Land Scrip, Homesteads*; R. J. Rosenbaum, "Mexicano vs. Americano: A Study of Hispano-American Resistance to Anglo-American Control in New Mexican Territory, 1870–1900"; Ozzie G. Simmons, "Anglo-Americans and Mexican-Americans in South Texas: A Study in Dominant Subordinate Group Relations"; and Victor Westphall, *The Public Domain in New Mexico, 1854–1891.*

American writers. The very inequities that offended their democratic values also gave a tempting, forbidden flavor to the great house. That it was as faint a threat to the stereotypical American Way as the plantation order of the Old South which it remotely resembled only added to its charm. Keen-eyed observers inevitably linked the hacienda order of the southwestern great house with the plantation order of the antebellum South. And in certain respects, as tantalizing as they are vague, the social order of the preconquest Southwest had indeed resembled that of the prewar South. The "Spanish" patron bore some similarity to the "blueblood" planter, the mestizo peon to the "redneck" farmer, and the Indian serf to the black slave. Like the antebellum South, the preconquest Southwest knew a landed aristocracy and a class of indentured or enslaved servants. Finally, both regions suffered conquest and occupation, dispossession and disinheritance. Like the postbellum South, the postconquest Southwest saw the gradual destruction of that landed aristocracy, with the attendant problems of racial and cultural adjustment. In short, the two regions and cultures conjured similar images of exotic ways of life lived in pastoral serenity before the Yankees drove their machines into these semitropical Edens. The southern plantation and the Hispanic great house presented similar appeals: families living for generations in the same house, tilling the same lands, holding the same relationship of class to class, race to race, man to woman.

That the story of the great house remained untold further enhanced its attraction. Early American visitors to the Southwest did little more than record mixed wonder and dismay at the unfamiliar nature of the alien institution. It remained for twentieth-century authors to excavate the decayed foundations of the great houses and show how and why they were brought down.

Fictional treatment of the great houses of the Southwest varies greatly from region to region. Variations in the manner in which the Mexican is treated seem to hinge on what authors regarded as the most suitable formula to attract readers of popular fiction. As with conquest fiction, once the formula was established, it tended to be self-reinforcing. There are, for example, no great-house novels set in postindependence Texas. Apparently the extreme feelings of racial hostility generated by the Texas Revolution, followed by decades of bitter border skirmishes, discouraged writing about the "romantic" and peaceful institution of the great house in a manner that might appeal to readers of fiction set in Texas. In an era of Texas history characterized by spiteful race relations, there was little market for fairy-tale novels about pale-skinned great-house aristocrats.

If the fictional method of dealing with the great house in the Texan romances is to ignore it altogether, the preferred method in the New Mexican novels is to raze it. The great houses of New Mexico are almost invariably seized by enterprising Yankee usurpers who gain them through financial manipulations that rarely include the marriages between male American commoners and female Castilian aristocrats which gave some aura of romance to conquest fiction. Once the great houses are acquired, the Anglo intruders set about altering the physical structure of the house itself at once—sometimes by eliminating it entirely—and replacing eroded "feudal" institutions with Yankee systems of enterprise and economy.

This attitude has been reinforced by timing. Most of the New Mexican great house novels written since the Great Depression tend to stress economic realities over guitar-strumming romance. Unlike most conquest fiction, however, the collapse of the New Mexican great houses is depicted overwhelmingly from the viewpoint of the conquered rather than the conqueror. The only significant exception is William McLeod Raine's *A Daughter of the Dons*, whose hero, a Colorado mining engineer, does not think particularly highly of the New Mexican gentleman. When Manuel Pesquiera, a foppish descendant of the *ricos* whose once-privileged status as a great-house owner has been reduced to that of a propertyless lawyer, prevails upon Gordon's sense of chivalry to give up his claim to one-half million acres in northern New Mexico, also claimed by Pesquiera's client, Gordon replies that he does not see "what chivalry has got to do with it." Challenging the American to a duel, Pesquiera receives an Anglo-Saxon putdown:

> "I offer you, sir, the remedy of a gentleman. You, sir, shall choose the weapons."
>
> The Anglo-Saxon laughed in his face.
>
> "Good. Let it be toasting-forks, at twenty paces."
>
> The challenger drew himself up to his full five feet six.
>
> "You choose to be what you call droll. Sir, I give you the word, poltroon—*lache*—coward."
>
> "Oh, go chase yourself."

When Pesquiera, beside himself with rage, slaps Gordon in the face, the Coloradan tucks the dapper little descendant of the dons under his arm and dumps him into an irrigation ditch.

In *Red Chili* (1940) by Myrtle Andrews, the American railroad is the villainous agent responsible for the invasion, subdivision, and dismemberment of the haciendas. The Hispano ranches are broken up, the great houses are gutted or sold to the railroad, and the New Mexican family structure is split asunder. Women take up with blond section hands. Men desert the ways of their fathers, go to work for the railroad, and become corrupted.

Those *ricos* who survive into old age in the new American order suffer even deeper traumas. Great-house fiction set in Arizona and New Mexico is liberally peopled with ancient aristocrats who live out their last years in private rage, public remorse, or garrulous self-pity. In *Adobe Walls: A Novel of the Last Apache Rising* by W. R. Burnett, old Don Sebastiano Unamuno is an example of the gracefully declining *rico*. Once the owner of a sizable part of Arizona, he now divides retirement between his run-down great house and a hotel in downtown Tucson, where he feels himself "to be a civilized man living on in another age, an age of wild barbarism inaugurated by the pushing, ignorant, ruthless Anglo-Saxons" (p. 169). In Frank O'Connor's *Conquest: A Novel of the Old Southwest*, a less fortunate *rico* ruminates on his fallen condition: "His great-grandfather had accumulated countless acres in the West by royal grant. . . . But the acres and the cattle had been wasted by his impecunious descendants, and now [Padierna], the last of the line, dwelt in tarnished splendor in a tattered *hacienda*" (pp. 251–252). In the final portion of the novel the callous and unsympathetic American protagonist, Ward Pendleton, prods Padierna into selling his Arizona land. Padierna collapses into final ruin, and Pendleton, tearing down the decayed great house, turns the bulk of the hacienda into a timber and cattle empire.

One salient feature of New Mexican great-house fiction is that the old Hispanic order undergoes complete destruction. Neither Anglos nor Mexicans make any effort to maintain even a few of the "Spanish" customs. Yet at the same time, most of the great-house owners or their descendants are depicted sympathetically. They are often effete, sometimes degenerate, and always helpless in the grasp of the Americans. But these usurpers lack compassion. They are greedy and cruel. They acknowledge few moral constraints. This callousness on the part of the American conquerors is by no means universal, nor does it automatically make heroes of the conquered. Instead, it is the Yankee conqueror who is no longer automatically an admirable person. In the evolution of southwestern fiction, the New Mexican great-house novels take a middle position between the blatantly racist conquest works discussed in Part I and the fiction focusing on Anglo guilt, which will be analyzed in later chapters.

No author is more representative of these trends than Paul Horgan. His writing about the decline and fall of the New Mexican great house is marked by a degree of compassion, subtlety, and sophistication unmatched in southwestern literature. *The Common Heart*, set in Albuquerque at the time of writing (1942), introduces one of the few declining dons who gains dignity as he loses property. Lean and gracefully aging, Don Hilario Ascarete has assumed a timeless quality. His name —Hilario—suits him well. He is a man of humor, a historian, a poet, and in his own way a prophet. Once a wealthy lawyer who educated his sons in Paris, Don Hilario lost his hacienda long ago and now prefers his own company. Sunning himself against the wall of his modest house, he gazes across the meadow towards the river, following the movement of the blackbirds and comparing their flitting course to that of his children, grandchildren, and great-grandchildren who try to imitate the Anglos with fancy clothes, repainted Fords, Saturday-night movies, and updated slang. Hilaro is the timeless and dignified survivor—the aged seer, "worn like an old man's shoulder, bent and drooping from carrying the weight of years; but still vital with duty's residue."[2]

Don Hilario, however, is an atypical New Mexican *rico*, one of the few who elicits our respect for his dignity rather than our sympathy for his dispossession. Horgan himself offered a more characteristic postconquest don in one of his finest short stories, "The Hacienda" (1936). Don Elizario is first introduced as a decrepit hanger-on in one of the run-down hotels in modern Albuquerque; in a series of narrative flashbacks Horgan recounts the old man's past. Once a young man of promise who served as delegate to Washington from the Territory of New Mexico in the 1880's, Don Elizario returned to the family's great house on the Rio Grande to find it washed away in a flood. The family disaster coincided with the arrival of the railroad, which offered Don Elizario a good price for his unused lands. Like an emperor moving his capital to a new location, the don moved his train of servants and caravan of fine furniture to Albuquerque. Unable to compete with "the exhausting Gringos," he followed the path of least resistance. He took an Anglo business partner and married a blonde gringa. She overlooked Don Elizario's dark complexion because he was still rich, but abandoned him when his partner made off with the last of the inheritance.

Reduced in less than a decade from rich and elegant "Spaniard" to fat and landless "greaser," Don Elizario's misfortunes are exceeded only by his self-deception. Confined to a small rented room at the run-down Elks' Club in the Anglo section

[2] Paul Horgan, *The Common Heart*, pp. 498–500.

of Albuquerque, he does his best to live like "a real Americano." Each afternoon, as the fading light conceals the club's
in a battered chair in the lounge addressing by name all who
pass, shaking his quivering jowls and waving his pudgy hands.
Passersby acknowledge Don Elizario's elaborate greetings only
when time is hanging heavy on their hands. Then businessmen
trot out the club's bootblack, a "nigger" named Chicken, who
addresses Don Elizario as an equal and hands him a bottle of
bad bootleg whiskey. Believing that blacks were created to
serve the Spanish race, Don Elizario orders the chuckling
negro to bring glasses for his faithful American "friends," who
proceed to bait the don while drinking his liquor:

> "You're a right busy man, Don Elizario," said the laundry-
> man with a gleam of his eye across his thin nose at the insur-
> ance man. "Sittin' here all day and workin' at your likker."
> The Don leaned back and rolled a gurgling laugh deep
> down in his contented throat.
> The insurance man said,
> "Well, it's a job you can do better than most, Don Elizario,
> eh!—You just better keep at it, we'd never get anything done in
> this town if we waited on the earliest settlers, now would we?"
> "No, no," said the old man, "My people have no gift for
> business. They are too fond of life.—Your glass."

Far from seeing himself as a babbling bore, Don Elizario
fancies himself a man of charm and wit. Placing a quivering
hand on his stomach, which he fancies to be his heart, Don
Elizario launches into a sodden history of his family's great
house that stood for centuries on the banks of the Rio Grande
—a huge fortress furnished with the finest Old World furniture
and surrounded by peons, cultivated fields, acres of orchards,
and leagues of unused land. When the laundryman reminds
him that the once-grand house is now a mound of mud, the
don breaks into tears. To fend off the cruelty of the laundryman's remark, he falls back on relating the small niceties of
life in the halcyon days of the great house. "When I was ten

years old," he babbles drunkenly in the last sentence of the story, "it was on my birthday, I planted a tree in the patio."[3]

If Paul Horgan began the sympathetic discussion of the fall of the great house, no modern writer has excavated its crumbling ruins with more thoroughness than Harvey Fergusson (1890–1971). The central theme of his great-house novels is familiar: the social and financial takeover of New Mexico by the Anglo-American trapper or trader turned rancher or merchant capitalist. The complexities of his argument and the sheer bulk of his writing on the subject, however, merit consideration in a separate section. In *Wolf Song* (1927), the first —though not the first written—of a trilogy spanning a half-century in historical time, the hero, Sam Lash, rides into Taos about 1830 with a year's cache of furs. Barging through a cock-fight in the jammed main street, scattering chickens and Mexicans right and left, Lash shouts: "Out of the way, you greasers! . . . get ready for the big doin's." Thrown into panic by this "hard-bitten, hazard-loving" gringo, the soft, fat natives of Taos can do nothing but take shelter behind the town's thick adobe walls, which give off a "peculiar defiant stench of life lived in sensuous untroubled squalor" (p. 25), and pray for the day when the blond barbarian will ride out of town.

One of the families so afflicted with moral rot is the wealthy Salazars. The daughter of the house, Lola Salazar, meets Sam at a fandago. They fall in love. Lash abducts the girl and carries her north to Bent's Fort, where they are married. While he is away on a hunting trip, the male Salazars ride north and repossess Lola. Outraged, Lash demands his wife back. At this point the novel breaks decisively with the conquest genre. On the surface Lash pays a heavy price for his marriage. The Salazars stipulate that in exchange for Lola he must embrace the Catholic faith, become a loyal Mexican citizen, and renounce

[3] Paul Horgan, "The Hacienda," in *The Return of the Weed*, pp. 67–81. The book is a series of brief sketches, each prompted by the description of a ruined building—a mission, a ranch house, a mansion, a windmill, a hacienda, and a filling station.

his wild ways—requirements that would not have been tolerated by the adventurers and traders who populate most conquest fiction. Lash, however, gains far more than he loses. The Salazars, believing that the large tracts of wilderness land granted them long ago by the Spanish Crown are useless, deed to Lash what they regard as a worthless reconciliation gift: full ownership and control of these far-reaching lands. In doing so they hand over to a gringo upstart their last hold on a sizable part of the Mexican Southwest.

Two years after he wrote *Wolf Song*, Fergusson published *In Those Days*, set in Albuquerque in the 1870's and 1880's. If the military conquest of New Mexico is a thing of the past, the socioeconomic conquest is proceeding apace. While Anglos sweat in the sun, Mexican aristocrats wallow in laziness and self-pity. Young Diego Aragón, heir to more acres than he has bothered to count or see, passes his days drinking, gambling, and racing a black stallion up and down the city streets. His one redeeming trait, foolhardy courage, gets him elected sheriff. His occasional feats of prowess, however, are offset by long periods of stagnation and ineptitude. Bestowing jobs on relatives and refusing to jail any New Mexican citizens who bear the remotest connection to the prolific clan of Aragón, Diego is beaten badly at the polls when he seeks reelection. Trying to compete with the Anglo in romance as he earlier competed in courage, he courts and marries a blonde gringa who helps him run through the rest of his inheritance in a matter of months and then divorces him. At the end of the novel this once-proud descendant of the dons is reduced to a fat greaser squatting beside a potbellied stove, telling lies about the golden age of the *ricos* to anyone fool enough to listen.

In a parting word to the reader, Fergusson makes it plain that the decline and fall of Diego Aragón symbolized the decline and fall of the great houses and the *ricos* who fell with them. Like the mighty adobe walls of the haciendas, Diego and his kind melted and crumbled "like sugar." They fell prey to the Anglo, according to Fergusson, because they had no heads for business. Therefore, the *ricos* of New Mexico had no functional place in the new southwestern order.[4]

The first great-house novel Fergusson wrote, *The Blood of the Conquerors* (1921), is also the last of the trilogy. Located in a small southwestern city that resembles Albuquerque in the early years of the twentieth century, the novel focuses on Ramón Delcasar, scion of a *rico* family which lost most of its land to the gringos through gambling, debt, and foreclosure. The Delcasar strategy in the new, booming century is to employ Ramón to defeat the Anglos at their own game by adopting Anglo principles of labor, thrift, and emphasis on material gain. The process begins when Ramón is sent to law school—the first Delcasar reduced to practicing a profession. He returns to New Mexico with a burning desire to "show the gringos what he could do." As the first step in his personal "conquest" of the conquering Anglos, he courts a lovely and empty-headed New York belle. Standing between Ramón and the money needed to sue for Julia's hand, however, is Uncle Diego Delcasar, a Falstaffian figure, once a respected sheriff but now drinking and wenching his way through the remains of the family fortune with alarming speed. Ramón has a peon kill his uncle from ambush, then embarks on a power struggle with a land speculator named McDougall. Ramón wins his fight by rolling through remote Hispano villages shouting, "Death to the gringo!" At the same time, he informs his wife's parents that he is not to be confused with "the common pelados" of New Mexico, whose land he is "protecting" from McDougall.

Aware of the hypocrisy of publicly championing the poverty-striken Hispano while retaining the life-style of a great-house baron with an Anglo wife, Ramón breaks under the strain. Spurned by his Anglo in-laws as a member of a "tainted" race, he abandons all pretense to being a man of the people and loses his Hispano followers overnight. As compensation, he splurges on diamonds, fancy clothes, and a newfangled

[4] Harvey Fergusson, *In Those Days*, pp. 54–55, 145, 237–239, 240.

auto-car. When his wife flees to New York, Ramón follows the uncle he despised and killed into drink, poker, and dissipation. When we last see him, he is squatting on the sunny side of a crumbling adobe wall, in "a position any Mexican can hold for hours," reading a letter from Julia. Briefly, the letter stirs the embers of ambition, reminding Ramón of the distance between the blonde and rich New York lady and his homely mestiza common-law wife,[5] between the once-great house of the Delcasar family and his own shabby, eroding adobe shack. But the reminder itself taxes his eroding mental powers to the limit:

> He saw in imagination the endless unvaried chain of his days stretching before him, and he rebelled against it and knew not how to break it. . . . He had tasted high aspiration, and desire bright and transforming, and wild sweet joy. . . . These things had been taken away, and . . . he felt he ought to do something, that he ought not to submit. But . . . the spring sunshine soaked into his body. A faint hum of early insects lulled him. . . . He grew drowsy; his dissatisfaction simmered down to a vague ache in the background of his consciousness.[6]

More than either the Salazars of *Wolf Song* or Diego Aragón of *In Those Days*, Ramón Delcasar is Fergusson's personification of the decline of the New Mexican *ricos*. For Fergusson, always an outspoken champion of thrift and hard work, Ramón's decision "to trade hope and hazard for monotonous ease" was irresponsible, reprehensible, yet somehow inevitable. Having aspired to serious competition with the Anglo on the Anglo's own terms, he met defeat through what Fergusson clearly believed to be the economic and emotional limitations and liabilities of his race. Playing the Anglo game was as disastrous for Ramón Delcasar as it had been for his immediate ancestors during the conquest. Fergusson's *ricos* do not come

[5] In *In Those Days* an Anglo businessman in Albuquerque warns a friend of the dangers of associating too intimately with mestiza women: "a Mexican girl . . . don't egg . . . a man on—a white woman would. . . . It's a lazy country and it makes a man lazy. When everything comes easy you jest rot" (p. 44).
[6] Harvey Fergusson, *The Blood of the Conquerors*, pp. 51, 154, 187, 264–266.

by initiative and responsibility naturally.[7] Their spurts of energy are unleashed only by passing motives—blonde women, fancy cars and clothes, unrealistic dreams of recovering the privileged position they formerly enjoyed within their own race. Once the external source of inspiration is gone, they revert to their natural ways. Fergusson's descendants of the conquistadors finally reveal that in their veins runs more blood of the greaser than of the Castilian.

If Fergusson's early novels established the outlines of his theme, his argument is completed in his two finest works, *Grant of Kingdom* and *The Conquest of Don Pedro*. Like most of Fergusson's work, *Grant of Kingdom* is strongly allegorical. The novel's theme is the history of an immense Spanish land grant and of the four men who struggled to control it. The first, a half-French, half-Scots-Irish trapper named Jean Ballard, meets and courts Consuelo Coronel, daughter of one of the richest New Mexicans in the Taos region in the 1850's. The Coronels, as wary of Ballard as the Salazars were of Sam Lash, try to discourage the upstart gringo by subjecting him to tedious hours of chaperoned courting:

> They did not hate him as a person but they hated anything alien. Family was everything to them. Their whole society was a great family and it was organized to repel intrusion. They did not have to insult him or reject him or even close a door to him. They could freeze him out and wait him out. . . . When it came to creating a situation full of vague promise and polite delay, the Mexicans were artists. In this respect, as in others, there was something feminine about all of them.[8]

Fergusson's concept of male New Mexican incompetence

---

[7] In his history of New Mexico, *Rio Grande*, p. 116, Fergusson elaborates on New Mexican dependency: "If you hire a Mexican to work for you he is likely to regard you as a potential source of all things needed and to become a somewhat importunate solicitor of favors. Give him half a chance and he will get himself into your debt and stay there. In a word, he will relapse into peonage."

[8] Harvey Fergusson, *Grant of Kingdom*, pp. 4–6, 12–13, 30–49.

was based on his notion of three racial traits: fondness for leisure, emphasis on the "feminine" family unit, and business ineptitude. The male Coronels fit the pattern perfectly. Lounging about the great house most of the day, they let the family hacienda go to seed and are eventually brought to their knees by Ballard with the one thing holier to most of Fergusson's *ricos* than blood: money. Eagerly accepting cash from Ballard in exchange for Consuelo's hand in marriage, the Coronels deed to the former trapper a "grant of kingdom" bestowed upon one of their ancestors by the King of Spain, encompassing two thousand square miles of wilderness. With Consuelo in tow, Ballard leaves the easy life of the Coronel hacienda to carve a cattle empire out of the harsh wilderness and to build his own version of a great house. Raising beef to feed the Anglo miners, cowboys, and store owners who soon filter into the region, Ballard becomes a wealthy man, exercising absolute though benevolent dominion over the Anglo ranchers and Hispano sheepherders who settle nearby. In its heyday the house of Ballard becomes a social center for the entire Southwest, presided over by a smiling despot and his wife, who oversees the great house in the style of a great lady.

Yet Ballard eventually finds that the conversion of his grant of kingdom from wilderness to garden has its bitter side. The early years of building the kingdom, with its simple pleasures of work and thrift, were the best. The later, soft years that bring power and responsibility are correspondingly less satisfying. Consuelo grows fat and is replaced in bed by a mestiza mistress. Beans and cheap wine give way to imported Havanas and French cognac. Increasingly as Ballard finds himself longing for the younger and harder days, he realizes that he spent twenty years "destroying one thing while he was building another." In the name of progress and change he had done what he could to dismantle the traditional New Mexican way of life only to find that he sorely missed it in old age. Shortly before his death he begins to fantasize about an idyllic past which, to his chagrin, he recognizes as the New Mexican great-house past that he helped to destroy. On his deathbed Ballard pronounces himself a fool.[9]

The disillusionment of Jean Ballard illustrates a turning point in Fergusson's concept of the assets and liabilities arising from the Anglo-American's overthrow of an "inferior" race. In challenging the clichés of progress on Anglo terms, Fergusson placed himself in the tradition of the other great-house novelists who implied that the American takeover of the Hispanic Southwest, however natural and inevitable, had its price. Yet Fergusson did not for a moment doubt that the American way was indeed superior. However much his conquerors ultimately question their motives, they *are* the masters of change, the architects of a new destiny. Ballard pines for the past only in the twilight of his career, and he is honest enough to admit that if he had his life to live over—without the gift of prophecy —he would act precisely the same way because his "genetic" drive would permit him no other course of action.

A more sophisticated treatment of the dilemma posed by racial destiny occurs in Fergusson's last and most distinguished novel, *The Conquest of Don Pedro*. The story of the mercenary "conquest" of the drowsing New Mexican village of Don Pedro by Leo Mendes, Jewish peddler turned storekeeper, is a rare tribute to the merchant who played a decisive role in developing the Far West. It is also Fergusson's most ambitious effort to explain how and why the great-house economy of postconquest New Mexico was overthrown by the American entrepreneurial ethic. Leo Mendes, a Portuguese Jew born on Manhattan's East Side, is a gentle and reflective man of infinite patience and perseverance. He lacks the bravado of the stock western hero. In a land where success is measured by skill with horses, guns, and women, Mendes rides a burro, shuns violence, and avoids women most of the time. Instead, he gets unobtrusively rich selling merchandise behind a counter. This mild-mannered man is a new kind of western hero, the Jew whose personal attributes, as Fergusson sees them, include a dark

[9] Ibid., pp. 50–55, 60–87, 108–112, 150–155.

skin, a capacity for "taking on the color of his environment," and an ability to speak Spanish like a native—but he also embodies, like so many immigrants of all backgrounds, the characteristic Yankee drive for material success.

Arriving on the outskirts of southern New Mexico shortly after the Civil War, Mendes begins his economic conquest innocently enough. Stopping short of the town to await the end of the long siesta hours, he then trots into town with burro and trade goods instead of horse and rifle. Against his "alien" combinations of patience and persuasion, resistance and resilience, the local great-house barons stand little chance. Setting up a *tienda barata* (cheap store) to rival the *tienda de raya* (company store) operated by the region's leading great-house grandee, Don Augustín Vierra, Mendes undercuts his competitor by lowering prices and extending long-term credit. He makes up his temporary loss by selling supplies to local ranches and beef and grain to the soldiers at the nearby fort. By the mid-1870's his store is serving fully one-third of the territory of New Mexico, and he has become "Don" Leo. Building a modest great house on the edge of town, he rides a Kentucky pacer and dines alternately with the Anglo soldiers at the fort and with the great-house *ricos* of the Rio Grande Valley. Eventually even the Vierras fall under Mendes' financial control. The conquest of Don Pedro has involved by the early 1880's the social and financial transformation of a sizable part of the Old Mexican Southwest.

Not content to confine his conquest to the economic overthrow of the great house, Mendes adds insult to injury by taking Don Augustín Vierra's wife, Doña María Guadalupe Vierra, as his mistress—a bit of romantic intrigue which enables Fergusson to add sexual degeneracy to economic ineptitude as explanation for the decline and fall of the New Mexican social order. A woman of good family from Mexico City, married in the full bloom of youth and set down in the midst of the "heat, flies and Indians" of the sterile borderlands, Doña Lupe has become hard and bitter herself, taking on the harsh and wrinkled outlines of the landscape. To beat back the erosions of age and boredom, she takes up with Leo Mendes, the town's single source of energy. The affair is a stormy one. Unfettered by puritanical restrictions, Doña Lupe is an artist of love, the heir of a "great and ancient erotic tradition" that begins with "the first faint smile of flirtation" and ends with "the final spasm."

She is by no means unique. The turbulent romance of Leo Mendes and Doña Lupe Vierra serves as Fergusson's excuse for some sweeping generalizations about New Mexican promiscuity and sexuality. He interprets the sexual "conquest" of New Mexican women by American "penetrators" as nothing less than a symbolic repetition of the earlier military conquest —the active male role representing aggressive American entry, the passive female role reenacting the "nonresistant" New Mexican reception of the conqueror. Their respective sexual behavior resembles a see-saw pattern of love and hate, desire and disgust. Of the two races, however, it is the conquered New Mexican which Fergusson ultimately condemns. The young and robust male Americans who invade the Southwest in the earlier conquest fiction were alternately attracted and disgusted by what they regarded as Spanish Mexican promiscuity. This is also true of Fergusson's male American heroes. Arriving in the Southwest decades after the conquest, they are drawn to and repelled by the "loose" sexual habits of all native New Mexicans, female and male alike. This licentiousness disturbs men of principle such as Leo Mendes—even as he joins in— but bothers no one within the native New Mexican order, including the clergy. Fergusson's novels are replete with priests who, themselves guilty of several transgressions, encourage their rollicking parishioners to strike a reasonable compromise between passion and piety by sinning six days a week and repenting the seventh. This convenient custom constitutes a mutually advantageous social contract between the shepherds and their flocks, bringing pleasure to the people and patronage to the Church.

The problem with *The Conquest of Don Pedro*, as with much of Fergusson's writing, is that its tendency to sermonizing eventually prevents the principal characters from being free agents. Such is the burden that Leo Mendes ultimately bears. As banker, broker, and lover to the house of Vierra, Mendes soon finds himself "deeply entangled in a prickly thicket of need and desire, of obligation and demand." The conquering peddler has become the prisoner of his own conquest, and he pays for it dearly. After a decade of unbroken prosperity, Mendes rejects Doña Lupe and marries her sixteen-year-old niece Magdalena, whom he had educated as a child into the American way of doing things. The result is more than he bargained for. A complex woman whose physical and emotional traits combine New Mexican beauty and passion with Anglo intelligence and ambition, Magdalena is a freak of her husband's own making. Using her liberated status as the wife of a gringo Jew to rebel against the double sexual standard of New Mexican society, she openly flirts with her many admirers and eventually runs off with a gun-toting, greaser-hating cowboy. Faced with his wife's infidelity, Mendes is also faced with the irony that his career as conqueror has come full circle. Having once "conquered" the wife of the town's leading aristocrat, he has now been "conquered" by an upstart who, in seducing his wife, replaces Mendes himself as the new ruler of the old New Mexican order—and also embodies more typical Anglo attitudes towards Mexicans. Finally rejecting the great-house society of the *ricos*, Mendes flees to the Anglo boomtown of Las Vegas, New Mexico, and buys into a large merchandising firm.

If Fergusson's heroes question their motives, deeds, and achievements, Fergusson nevertheless ultimately affirms that the benefits of Anglo conquest outweighed its cost. His empire builders experience self-doubt, but only because they realize that the creation of a new order is frequently attended by the destruction of other things worth preserving. For Fergusson this process is the replacement of Mexican indolence by Anglo industry. His great-house fiction focuses on an inevitable social and economic turnover that was only accidentally an ethnic one as well. He scrupulously avoids color distinctions. He has little to say about the Mexican's complexion. His most admirable great-house conquerors, Jean Ballard and Leo Mendes, are men with dark complexions. He was concerned primarily with the special gifts of the Anglo-Saxon race as he saw them and only secondarily with the corresponding defects of the New Mexican *ricos.*

Fergusson does not possess deep sympathy for the New Mexican people because he believes that regions, like men, have their life cycles. In the case of New Mexico, one ethnic group stood in the path of another and was removed from power. He seems to deny the possibility that as the Hispanos became Anglicized, they might have begun competing with the Anglo-Americans on their own terms. Nor did he write or live long enough to watch his ethnocentricity challenged in the late 1960's, when a sizable number of young Anglos began to exhibit what Fergusson surely would have regarded as economic lassitude and social decay—behavior characteristic only of New Mexican *ricos* in his value system. The focus of Fergusson's work remained his conviction that the New Mexican *rico* lacked the competitive spirit Fergusson viewed as an Anglo-Saxon monopoly. That the native New Mexican stood in the path of Anglo "Destiny," "Conquest," and "Kingdom" was not his fault. It was merely his misfortune.[10]

The fictional seizures of the California great houses differ markedly from those in Texas and New Mexico. California dons were treated more compassionately in conquest fiction than were their Texan and New Mexican counterparts. This more understanding treatment in turn opened the way for a series of works in which the Americans still gain land, houses, and ladies but win the love and friendship of the conquered race as well. Fiction about the takeover of the California great houses represents the American invaders less as invaders than as invited guests. Indeed, the fall of the California great house is no fall at all, but rather the semiresurrection of a dying institution through the graceful mixing of American democrats and Californio aristocrats as near-equal partners in a common

[10] The best complete biography of Fergusson is William T. Pilkington, *Harvey Fergusson.*

cause. The effect is twofold: to keep the mass of lower-class Californios where they have always been, and to build a new economic and social order upon the decaying foundations of the great house without demolishing it. The viable Californio trappings of the great house are retained—the architecture of the house itself, the landscaping, the cattle herds, the vineyards, and even some of the polite social graces that ornamented the old-time houses. The "feudal" elements of the great house, Indian serfdom, and medieval agriculture are replaced by Yankee husbandry and mechanized farming. When the modernized great house is finished, it combines Yankee energy and Californio leisure, scientific agriculture and slow-paced living, plows and promenades.

One of the earliest great-house novels set in postconquest California, *Tide of Empire* (1927) by Peter Kyne, illustrates several of these formula devices. Arriving in the gold fields in 1850, Dermod D'Arcy, an Irish-American, courts a "pure-bred Castilian" named Josepha Guerrero, whose ivory complexion suggests "not a drop of native Indian blood." When D'Arcy learns that the U.S. Federal Commission on Land Titles has rejected Josepha's claim to eight square leagues of land on the Sacramento River, he tells her that he is delighted with the loss, as it is not the American way to accept dowries. However, when the land commission reverses its decision, D'Arcy accepts the burdens of property ownership with gentlemanly resignation, and the novel departs radically from the formulas of the conquest genre. Out of patience with the money-minded Yankee squatters who have settled on Josepha's estate and are rapidly converting the grasslands into irrigated pastures, D'Arcy summarily evicts his fellow-countrymen. Once D'Arcy and Josepha are married, they turn the vast acres of their Sacramento River estate back into the peaceful cattle country it was before the American conquest. Even the family great house is preserved intact. So, except for a few American-style practical improvements, is the old order of the Californio dons.

A far more sweeping renovation attends the takeover of another California great house in *The Ranch of the Golden*

Flowers by Constance Lindsay Skinner. Shortly after the start of the gold rush, two orphaned pioneers from Kansas, teenager Lank Hardie and his sister Tess, arrive at the De Soto hacienda in southern California and are adopted as members of the family. Though the De Sotos set out to convert the Hardie children to the Californio way of life, the Kansas orphans quietly but quickly turn the tables. Lank, a sixteen-year-old farm boy, wonders how the De Sotos make their living. When he learns that they rarely bother to plant and do not know what plowing means, he concludes that the De Sotos are in a crisis. Lank quickly learns the few necessary Spanish words to get the job done: "Like 'plow' an' 'horse' an' 'work' an' 'hurry up.'" Trying to inculcate a sense of time, he tells Munita De Soto, lovely teenaged daughter of the house, that she must no longer take the better part of an hour to fetch her school books each morning. Discarding the pointed sticks used by the Californios for centuries to poke holes in the ground, Lank introduces the plow. He mobilizes once-idle vaqueros and sends them into the fields bearing hoes and scythes instead of ropes and bridles. In no time at all the De Soto meadows, once rank with mustard weeds, are producing bumper crops of fruits, vegetables, and grains. By the end of the novel the feckless De Sotos and the enterprising Hardies have reached an understanding: the De Sotos agree to become full-fledged "Kansoos" farmers, and the Hardies agree to take on a few of the less harmful trappings of the California great-house culture. The final message in this novel is that once Lank and Munita are married, they will accomplish genetically what has already been accomplished economically. They will found a new dynasty in California, mixing Spanish leisure and romance with Kansas thrift and common sense, all without overthrowing the traditional privileged order.[11]

An even more extreme example of this cultural fusion occurs in *Mysterious Rancho* by Jackson Gregory. Business tycoon Benjamin Maxwell Whitney, ruined by a Wall Street rival

[11] Constance Lindsay Skinner, *The Ranch of the Golden Flowers*, pp. 21–49, 72, 89, 148–158.

in the 1920's, returns to his native California to find peace of mind and reorder his priorities. There, at the base of the Santa Lucia mountains in the southern part of the state, Whitney stumbles upon an ancient great house that has stood intact since the late 1700's. Few fences scar the land; few acres are broken to the plow. The prince of the estate, antique and elegant Don Mento Olivas, is a white-bearded gentleman of the old school who carries himself "with that graceful dignity which is a birthright" of the well-born Spaniard. Clinging stubbornly to the old amenities, Don Olivas dreads the single day set aside each month for "work," by which he means doing battle with his depleted bank accounts.

Whitney promptly sets about pulling Don Olivas out of approaching bankruptcy. Buying the adjoining ranch, he stocks the range with pureblooded cattle, puts in telephone and electricity lines, and builds concrete dams to irrigate his barley fields. When accused by his Californiana sweetheart Teresa of violating the beauty of God's acres, the two square off in a verbal duel symbolic of the postconquest relationship between the two cultures:

> ". . . America commercializes everything. You would take the valley . . . and coin it into dollars and cents!"
>
> "Not by a jugful," he laughed at her. . . . "What did your distinguished ancestor want with all these acres? You hold some forty-five thousand and that's just a fragment of the ancestral estate. . . . Why did he want all that? Just to look at? Just for the beauty of the scenery?"

Taking his lady love to a nearby hilltop, Whitney presents a Yankee vision of future California, transformed from untamed forest and runoff water into waving fields of grain and dams to nurture the thirsting land. Capping the image, he informs her that their own marriage will usher in a new era in California history, with Teresa's reverence for the past and Whitney's passion for progress uniting the best of feudal Spain and Coolidge's America to form a new elite society in the Far West of the twentieth century.[12]

[12] Jackson Gregory, *Mysterious Rancho*, pp. 17, 39–44, 166, 246–247.

Whatever its artistic merits and whatever its setting, great-house fiction continues and refines stereotypes established in the conquest genre. Great houses fall because Americans are energetic, virile, and practical, while Spanish Mexicans are lazy or degenerate. Even when the conqueror is greedy and rapacious—even when brute force, injustice, and economic exploitation accompany the destruction of the Mexican order —the American remains superior to his victims in physique, intellect, and ambition. The great-house owners for their part deserve their fate because they prove incapable of putting their property to its best and highest use.

Despite this affirmation of Manifest Destiny, a good many of the great-house novels suggest that while the Americans might have been invariably successful in overturning the old Mexican order, they did not always do it properly. Periodically the idea crops up that somehow there was something wrong with the postconquest takeover of the Southwest. Something was not entirely admirable about the American economic system. Something was hypocritical about American ethics. Try as they might to justify the destruction or renovation of the great houses of the Southwest, Anglo writers using this theme could not avoid suggesting that there had been something attractive about the culture their heroes feel compelled to destroy. Their works are filled with lyrical descriptions of the pastoral beauty of the Californian and New Mexican country-sides before the Yankees pushed into the garden. Even the conquering heroes are sometimes entranced by the great-house way of life before they recover their practical senses and set about their work of demolition or renovation.

This pattern of initial attraction followed by denial and destruction derives from polarities inherent in southwestern fiction. The frequency with which Anglos adapt to the great-house culture they set out to destroy suggests an attraction which gives way to censure and denial only after a considerable personal struggle. This attraction is at once more complex and more sophisticated than the blunt sexual appeals discussed in chapter 3. As self-conscious spokesmen of progress, the writers of great-house fiction could nevertheless envision the possibilities of a life free from what they somehow felt to be the dehumanizing demands of Yankee civilization and its obsessive preoccupation with order and system, energy and enterprise. Envisioning that other life, they could permit their characters to yearn for it, as their counterparts in conquest fiction had yearned for what they regarded as Mexican sexual freedom. Yet while longing for leisure, they had to reject it just as surely as they rejected Mexican "promiscuity." American writers allowed their characters to be tempted once again. This time, however, the temptation was so strong that the Anglos felt driven to destroy it by destroying the entire life-style, or at least remodeling it to fit Yankee patterns. They condemned the great house precisely because it was so attractive. They censured it because they were ashamed to be tempted, and they viewed their yearning for a restful, even idle, life-style as a desertion of the higher American way. The conviction that the great houses were destined to be destroyed by a superior people was grounded in all that writers of great-house fiction felt and assumed about both the Spanish Mexican's way of life and the Anglo's concept of himself, his history, and his future.

CHAPTER FIVE

THE LITERARY DEGRADATION
OF THE MEXICAN

THE LINE CONNECTING the conquest fiction of the nineteenth century to the modern pulp westerns set in the Southwest is direct and obvious. Action, plots, and characters remain the same: Anglo heroes best Mexican bandidos, blonde heroines compete with Castilian dark ladies for honorable marriages, and sexy halfbreeds more explicitly bed, but still rarely wed, the Saxon hero.

There is, however, a significant reason for separating the modern pulps from their literary ancestors. The twentieth-century works exist within an established matrix. The conquest is an accomplished fact. Unlike the Beadles and Buntlines, whose Saxon heroes again and again imposed North American order on Mexican chaos, the twentieth-century pulp tales have their pecking order established not only from their first page, but even earlier—in the minds and emotions of their readers. This established order is particularly significant in a cultural form that is essentially soft-core, designed to titillate rather than disturb its audience. Pulp works have no high purpose. They are intended to sell. They sell by entertaining a large and nondiscriminating audience. They risk alienating that audience at the risk of losing sales. Pulps may tantalize and even shock the reader's sensibilities in certain areas, usually sex and violence. They are not likely to offend the reader's sensibilities by strongly challenging what authors and publishers regard as conventional political, social, or economic beliefs and values.

Translated from the general to the specific, this approach has generated an endless sequence of novels and stories featuring the Mexican as either bandido or buffoon. The Anglo protagonist is more likely to represent establishment institutions than was the freebooting individualist favored in the Beadles. He may be a U.S. marshal or, frequently, a Texas Ranger.[1] But this fact only highlights his superiority over his villainous or simple-minded antagonists. Now it is official as well as personal and racial. In this context the Mexican male of the twentieth-century pulp has even less chance of making a good showing than his Beadle/Buntline prototype.

Stephen Crane and O. Henry are among the more respectable writers who have contributed to this process. Crane's flamboyant "Horses—One Dash" features a Texas Ranger named Richardson traveling in rural Mexico with a servant named José. He has just settled down for the night when he is disturbed by a dozen Mexicans who try to rob him. The drunken leader is on the point of attacking Richardson when he is stopped by the ranger's calm presence. Realizing that he "came extremely near to having eaten his last tamale," the bandit preserves his standing by beating the cringing José. Once the two are rescued by government troops, however, José switches from cringing coward to boasting buffoon: "exultant, defiant, and oh! bristling with courage."[2]

Crane's story was a one-time effort. O. Henry based much

[1] Most of the Texas Ranger works closely resemble the Beadle dime novels in characters and plot. In *Rio Rita*, by Harry Sinclair Drago, Ranger Jim Stewart solicits the aid of the heroine, Rita Fergusson, daughter of a Spanish mother and an American cattle baron, to capture an oily bandido nicknamed, in "the spiggoty tongue," The Kinkajou; then the two settle down on Rita's large ranch. In *Jess Roundtree, Texas Ranger*, by Dane Coolidge, Ranger Roundtree meets Alicia de Montana, whose delicate features and pale skin show her to be of "pure Spanish blood" and not to be confused with the "low-browed *pelado*" scum of the border. After joining forces to capture a gang of bandidos called the Vinagrones (Sand Scorpions), who specialize in stealing beautiful women and holding them for ransom, Alicia and Roundtree are wed. In *Clattering Hoofs*, by William Macleod Raine, a golden-haired cattle baron's daughter, Sandra Ranger, is kidnapped by a vicious bandido but is rescued by the blond hero Bob Webb, an Arizona Ranger.

[2] "Horses—One Dash," in *The Work of Stephen Crane*, XII, 203–220.

of his early career on a series of tales, collected in *Heart of the West*, whose Mexican males have no redeeming qualities whatever. Their behavior ranges from fawning servility to inept villainy. In "An Afternoon Miracle," a sooty-skinned *bandido* named Leandro García tries to assault a Saxon damsel as she is bathing in a Texas water hole. Bounding out of the brush, the swart greaser looks the lady over "with an ominous, dull eye":

> "I no hurt-y you, Senorita. . . . But maybeso take one *beso*—one li'l kees, you call him. . . ."
> "Vamoose, quick," she ordered preemptorily, "you coon!"
> The red of insult burned through the Mexican's dark skin.
> "Hidalgo, Yo!" he shot between his fangs. "I am not neg-r-ro! *Diabla bonita*, for that you shall pay me."

At this point a red-haired ranger named Bob Buckley appears and, observing that García has no gun, challenges his adversary to a fistfight. Frightened by the Saxon reputation in physical combat, the bandit draws a concealed knife. Before he can hurl it, Buckley delivers "the good old Saxon knock-out blow—always so pathetically disastrous to the fistless Latin races," thus rescuing the damsel with maidenhead intact.[3]

In his later poems and short stories O. Henry shifts the emphasis from the Mexican as villain to the Mexican as buffoon. In an ode to "Tamales," published in the collection *Rolling Stones*, Don José Calderón, a tamale vendor in Austin who lost a grandfather in the Mexican War, takes revenge by serving American customers tamales made from long-dead cats and dogs:

> This is the Mexican
> Don José Calderón
> One of God's countrymen,
> Land of the buzzard,
> Cheap silver dollar, and

---

[3] O. Henry, "The Caballero's Way," "Dry Valley's Indian Summer," "Hygeia at the Solito," "The Higher Abdication," "The Princess and the Puma," and "An Afternoon Miracle," in *Heart of the West*, pp. 101, 119–129, 153, 187–188, 248–249, 261.

Cacti and murderers.
Why has he left his land,
Land of the lazy man,
Land of the pulque,
Land of the bullfight,
Fleas and revolution . . .
This is the reason . . .
Listen and tremble
One of his ancestors,
Ancient and garlicky . . .
Died full of minié balls,
Mescal and pepper.
Dire is thy vengeance,
Don José Calderón.
For the slight thing we did
Killing thy grandfather.
What boots it if we killed
Only one greaser,
Don José Calderón?
This is your deep revenge,
You have greased all of us,
Greased a whole nation
With your Tamales. [Pp. 257–258]

Crane and O. Henry set a fashion. More and more twentieth-century writers added to their repertoire the comic Mexican, the funny man who provides comedy relief to—and sometimes from—the sober Saxon heroes and their ladies. Reflecting the established cultural pecking order mentioned earlier in this chapter, these chili-pepper bumpkins do not pose even a fabricated threat to Anglo society. The Beadle bandidos were at least potentially harmful figures who sometimes played important plot roles and whose position outside the law dictated the need to dispose of them. The slapstick greasers are entirely harmless characters—outsiders *within* the Saxon Southwest. Often they are riffraff who sometimes run small errands for Saxon citizens, but usually they can be found roosting against back-alley shanties, sleeping in stable haylofts, or sitting on segregated barstools. They hardly dare lift their eyes to a white woman. Yet the fate of these clowns is pathetically disproportionate to their "crimes." The new-model greaser need no longer be a bandit at all; it is enough that he is a greaser. He may be a drunkard, guttersnipe, a well-meaning jester, or simply an innocent citizen who happens to be in the wrong place at the wrong time. However lowly his station in life, whatever his ambitions to lift himself from the alley dust or the saloon floor, his efforts are doomed to failure. In the world of the pop and pulp western, a "reformed" greaser is a contradiction in terms. The genetic disease of greaserism is permanent.

The master of the Mexican as a figure of crude comedy was Alfred Henry Lewis, a turn-of-the-century humorist who based much of his career on tales pitting swart bumpkins against "white" cowboys. Occasionally Lewis' brown-skinned buffoons are violently dispatched in the manner of the Beadle bandidos. More often they are simply made the butt of crude jokes. In *Wolfville* (1897), a harmless Mexican walking the streets of Wolfville late at night carrying a monkey wrench is mistaken for a stranger with a gun and is shot dead by a leading citizen. The following day the *Wolfville Daily Coyote*, praising the high sense of civic duty that prompted the citizen's action, cautions the greaser population to be more careful. In *Faro Nell and Her Friends* (1913), Lewis offered a swarthy dipsomaniac by the name of Monte. To rid themselves of this embarrassing barfly, the local cowboys rope a live bobcat and chain the beast over the Red Light Bar. When the cat leaps at Monte, the Mexican goes into *delirium tremens* and almost dies but refuses to give up drink. Conceding defeat in their efforts to reform an unregenerate greaser, the cowboys assign Monte a segregated barstool, label him a tourist attraction, and appoint him "official drunkard of Arizona," a title which Monte bears with pride.[4]

[4] Alfred Henry Lewis, *Wolfville*, p. 138; Alfred Henry Lewis, *Faro Nell and Her Friends: Wolfville Stories*, pp. 99–125, 242. Another harmless greaser buffoon appears in Emerson Hough's *Heart's Desire: The Story of a Contented Town, Certain Peculiar Citizens, and Two Fortunate Lovers*. José Santa María Trujillo, a clownish jockey, charges ahead of his Texan rivals in a horse race but foolishly fans his hat-shy mount with a sombrero and is tossed high into the grandstands (pp. 217–218).

Whether victims of the bottle or of cowboy rough-housing, Lewis' greasers are tolerated only up to a certain point. If they dare to assert themselves in any significant fashion, they are summarily dispatched in the manner of the Beadle bandidos. In *The Sunset Trail* Lewis introduced a halfbreed nicknamed the Tomcat who initially serves as town clown of Dodge City, Kansas: "He was half Mexican and half Comanche, and the blend was unfortunate. . . . his heart became the heart of a hare whenever the cold, gray-eyed gaze of one of clean white strain fell across him in hostility." Annoyed that he cannot "face a white of the pure blood without turning craven to the bone," the Tomcat, suitably lubricated, leaves his barstool and sets out to prove himself as a man of courage by killing and scalping Bat Masterson, sheriff of Dodge. En route to his rendezvous with Masterson, he pauses for a fortifying drink, fires at a saloon proprietor, misses, and kills a dancehall girl. Pursued by Masterson into the desert, the sobered Tomcat tries to bushwhack the sheriff, misses again, and is shot and left in the desert for the coyotes.[5]

When the new-style greaser does attempt to function as a badman, he tends to be conspicuously less bad and more "comical" than his dime-novel ancestors. In Jackson Gregory's *Riders Across the Border* (1932), for example, the governor of Sonora, a pompous figure named Don Carlos Toroblanco, suffers prolonged humiliation at the hands of the Anglo hero, Rogue Madden. When Madden, owner of ranches on both sides of the border, invites Toroblanco to join a privileged group of Arizona ranchers in a friendly card game at one of his manors, Toroblanco accuses his host of cheating. Madden delivers the predictable knockout blow, trusses up the governor, and discovers several pieces of dining-room silver that he has surreptitiously pocketed during the game. When the governor's "Mex" smell becomes too much, Madden contemptuously releases him, whereupon he promptly tries to abduct Madden's be-

[5] Alfred Henry Lewis, *The Sunset Trail*, pp. 22–23, 122–133, 168–191, 295.

trothed. Madden responds by stealing into the governor's tent, stripping him of his pants, and marching him across the border to the Arizona authorities for hanging.

The novels of Zane Grey and Max Brand contain many buffoon-bandits of the Toroblanco model. Like their dime-novel predecessors, they exist primarily to fumble the capture of the heroine or bungle the showdown with the hero. But this is not their exclusive function. Grey's and Brand's bandits come far closer to ravishing blonde heroines than did their Beadle predecessors. Zane Grey in particular specializes in "little swarthy-skinned greaser runts" who *almost* debauch the fair heroines. His novels are replete with tantalizingly unfinished sentences that tease the reader into expecting the worst while maintaining the rigid linguistic proprieties prescribed by the censorship standards of the 1920's and 1930's. In *Desert Gold,* the heroine describes to the two heroes, former college football players Dick Gale and George Thorne, what would happen to her should she fall into the clutches of the black-skinned bandit Rojas. On the first day of her capture, Mercedes explains, Rojas would reserve her for himself. On the second day he would turn her over to his brutal henchmen; on the third day he would toss her to the dogs of his bandit camp. To thwart Rojas' initial plan to capture and deflower Mercedes, Gale tackles the bandit in a border saloon and tosses him across the room in a forward pass with no intended receiver, thus permitting Thorne and Mercedes to escape unscathed. Later, when the persistent Rojas actually captures Mercedes, Thorne, temporarily indisposed by a cactus thorn embedded in his gun hand, begs Dick to shoot Mercedes (*not* Rojas) before it is too late: "Kill her! Kill her! . . . Can't—you-see-Rojas———." Dick, paralyzed by Rojas' obvious intent, is slow to act. Just as Rojas is "about to ———," a Yaqui Indian guide, whose pure strain of blood places him above the halfbreed bandidos, at least in Grey's racial hierarchy, forces Rojas over the edge of a cliff. Tumbling downward, the bandido is brought up in mid-flight by a bunch of *cholla* cactus, there to twist in agony until he breaks free and continues his plunge into the bowels of the canyon.[6]

This pattern has continued unabated in the second half of the twentieth century. Selections of images could be made from among dozens, perhaps hundreds, of examples. Among the most useful is Frank O'Rourke's *A Mule for the Marquesa* because of the significant differences between the treatment of Mexicans in the novel itself and in its film version, *The Professionals*, made only two years later. O'Rourke's original work features a team of five men, each expert in a particular form of derring-do, hired by wealthy rancher Augustus Grant to penetrate the stronghold of a revolutionary turned bandit and to rescue the rancher's kidnapped Mexican wife. Some progress has been made in fifty years. The group accomplishes its task expeditiously, but without moralizing about the Saxon mission. Their superiority over their adversaries is technical rather than ethnic. But it is nevertheless superiority. As trackers, thinkers, and fighters, the Mexicans never have a chance.

This approach can be explained at least partly in terms of a need for targets characteristic of all adventure fiction. Cultural prejudice, however, also seems to play a significant role in the images of Mexicans in *A Mule for the Marquesa*. Admittedly, one of the rescue team, son of a Mexican father "of good blood" and an Irish mother, is described as a tracker and a bowman fit "to ride the war trail with the Comanches." But he is on the right side. He is also a taciturn character who tends to fade into the background compared to his more voluble Anglo comrades. The Mexican characters who stand out in the reader's memory are the villains. And they stand out as being beneath contempt. The marquesa of the title is a scheming whore who betrayed her loving, trusting husband for a high-born Mexican lover. He "blew the family fortune gambling on the revolution. . . ." He is nothing but "one of a long line of plunderers" who now seeks to buy a pardon from the current government with ransom money for a "kidnapping" that never

[6] Zane Grey, *Desert Gold*, pp. 28–50, 162–176, 221–223.

took place. The bandit leader himself, Jesús Raza, has a mind that is "a direct, uncomplicated extension of elemental desires . . . holding no devious intelligence, no grasp of reason." The other members of Raza's band are primarily of the same stamp: drunkards, brutes, degenerates. The best than can be said for them is that they are the products of years of fighting, survivors whose humanity has been eroded by a harsh land and a harsh war.[7]

If the degradation of the Mexican male remains a fact of life in pulp westerns, he at least has seen the Saxon hero crawl into the mud with him. The process of abandoning the white man's burden was gradual. It began by his humanization—by allowing him to fall in love with someone besides his horse, to take a nip from a jug now and then, and even to make mistakes in judgment. This process, common to westerns as a genre, was in full swing by the 1940's. It has affected white-brown relationships primarily by introducing Saxons who may be protagonists but are scarcely heroes. They are bound by no discernible moral code. They spill blood and bed women with little mercy or moderation. The distinguishing mark of the new pulps is that their authors feel no need either to explain how these men became what they are or to defend their behavior. The conduct of the new-style Saxon as described in the course of a short story or novel is our only guide to his past. It is no longer necessary to show how formerly upright farmers, soldiers, or cowboys went astray. It is now considered enough for the reader to know that the hero is quite frankly without moral motivation and has no intention of starting a new life unless changing times make it too difficult to sustain the old one. The conventions of the contemporary pulpster generally involve avoiding questions of morals and motives, concentrating instead on the Saxon protagonist's "badness."

Such central characters are by no means confined to westerns with a border setting. Given the comprehensive negative images of Mexicans already existing in popular culture, it is,

[7] Frank O'Rourke, *A Mule for the Marquesa*, reissued as *The Professionals*, pp. 25–26, 64, 80, 101. References are to the latter edition.

however, hardly surprising that authors seeking a backdrop for the actions of their antiheroes gravitate towards the Rio Grande. In particular, the Mexican Revolution of 1910–1920, with its comprehensive spectrum of violence, established Mexico as a last fictional frontier, a barbarous land offering endless possibilities for killing bandidos and seducing señoritas whose respective fates mattered little even to themselves. Dane Coolidge's *Yaqui Drums* (1940) offers a hero, Milt Seabeck, who joins the Sonoran rebels for no other reason than that he loves to kill and is good at it. When the tide of battle turns against the Villistas, he boots friends from his high-powered getaway car and races to the border to save his own skin. Stumbling upon a lost gold mine en route, Seabeck momentarily considers telling his rebel friends about the find so they might use the gold to purchase arms and win the revolution. Instead, he keeps the secret of the mine to himself.

Yaqui Drums is, in short, a watershed novel. It announces the arrival of the American mercenary who fights not to advance the Saxon race or the concept of Manifest Destiny, but for money, adventure, or simple bloodlust. The only difference between Milt Seabeck and the dozens of soldiers of fortune who follow him in three decades of pulps with a southwestern setting is that the more recent freelancers are as formidable in the boudoir as their Beadle and Zane Grey predecessors were on the battlefield. The plot lines of these works are virtually indistinguishable. Their primary requirement is a sufficiently brutal protagonist. He need not even be of pure Saxon stock. One series hero, Jim Sundance, is half Indian. Another, Josiah Hedges, created by George Gillman and featured in over twenty novels, is actually half Mexican. He demonstrates, however, no significant "Mexican" characteristics. He is simply another grotesque creation designed to appeal to the kind of reader C. L. Sonnichsen aptly dubs "Felix Lapgore"—a man with a seemingly insatiable appetite for extreme forms of vicarious violence.[8]

[8] C. L. Sonnichsen, "The Wyatt Earp Syndrome," in *From Hopalong to Hud: Thoughts on Western Fiction*, pp. 28 ff.

The novels collectively titled *Fargo* can be presented as reasonably representative of this type of western. Neal Fargo, the title hero of the series, shoots and ruts his way through the Southwest in the early years of the twentieth century with little of the well-intentioned innocence that made some of the Beadle heroes amusing. He is a hired killer who signs on the dotted line to the highest bidder. Known and feared from South America to Alaska, from the Philippines to Wyoming, in *Bandolero* (1973), by John Benteen, Fargo takes his talents into revolutionary Mexico, running guns for Pancho Villa. In the opening sequence he turns seven hundred Mexican federal troops into "a bloody, writhing mass of flesh" with a single machine gun. After exterminating several more detachments of government troops and bedding a proportionate number of loose-principled señoritas, Fargo lights out for the last New World frontier in Australia. In Benteen's *Apache Raiders* (1973), Fargo fires notched bullets between the eyes of greaser victims, reducing their heads to brown pumpkins "dissolving in a red spray." In *Sierra Silver* (1974), written by John W. Hardin, he obliterates bandidos and Federalistas alike with firebombs made from tequila bottles and in spare moments leaps from the bed of a New England schoolmarm to the *sala* of a great-house señorita named Isabel Fernández. Examining Fargo's sexual equipment critically, Isabel pronounces him a boar. Fargo replies that he will make a sow of her, and proceeds to do so in explicit detail.[9]

To achieve maximum impact, however, a hard-boiled hero —or antihero—requires a suitable adversary. An author can

---

[9] For another sample of this genre, the reader with a strong stomach might try the Lassiter series of pulps, featuring as the title hero a black-dressed loner similar in appearance and behavior to "The Man with No Name" created by Clint Eastwood. In Jack Slade, *The Man From Tombstone*, a greasy *pistolero* who guzzles whiskey for breakfast and clamps his oily hair tight in his teeth, tries to shoot it out with Lassiter and receives a bullet up the nose. In Slade's *The Man from Del Rio*, Lassiter disposes of a band of "scrounging, scrummy little greaser rats" just as they are on the point of gang-raping the bosomy blonde heroine. In *Sidewinder*, also by Slade, Lassiter dispatches no fewer than sixty greaser gunmen—smashing skulls, crushing throats, and blowing bandidos skyward with dynamite as they shriek to the saints for help.

hardly oppose bandit-buffoons of the O. Henry model to someone with the combat skills of a Neal Fargo and expect to sustain reader interest in what is supposed to be an adventure
story. As a result, the modern pulps, almost by necessity, have
begun restoring some dignity to their Mexican villains. An early example of this process appears in William MacLeod Raine's
Beyond the Rio Grande. Manuel Megares, "the bogy man of
the border," is a talented thief and willing murderer gifted with
fair skin and an impeccable command of English. His most
winning trait is that he admits he is a fraud. Fond of mouthing
patriotic platitudes about his commitment to the Mexican Revolution, Megares privately rants against the rabble and plots
to enrich himself at their expense. Yet his frankness by no
means compensates for his underlying wickedness. When he
captures the two Saxon protagonists, petroleum baron Jack
Hadley and fair-skinned lady cattle rancher Lee Reynolds, he
decrees death for Hadley and concubinage for Lee. In that as
in everything else, he is mistaken. A complex plot contrivance
enables Hadley to capture Megares. Here, however, Megares
proves his difference from the cringing cowards of the dime
novels and the clowns of the Lewis type. Refusing to beg or
bargain for his life, Megares faces a firing squad with courage,
humor, and a Shakespearian quotation.[10]

The Mexican villain can become virtually lost in the shuffle
of degenerates that stalk the pages of the new-style pulps. John
W. Hardin's *The Comancheros* pits Jim Sundance against a
gang of fifty hand-picked grotesques prefiguring the group as-
sembled for the denouement of Mel Brooks's *Blazing Saddles.*
But the leader is an Anglo deserter from the U.S. Army, a sadistic butcher, and a backslidden Baptist to boot. As for Sundance, he gains credibility with the gang by shooting a Mexican priest who refuses to pray over the leader's dead brother—previously hanged surreptitiously by Sundance himself.
When we finally meet a Mexican bandido named Ramírez, it

[10] William MacLeod Raine, *Beyond the Rio Grande,* pp. 146–158, 175, 218, 250.

is in a verbal confrontation with, of all things, a homosexual Anglo gunman:

> The gun in the nance's hand came up slightly; there was a shake in his whiney voice . . . "You got a dirty mouth on you, greaser."
>
> Ramírez threw back, "You too, Flossy, but not from talking."

In this context, Ramírez seems something of a relief. At least his teeth are perfect and he has a sense of humor.[11]

More typical of the new model of Mexican villain is the character of Rodolfo Fierro, Neal Fargo's frequent antagonist in those works in the series with a border setting. While Fierro has some of the characteristics of the Beadle greaser, he is anything but a grotesque foil for the Saxon soldier of fortune. He is portrayed with some fidelity to his historical prototype—a ruthless killer, hardly less skilled in the broad spectrum of martial and military arts than Fargo himself. A dangerous man in every way, he sustains the respect if not the affection of his immediate followers. On several occasions he comes uncomfortably close to ending Fargo's career permanently. Certainly Fargo himself speaks and thinks of Fierro in terms of respect which would have been incomprehensible to Young Wild West or a Texas Ranger. Similarly, the Comancheros who come closest to ending Sundance's career are Mexican—renegade *rurales* whose parent corps is described with respect as tough and smart and whose own behavior is intelligent and courageous even if ultimately fatal.[12]

If the Mexican male is in the process of recovering at least some of his dignity as a pulp villain, the Mexican woman, whether halfbreed harlot or Castilian dark lady, is facing increased competition as a sexist stereotype. At the beginning of the century the greaser hussy still held her place. O. Henry specialized in creating dusky temptresses with misspelled names denoting half-breed status: Pancha Sales, Tonia Pérez, Pan-

[11] John W. Hardin, *The Comancheros*, esp. pp. 101 ff.
[12] Ibid., pp. 138ff.

chita O'Brien. Zane Grey's border novels generally included dark-hued sluts whose sole function in the story line was to tease the Saxon heroes close to or beyond the brink of sin. Margarita Arallanes, the half-caste queen of seduction in *Wanderer of the Wasteland* (1920) is a "damn leetle wild cat—mucha Indian—on fire all time" who explores the anatomy of hero Adam Larey with such persistence that Adam finally abandons his Sunday school principles. When Adam's devilishly handsome and unprincipled brother arrives unexpectedly from the East, Margarita switches siblings with absolute lack of moral scruples. Adam, beseeching the "swart vixen" to remember his lovemaking, receives the classic answer of the one-night stand: "Ah, señor—so long ago and far away!" Shocked by Margarita's betrayal and even more by his own fall, Adam goes into exile in the Arizona desert. There he is discovered in a sequel, *Stairs of Sand* (1928), by a rancher's daughter, "of a blond type seldom seen in the Southwest," who persuades Adam to forget his long-ago affair with the "little slip of a greaser girl."[13]

Unlike Grey's halfbreeds, Max Brand's dark ladies usually tend to be highborn and therefore proportionately more qualified to wed the Saxon hero. Indeed, as in conquest fiction, they sometimes turn out to be all-white heroines temporarily disguised. In *Border Guns* (1928), "Francesca Laguarda," a dark-skinned, gun-toting moll who runs liquor, Chinamen, and opium across the border in the 1920's, finally removes her black wig and brown stain and reveals her true identity as Helen O'Mallock, a "pure, unmixed Irish" lass who only posed as a halfbreed bandida to bring the smuggling racketeers to justice. Usually, however, Brand's updated dark ladies simply act more sensually than their predecessors in the conquest genre. Thus, in *Silvertip* (1933) the title hero courts Julia Monterey, a lovely, high-caste heiress who loses Silvertip only because he is a

[13] Zane Grey, *Wanderer of the Wasteland,* p. 50; *Stairs of Sand,* p. 57. In Grey's *Majesty's Rancho,* Majesty Stewart, golden-haired sorority girl from New York who buys an old Spanish-grant ranch in Arizona, is opposed by a hard-drinking halfbreed vixen "on the make" named Bonita, who aspires to win the hero, Lance Sidway, but must settle for "several *vaquero* beaus" who seduce her one by one.

serial hero who must ride out of the last page into the next novel. By contrast, Les Tarron of *Flaming Irons* (1948) is a single-episode hero and pays permanent suit to Anna María Alvarado in an explicit fashion that would have shocked his fictional Saxon ancestors.

Popular literary treatments of the Mexican woman as slut face an increasing problem of what to do for an encore. Even Neal Fargo fails to exhaust Isabel Fernández by the end of *Sierra Silver*. Finding her still "hot as a busy machinegun," Fargo takes her to New Orleans to enlist her in a high-class whorehouse. The most obvious alternative is provided by the sexual liberation of the Saxon heroine. Here too, *Yaqui Drums* is a watershed in its introduction of Becky Bayless. Not only is she Seabeck's open and unabashed mistress, she is also a pilot who swoops over enemy troops and heaves homemade bombs from the cockpit of her light airplane, decimating entire battalions with a single toss. Ms. Bayless is the first in a long run of Norteamericanas whose pale-skinned beauty and pure racial heritage act as no barriers to performance both on the field of battle and between the sheets.

The brown whore may compete by increasingly overt sexual behavior, strikingly portrayed in dust-cover illustrations, in "dirty" language, and in explicit bedroom athletics. This reflects no essential moral difference from the nineteenth-century mixed-blood tart. The appearance of the soiled white dove, however, has eliminated the most obvious and dependable distinction between dark and light ladies: the gap between sexual potential and bedroom achievement. Since nearly all pulp heroines of whatever hue are now known of men, there is no longer an automatic need to field a battery of off-color trollops to offer more or less obscene contrasts to the snow-white and virtuous heroines. In the liberated atmosphere of the modern pulps, brown beauties offer no more than color variation to break the monotony. This startling degree of sexual leveling has rendered unnecessary, if not obsolete, one of the primary Mexican characters in the traditional border western: the half-breed whore. The other three—the dark lady, the Castilian don, and the greaser bandido—are still essentially irreplace-able. They have no white-skinned counterparts who behave *exactly* as they do. Once the white heroine was permitted to trespass on sexual territory formerly the province of the brown harlot, the essential difference between the two became part of our pop-cultural past. With all pulp heroines sexually active, the halfbreed daughter of joy has lost her earlier, unique func-tion.

Equal-performance sex, however, raises another question about the relationship between the races. Did the sexual "liber-ation" of the white woman lead to a basic change in status for the brown woman as well? Did the "lowering" of all-white women onto the ranch-house sofa or the desert bedroll lead to the lifting of *truly* brown women—as opposed to off-white Castilian ladies—to full heroine status? With a few notable exceptions, the answer is no. The color bar has survived the sexual liberation of the white woman. If white heroines are now free to bed white heroes, brown ladies are not correspond-ingly free to become wives to their Anglo lovers. The new race-sex equation seems to be one in which white or near-white Castilian ladies qualify both as mistresses and life-mates. Their loss of virginity no longer precludes marriage. Brown women, on the other hand, "freed" sexually since the first con-quest novels, are still held in racial if not sexual bondage.

Extensive research has unearthed only three novels in which the Anglo-Saxon hero actually marries a mestiza. In each case a conscious decision to marry a woman traditionally considered genetically polluted combines a tribute to the power of young love with the back-to-nature movement characteristic of cer-tain elements of mid-twentieth-century popular culture. In-stead of being a halfbreed whore, the brown woman becomes a kind of earth mother. Her Saxon husband is a man who con-sciously rejects the values of his conquering brethren. Frank Yerby's *The Treasure of Pleasant Valley* features a South Caro-lina planter, Bruce Harkness, who migrates to the gold fields in 1849 and falls in love with a mestiza named Juana. The reader must agree with Harkness, however, when he declares that Juana is no common halfbreed. Neither a pale-hued Castilian nor a dark and "coarse-featured breed," she is apparently descended from an Aztec princess who mated with a Spanish conquistador. Juana, therefore, is graced with "Spanish" features and "Indian" coloring, a combination that makes her look vaguely Grecian or Egyptian. Yet for all the author's hedging on the subject, this woman's darkness is permanent. There is no wig, mask, or stain that might be removed at will to reveal yet another disguised Castilian posing as a halfbreed for purposes of plot. And Harkness, descendant of slaveowners, admits his attraction, marries Juana, and settles down to a simple life of subsistence farming as close to nature and as far from the bigotry of Anglo-dominated California as possible. When Harkness discovers gold on his Pleasant Valley farm, he acts very differently from the Saxon heroes of the conquest and great-house novels. Tossing the ore back into the earth, he keeps the whereabouts of the mine a secret. And after some misgivings about what sort of "off-color halfbreed brats" he might expect from union with Juana, he even welcomes their forthcoming child.[14]

Bruce Harkness' willingness to marry a halfbreed is not taken for granted. Yerby takes pains to establish him as smarter, stronger, and more handsome than any other Anglos in the novel. Harkness can afford to be a "halfbreed-lover" for the same reasons of prowess that enable other Saxon heroes of the Beadle type to lynch or shoot halfbreeds by the score. Like them, he is master of his destiny. He simply chooses a different destiny than most Saxon heroes.

The same can be said for the second hero who chooses a halfbreed wife in a nineteenth-century pastoral setting: Irish-American mountain man John O'Brien in Frank O'Rourke's *The Far Mountains* (1959). O'Brien takes brown-skinned Luz Trujillo as wife only after his first love, a wealthy Castilian named Linda Lucero, is given by her father in marriage to a suitor of her own race and class. When Linda's husband drinks

[14] Frank Yerby, *The Treasure of Pleasant Valley*, pp. 70–87, 133–145, 220–222, 274, 286.

himself to death, O'Brien briefly considers deserting Luz and renewing his courtship of Linda. Instead he remains loyal to his "breed" wife not through moral scruples but because he realizes that Luz Trujillo, so vastly inferior to Linda Lucero in pedigree, is correspondingly her superior in beauty, grace, and character.

The third hero who marries a mestiza is Kelley Adams, a disillusioned expatriate who crosses the Arizona border to join the Villistas in Robert MacLeod's *Six Guns South* (1970). Arriving at a large hacienda, Adams meets and courts Lidia Sánchez, daughter of a wealthy landowner. The reader prepares for yet another union of American commoner and Castilian aristocrat. Yet Lidia Sánchez proves to be a most unusual dark lady. She boasts that she is a mestiza and is proud of it; her cinnamon complexion offers visual support of this shocking revelation. This short novel manages to violate most of the other unwritten laws of the pulp western. Lidia Sánchez is indeed wealthy, but she channels her wealth in a unique direction. Unlike most Mexican heroines, who side with the Saxon heroes, Lidia joins the rebels and turns her hacienda into a giant cooperative farm run by the rebel-peasants. Her radical views, her incisive intellect, and, above all, her complexion mark her as alien to the mass of dark ladies and halfbreed whores who crowd the pages of contemporary southwestern pulp literature. And when Kelley Adams marries this unlikely heroine, he assumes management of a communal farm instead of a great house. He also becomes one of the few Saxon heroes in literature who commits double treason by rejecting both the privileged economic order and the time-honored pattern of union between Yankee commoner and Castilian aristocrat.[15]

---

[15] In an earlier novel, *The Appaloosa*, set in Mexico in 1874, MacLeod settled for the traditional resolution of a white male–brown female affair. Matt Fletcher, an American drifter with a small amount of Mexican blood, pursues a thief named Jesús Medina Mora into Mexico to recapture the Appaloosa horse that Medina stole from him. When Medina sadistically breaks his arm and leaves him to die in the desert, Matt is rescued by a dark-skinned, gold-toothed whore named Trini who falsely boasts of "Spanish" blood and sacrifices herself so Matt can kill Medina—thus leaving Matt free to return to his true love, a Plains Indian woman named Wo Ista.

Given the built-in restrictions of formula westerns with a border setting, the wonder is not that so few lovely and talented mestiza heroines appear in these novels, but that any appear at all. In a medium dedicated to giving the least possible offense to the greatest possible number of readers—most of whom are Anglo—it would be foolish to expect much in the way of controversy. Certainly the conventions of formula westerns preclude the possibility of stressing Anglo-Mexican racial mixtures, much less analyzing the revolutionary overthrow of the old order in Mexico or the miserable lot of the peasantry. Such material is considered too intellectually and emotionally demanding for the pulp reader seeking recreation. There is, moreover, nothing especially provocative about the few mestizas who do manage to gain full heroine status. To a lady, they all look "Egyptian," "Greek," or perhaps Hawaiian or Tahitian—all within the accepted pulp canon of acceptable features and complexions. Finally, the formula western as yet features no male Mexican "breeds" who dare to marry "white" women. When the color line is crossed, it is Anglo males who do the crossing. Doubtless this reflects the desire so characteristic of popular culture to avoid unorthodox subject matter. From a dramatic viewpoint, this need to shun controversy commits even the modern author of formula westerns to an Anglo-Saxon world that is intrinsically hostile to *all* greasers, be they bandits or buffoons, whores or Amazon dark ladies.

The few novels cited as exceptions are just that. They are mentioned here because it is assumed that such novels are less familiar to most readers than the conventional works that dominate the genre. These exceptions simply point up the overwhelming similarities between the conquest fiction of an earlier era and the typical pulp western of our time. The brown whore as sex object, though no longer holding a monopoly on promiscuity, is still available to reinforce the dictum that white heroes may bed brown, but usually marry white. And of course the bandido remains one of the permanent fixtures of the border western. From the Beadles to the present-day pulps, the greasers and the *cholas* have maintained a degree of popularity and predictability unmatched by any other ethnic stereotypes in American fiction. The recent border westerns explore no new possibilities for the treatment of Mexico, Mexicans, or Mexican Americans of the Southwest. Instead, they simply expand the ways in which Mexican bodies tumble gymnastically into bed or topple grotesquely on the battlefield, in both cases only abetted by the emergence of the Anglo antihero. In the foreseeable future there does not seem to be much reason to expect a dramatic shift in moral tone or direction. As long as the market for Mexican stereotypes exists untouched by the kind of demand to alter ethnic stereotypes that has almost obliterated the savage redskin and the shuffling Sambo, we can expect the bandido and the brown lady to remain as popular mainstays of the border western.

CHAPTER SIX

THE CINEMATIC DEGRADATION OF
THE MEXICAN, 1894–1947

FROM ITS INCEPTION, the popular cinema, particularly in the United States, has combined critical disdain with public approval. More Americans watched movies than read books at mid-century.[1] It is reasonable to consider that movies reflect certain attitudes and concerns of their viewers. For ninety minutes it is possible to enjoy the reenactment of one's more acceptable fantasies—relishing triumphs, overlooking faults and failures, and tolerating prejudices. And the greaser has been the subject of one of those prejudices from the beginning.

In contrast to the earlier discussion of printed works, it seems unnecessary to distinguish films set north of the Rio Grande from those set south of the border. The stereotypes are too consistent, the differences too obscure, to make any significant difference. The first movies with Mexican settings were

[1] Russel B. Nye, *The Unembarrassed Muse: The Popular Arts in America*, p. 2, notes that by the mid-1940's average weekly attendance at American movies was ninety million and that the average American between his second and his sixty-fifth years spends three thousand days, almost nine years of his life, watching movies and television programs. Scholarly studies of the early motion picture industry are few. For general information regarding this period, see Fred J. Balshofer and Arthur C. Miller, *One Reel a Week*; Benjamin B. Hampton, *History of the American Film Industry from Its Beginnings to 1931*; Lewis Jacobs, *The Rise of the American Film: A Critical History*; Gerald Mast, *A Short History of the Movies*; Joseph H. North, *The Early Development of the Motion Picture, 1887–1909*; Terry Ramsaye, *A Million and One Nights: A History of the Motion Picture*; and Anthony Slide, *Early American Cinema*.

innocuous enough: short-subject bullfights produced in the 1890's. These vitagraph peep shows were followed by an increasing number of full-length features including Mexican characters. Prints of these early films are rarely available. However, with the help of a painstaking unpublished study by George H. Roeder, which lists and summarizes three hundred "Mexican movies," it is possible to establish a rudimentary set of Mexican stereotypes presented during Hollywood's first half-century.[2] Most of the early films simply follow patterns established by the Beadles and their literary successors. The Mexican is portrayed as bandido, clown, or dark lady. By the 1930's he adds two variations to his repertoire: the caballero and the gangster. On the whole, however, he remains a subject—someone to be killed or mocked, seduced or redeemed by Saxon protagonists.

Whatever his role, film titles and advertising make open use of the word "greaser," at least up to the 1920's: *The Greaser's Gauntlet, The Girl and the Greaser, Broncho Billy and the Greaser, The Greaser's Revenge, Guns and Greasers,* or, bluntly, *The Greaser.*[3] The artistic quality and cultural sensitivity of

[2] I am deeply indebted to George H. Roeder, Jr., "Mexicans in the Movies: The Image of Mexicans in American Films, 1894–1947." He includes documentaries as well as fictional films and summarizes the history of the film industry. Although Roeder viewed only thirty of the three hundred films listed, he provides summaries of all of them, culled from magazine reviews, in the thirty-nine-page appendix, which is the most useful part of the manuscript, since the text drops off sharply at 1922. A much less ambitious but more carefully structured summary of the Mexican in movies between 1908 and 1914 is Blaine P. Lamb, "The Convenient Villain: The Early Cinema Views the Mexican-American," *Journal of the West* 14 (October, 1975): 75–81. A list and description of early films made in the Southwest can be found in Kemp R. Niver, ed., *Motion Pictures from the Library of Congress Paper Print Collection, 1894–1912.* For further information regarding the depiction of Mexican Americans in silent films following World War I, see Kenneth W. Munden, ed., *The American Film Institute Catalog of Motion Pictures Produced in the United States: Feature Films, 1921–1930.*

[3] *Guns and Greasers* (1918) was the last film to use *greaser* in the title, though the term was still used occasionally in advertising. To appreciate fully the brown-white moral dichotomy established in these early movies, one would probably have to be able to view them with a contemporary audience. *Moving Picture World,* the leading trade journal of the first two decades of the century, reported that audiences viewing *Across the Mexican Line* applauded almost every move made by the good Americans, while the actions of Castro, the bandido, met with loud hisses. Lamb, "Convenient Villain," p. 80.

these films match their titles. If adventure stories, they feature no-holds-barred struggles between good Americans and bad Mexicans. The cause of the conflict is often vaguely defined. Some greasers meet their fate because they are greasers. Others are on the wrong side of the law. Others violate Saxon moral codes. All of them rob, assault, kidnap, and murder with the same wild abandon as their dime-novel counterparts. The celluloid Mexican dresses the dandy, with broad sombrero, gaudy short jacket, intricately embroidered trousers, and tooled leather boots. The Saxon hero wears ordinary Levi's, plain shirt, and boots, with only his white Stetson to mark his status.

Greed plays a primary role in the early movie greaser's misconduct. Occasionally, as in *The Mexican*, a covetous Mexican landlord demands too much rent from the heroine and gets his "yellow cheeks" slapped by the girl's fiancé. More often, the greaser attempts to steal horses or gold. Some greasers even pocket money intended to succor the sick; in *Broncho Billy's Redemption*, a minor Mexican character who is entrusted with money to buy a prescription for a dying man tears up the prescription and makes off with the cash. In *The Girl and the Greaser* the Mexican servant of a poor homesteading family steals money which the family had been using to treat a sick woman. *The Lost Mine* features a Mexican who teams with an American saloon owner to defraud the hero of a mine which is rightfully his. In *The Black Sheep* a greaser thief is shot by rival gamblers who feud over the stolen money. *Man's Lust for Gold* and *The Eldorado Lode* both feature Mexican gold thieves, and *Slim Gets the Reward* has a bit role for a greaser horse thief.[4]

The greaser of the early films is as lustful as he is greedy. In *The Pony Express* a bandido abducts the Saxon heroine. The hero summons a posse and in one of the first of many cinematic chases, pursues the bandido and his henchmen, shooting them down one by one without sustaining casualties. In the final showdown the greaser leader tries to stab the hero several times but is overcome by a knockout blow. A comic

[4] Roeder, "Mexicans in the Movies," app., pp. 7, 14–15, 18.

treatment of the theme of attempted seduction followed by retribution is *His Mexican Bride*, in which a New York engineer rescues the daughter of a wealthy "Spanish" mine owner by turning the would-be greaser seducer over his knees and spanking him. Far more vicious in its treatment of the greaser villian is the 1909 epic *The Mexican's Revenge*. Don Ramón Molina, rejected suitor of a girl named Rosita who loves an officer from a U.S. warship anchored off the southern California coast, kidnaps the officer and binds him securely beneath the limbs of a large tree. Since "there is a strain of Indian blood in Molina's veins and he would first torture and then kill his victim," he suspends a boulder above the officer and sets a fire to burn slowly through the rope. His actions, however, are discovered, and Rosita leads a party of American sailors to the rescue in the usual nick of time.[5]

As these examples indicate, dozens of movies followed dime-novel patterns. There is, however, one difference worth observing. In the films the lustful greaser is sometimes allowed to reform, usually by saving the Anglo heroine from defloration. In *The Greaser's Gauntlet*, José, the Mexican protagonist, is spurned by his American innamorata. He then recruits another Mexican and a degenerate American to help him kidnap the girl. Just as the American accomplice reaches the point of rape, José's conscience awakens. He kills the American, returns the girl to her home, and retreats into the mountains of Old Mexico, there to live a lonely but morally satisfying life with his dear mother. In an even more extreme version of this theme, *Tony, the Greaser* is a ranchhand who makes advances to the boss's daughter. After she explains that she could never love him, he rejects revenge and, at the cost of his life, saves

[5] Roeder, "Mexicans in the Movies," app., pp. 7–9. Examples of near seduction of heroine and near stabbing of hero by greaser villain number in the dozens but vary little. In *Mexican Bill* the title villain accosts an American girl and almost stabs her American lover before he is finally "strung up" by a vigilante posse. In *A Thwarted Vengeance* a drunken greaser evicted from a bar by a cowboy binds the cowboy while he is asleep, kidnaps the cowboy's girl, and is about to ravish the girl and kill the cowboy when the cowboy's sidekick enters and stabs the Mexican.

the girl, her father, the father's ranch, and the American flag flapping atop the ranch house from a gang of greaser "insurrectionists" bent on rape and murder. As he dies, he kisses the girl's handkerchief.[6]

The fates of José, Tony, and their cinematic counterparts suggest that early silents add a new element to the existing set of stereotypes. In conquest fiction and great-house novels, Beadles and pulps, color determined character, particularly for males. Now we meet for the first time the Mexican male of low blood but good heart. His is an unenviable lot, as he is doomed to wander between the longed-for world of the Anglo and the stigmatized world of the Mexican, held forever in a middle position between Saxon heroes and greaser villains. It is the faint beginning of a pattern to be developed more fully in a later generation of books and films.

The Mexican Revolution of 1910–1920, coinciding exactly with the first decade of full-length films, provided inspiration for a number of "revolutionary" movies, Hollywood-style. Of the fifteen films with Mexican settings released between 1913 and 1916, five deal more or less with actual events of the revolution and involve no Americans at all,[7] five more simply show the U.S. Army in pursuit of bandit-"rebels," and five are adventure films portraying American citizens embroiled in events that touch only tangentially on the revolution. Typical of the last category are three movies starring Tom Mix, who saves the golden heroine from bandidos masquerading as rebels in *An Arizona Wooing* and *Along the Border* and brings to justice

[6] Roeder, "Mexicans in the Movies," app., pp. 7, 20, 21. In *The Two Sides* a humble Mexican rescues the ranch owner's daughter from a fire and is duly rewarded; in *The Mexican* (Selig, 1914) another Mexican ranchhand saves the ranch owner's daughter from death from a rattlesnake bite and is justly compensated. Cited in Lamb, "Convenient Villain," p. 79.

[7] For example, *The Mexican Joan of Arc* opens with a scene in which a father and son are arrested under suspicion of being *insurrectos* and are executed by order of a corrupt judge. The bereaved widow turns herself into the title heroine, leading a band of Mexicans into the rebel movement and executing the colonel of the federal troops in her area. *The Mexican Revolutionists* features a rebel named Juan, who is captured by federal troops but escapes and helps the rebels capture Guadalajara. Cited in Roeder, "Mexicans in the Movies," app., pp. 12, 15.

a band of "insurrectionist" stagecoach robbers in *The Sheriff's Blunder*. The five films in the second category feature bandidos who pose as rebels, covering their illegal activities with patriotic cant about uplifting the masses and unseating privilege —an ideological position that does not endear them to the conservative Saxon heroes. The treacherous conduct of a rebel chief named Longorio in *Heart of the Sunset* is typical. A "beastly Mexican Villain" who kills a gringo, steals a herd of cattle, kidnaps a woman, and tries to torture a Texas Ranger— all in the name of revolution—Longorio is on the point of "marrying" the girl and killing the ranger when he is warned by a priest that such conduct might jeopardize his plan to become president of Mexico. He therefore temporizes, vacillating so long that he is finally outwitted by the heroine.[8]

Hollywood also played the Mexican Revolution for laughs. The "hero" of *The Mexican's Chickens* is a small-time chicken farmer named Señor Sourface, who joins the federal army because the rebels are stealing his chickens. Captured by the rebels, Sourface is sentenced to be fired from a cannon. Summoning his expertise as a former circus performer, Sourface changes direction in mid-flight and nose-dives into a blanket held by his wife and daughter a mile away from the firing point. *Shaved in Mexico* stars a buffoon barber named "Señor La Bullio," who fancies himself a ladies' man and is just on the point of making "the big hitio" with a sexy señorita called Hitchey Koo when a traveling Saxon salesman named Perkins steals Hitchey Koo away from him. The film ends with Señor Bullio chasing Perkins with a razor while Hitchey turns her well-rounded behind on both suitors.[9] Perhaps the most fully developed character among these brown buffoons is Pancho

---

[8] Roeder, "Mexicans in the Movies," app., p. 22. Roeder also makes the distinction among the three sets of revolutionary films that I have adopted (Roeder, "Mexicans in the Movies," text, p. 20). Other examples of Saxon heroes who battle bandidos posing as *insurrectos* are *The Honor of the Flag, The Mexican* (Lubin, 1911), *Mexican Filibusterers, Down on the Rio Grande, Mexican Conspiracy Out-Generaled, The Mexican's Defeat, Across the Border,* and *Arms and the Gringo,* all cited in Roeder, "Mexicans in the Movies," app., pp. 11–12, 16–19.

[9] Roeder, "Mexicans in the Movies," app., pp. 25, 28.

López of *The Bad Man*. He is more jester than villain—a half-menacing, moustache-tweaking clown who boasts that he kills a gringo for breakfast and spouts bad verse delivered in a greaser accent: "I keel ze man ziz morning, / Heem call me dirty crook. / I keel some more zis noontime / And steal ess pocketbook." But he also returns stolen cattle to Anglo owners.[10]

More enduring and more popular than feature-length greaser comedies have been short subjects and animated cartoons with Mexican themes. Once more some distinctions can be made between Mexico as a setting and the Mexican as a stereotype. When Mutt and Jeff defeat a bull that has previously survived battles with Mexico's best toreadors in *Mixing in Mexico*, or when Daffy Duck is temporarily paralyzed by a shot of tequila in *Mexican Joyride*, then bests another bull by reminding him of the Good Neighbor Policy, their antics cannot reasonably be described as maliciously racist. Toreadors, sombreros, and cacti function as backdrops to comedy.

Some negative cartoon images of the Mexican, however, are both overt and insensitive. One series produced by Warner Brothers during the 1950's is still regularly seen on early-morning television and is available for private rental. It features Speedy González and Slowpoke Rodríguez, two mice whose accents and usual garb of sombreros and white cotton clothes easily mark them as animated versions of the greaser clown. As for their behavior, Slowpoke Rodríguez is a stereotyped lazy Mexican. And if Speedy González is energetic enough, neither his frenetic activity accompanied by shouts of *"Arriba, arriba, arriba!"* nor his constant triumphs over such characters as Sylvester Pussycat ever quite overcome his greaser image. Perhaps his name, which is probably by coincidence also the name assigned to the protagonist of dozens of obscene jokes focusing on Mexican sexual prowess, reinforces this image for adult viewers in a way that might well be meaningless to the cartoons' current preadolescent audience. The popular Hanna-Barbera stable also includes a sombrero-wearing burro, com-

[10]Ibid., app., p. 21.

plete with "Mexican" accent, who acts as a sidekick to Quick Draw McGraw, the gunslinging horse.

It would probably be a mistake to exaggerate the significance of these films and the equivalents made by other studios. Above all they are not, as were their live-action predecessors, part of a genre specifically designed to present Mexicans as ridiculous. Mice outwit cats in a wide variety of cartoon locales. Nevertheless, on the whole those cartoons employing Mexican characters and situations reinforce even at their best a set of stereotypes hardly needing reinforcing. They do so, moreover, in an apparently innocuous fashion. Their audience is arguably young enough to internalize the stereotypes to the point that more serious or more vicious versions do not give enough offense to generate rejection—particularly since these cartoons now appear almost exclusively on television. It is reasonably safe to assume that fewer adults watch "The Bugs Bunny–Road Runner Show" than saw its component elements when they were originally shown in theaters as antecedents to feature films.[11]

In sharp contrast to the greaser clowns, the dark-skinned bandidos, and the Mexican victims of the early cinema were the caballeros. These light-skinned Castilian gentlemen played leads and title roles, often in the process mocking or snubbing their darker-hued brethren. While no match for Anglo heroes, when permitted to operate within the parameters of their own race they tower far above the mixed-blood mestizo.

One of the first Castilian caballeros was Zorro, who matched his impeccable pedigree against lesser members of his race in the setting of Mexican California. In both versions of *The Mark of Zorro*, one made in 1920 and the other in 1940, Don Diego Vega poses in public as a simpering dandy who per-

[11] Ibid., app., pp. 26, 33, 37–38. Representative titles in the extensive Speedy González series include *Go Go Amigo*, *González González*, and *Tortilla Flats*. The impact of televised cartoons on their juvenile audience has generated a vast amount of literature, much of it polemic. A good beginning for students of the question in *Television and Growing Up: The Impact of Televised Violence: Report to the Surgeon General from the . . . Scientific Advisory Committee on Television and Social Behavior* (Rockville, Md.: National Institute of Mental Health, 1975).

fumes his hair, prefers the company of women in the parlor to that of men on the battlefield, and refuses to come to the aid of his father, the aristocratic former governor of Spanish California who has been unseated by mestizo mobocracy. In his secret identity, Don Diego becomes Zorro—a black-clad masked wonder with flowing cape and flashing blade who almost single-handedly defeats the Mexican *canaille* and then reveals his identity to his father, who is reinstalled as the rightful governor. Like the conquest and great-house fiction from which these films derive, they are strongly elitist. There is no suggestion that the peasants Zorro defends against the mestizos might be able to mount their own resistance movement against their oppressors or that the best interests of the Spanish nobles might not always coincide with those of other Californians. These points, however, must be balanced against the fact that the Zorro films are intended as adventure stories, not quasi-Marxist social commentary. And in this respect they succeed quite adequately.[12]

Zorro's leading caballero rival was the Cisco Kid, who rode the Southwest in a series of films set in the decades after the American conquest. In the movies *In Old Arizona* and *Return of the Cisco Kid*, the Kid is played by Warner Baxter as a boisterous and swashbuckling Robin Hood who robs the rich and sometimes gives to the poor. Another and more familiar Cisco Kid series stars César Romero as a dashing and debonair border Romeo who outwits the U.S. Army, aids widows and orphans, and dallies with señoritas in no fewer than five films produced in a three-year period: *Cisco Kid and the Lady, The Gay Caballero* (1940), *Lucky Cisco Kid, Viva Cisco Kid*, and *Ride On, Vaquero*. Each film follows the same formula. Romero appears from nowhere, rights wrong at the point of his gun, dallies with a pretty lady, and disappears into the horizon. The Kid's behavior matches perfectly that of his Anglo counterparts in the western sequences so popular in the 1930's:

[12] *Mark of Zorro* set a plot pattern followed in all subsequent movie and television treatments of the Zorro story. Other California don films include *Don Mike, Bold Caballero, California Mail*, and *In Old Caliente*, all cited in Roeder, "Mexicans in the Movies," app. pp. 25, 27, 30, 35.

ride in, destroy evil, and ride out, leaving a broken heart or two behind. If he flirts with Anglo women, his status as a serial hero precludes marriage. His fair-skinned good looks, moreover, clearly marks him as more "Spanish" than Mexican.

Only one caballero hero actually gets the girl. Don Arturo Bodega (Cornel Wilde) is a silk-suited grandee who joins Fremont's Freedom Forces in *California Conquest* to defeat the greaser scum of the Pacific province and wins an Anglo bride in the process—the daughter of a humble drugstore keeper. Mulling over Don Arturo's proposal of marriage, the lady pops a qualifying question of her own: "You *would* give a lot to be an American, wouldn't you?" The implication that a highborn Spaniard is just barely good enough for an American commoner can hardly be missed by the least sensitive viewer.

The gay caballero who battles the degenerates of his own race, fights on the right side of the California conquest, or outwits the U.S. Army apparently had limited appeal. Zorro, Don Arturo Bodega, and the Cisco Kid have had no successors in the past quarter-century of Hollywood cinema. Even before their demise, they were outstripped in popularity by another Mexican character who competed with the bandido and the buffoon for top Hollywood honors: the dark lady. In most films the role is as impersonal as it is forgettable. A common version is the halfbreed shrew, a Mexican Jezebel who seeks vengeance on an unfaithful lover by stabbing the cad, poisoning him, or conniving to have him punished for a crime he did not commit.[13] Lupe Vélez, however, elevated the stereotype to star billing. During the thirties and forties she won fame as a short-

[13] Several films place heavy emphasis on coed villainy or violence among Mexicans: *The Ranch Man's Daughter, An Arizona Escapade, The Bandit's Spur, A Mexican Romance, Through a Higher Power,* and *Juggling with Fate,* all cited in Roeder, "Mexicans in the Movies," app., pp. 13–16; and Lamb, "Convenient Villain," p. 77. Only once, to my knowledge, does an Amazon shrew actually desert an American male for a Mexican lover. In *Broncho Billy's Mexican Wife* Broncho Billy marries a Mexican dancer, Lolita, who then falls in love with an effete singer named Manuel. The two conspire to have Broncho Billy arrested for a crime he did not commit. Broncho Billy also has his hands full in a sequel, *Broncho Billy and the Greaser,* protecting an American postmistress from a lecherous "half-breed." Roeder, "Mexicans in the Movies," app., p. 14; and Lamb, "Convenient Villain," p. 78.

140

fused firecracker in such song-and-sex grade B quickies as *Hot Pepper, Strictly Dynamite, Mexican Spitfire's Elephant,* and *Mexican Spitfire's Blessed Event.* Lupe Vélez's appearance and behavior were always predictable. Much of the humor in the Spitfire series combines her hip-swaying pirouettings and her considerable difficulties with the English language. In *Girl from Mexico,* for example, Lupe blends craftiness and naiveté to hook a New York radio agent. She is a persuasive and funny sex kitten; even when she sits down to read the comics, she becomes hopelessly and endearingly entangled in the misadventures of "Donald Duke" and "Mickey Moose." Her cinematic blend of passionate nature, hot temper, bustling activity, and mercurial reversals of mood established her as the foremost example of the generously endowed and correspondingly fickle females of her race.[14]

Sometimes, as in conquest fiction, the dark lady has the good fortune not to be a dark lady at all. Presumed at the start of the film to be a fair-haired, blue-eyed "breed," she turns out to be of pure Saxon parentage. Or she is permitted to be of mixed American-Mexican ancestry—a hot-pepper, cold-cucumber combination that serves up a "dark" lady of extremely erratic behavior such as the Anglo-Mexican in *Rio Grande,* who is advertised as "passionate, revengeful, brave, unreasonable and most cussedly lovable."[15] When she encounters female Saxon competition, she goes down to defeat as surely as she did in the dime novels. If, however, she is permitted to operate with no blondes on the horizon, she can eventually win the hero—if her "Mexican" heritage is pure Spanish.[16]

[14] Dolores Del Río, born into an aristocratic Mexican family, usually played "Latin," "Spanish," or South American roles and therefore was considered to be in a higher category than the mestiza "spitfire," Lupe Vélez.

[15] See also *The Only Road.* Roeder, "Mexicans in the Movies," app., pp. 23–24. In the few love films featuring an all-Mexican cast, the dark lady usually rejects a rich but corpulent and corrupt Mexican suitor in favor of a poor but handsome Indian or mestizo love. Cf. *Love in Mexico, Papita,* and *When Hearts Are Trumps,* all cited in Roeder, "Mexicans in the Movies," app., pp. 10, 16.

[16] In *Border Cafe* for example, a hot-tempered song-and-dance nightclub performer named Armida is wooed by a rich Harvard graduate, the son of a

Since easy victories make for bad drama, by far the most popular type of dark lady is only half-Spanish and therefore must undergo a long apprenticeship before gaining the Saxon hero. These tests of loyalty invariably require the dark lady to desert her race, her native country, or both. Dozens of films exploit her precarious position. She may fall in love with a captured American and rescue him from imminent execution at the hands of the Mexican army. Perhaps she must turn against a member of her family—a brother, as in *Chiquita, the Dancer,* or a father, as in *His Mexican Sweetheart*—thus demonstrating both her loyalty to the hero and her allegiance to "the land of the free." Whatever the variations on the theme, the outcome is the same. The dark lady gains the hero only by renouncing her past. Even then, her unaided efforts are not always adequate. *On the Border,* for example, stars a U.S. Secret Service agent who breaks up a gang of smugglers with the combined aid of Rin-tin-tin *and* a beautiful half-"Spanish" shepherdess named Pepita—a threesome that leaves the matter of which assistant should receive second billing very much in doubt.[17]

By 1928, an estimated 98 percent of the films shown in Mexico were made in the United States. Mexican officials were

---

U.S. senator. When the senator tries to talk Armida out of marrying his son, pointing to the family's distinguished Brahmin ancestry, Armida claims that her ancestors, too, were bluebloods, and the senator lifts all restrictions on the match. Roeder, "Mexicans in the Movies," app., p. 32.

[17] Roeder, "Mexicans in the Movies," app. pp. 11–14, 27. Roeder also names *Across the Mexican Line* and *The Senorita's Conquest* as movies of this type. Films featuring señoritas who rescue the Saxon hero by deserting a member of their race vary in plot design but never in motive. In *The Ranger's Reward* a señorita helps a Texas Ranger capture a bandido and is rewarded by marriage. In *Curse of the Great Southwest* an American sheriff captures a rustler with the help of the head rustler's girl friend. *The Mexican Rebellion* traces the change of heart of a señorita who works for the federal cause in the revolution—until she meets an American who is working for the rebels. In *The Kick Back* a señorita saves an American, arrested on a smuggling charge, from execution. In *Hands Across the Border* the American hero breaks up a gang of smugglers with the help of a lovely "Spanish girl," and the same thing happens in *Border Romance.* In *The Gay Caballero* (20th Century Fox, 1932) the American hero defeats a vicious cattle baron named Paco Morales with the aid of Morales' niece, Adela. Roeder, "Mexicans in the Movies," app., pp. 15–16, 19–20, 24, 26–28.

filing an increasing number of complaints about the images of their land and people these films conveyed.[18] Yet Hollywood, not content with continuing to turn out bandidos, clowns, and dark ladies, began experimenting with a new negative Mexican stereotype as well. The greaser gangster is a product of the prohibition era and the depression but differs in several respects from the Anglo model established by such stars as James Cagney and George Raft. He is a coward. He is invariably treacherous, without even the in-group loyalties of his northern counterparts. He is oily and ugly, crude and overdressed, in no way a romantic figure even when considered as a man outside society.

No actor of the thirties and forties lived down to this stereotype more faithfully than Leo Carrillo. In more than two dozen films he portrays a man involved in the rackets: gambling, murder, extortion, pimping. He is sometimes sinister, sometimes comic, but always inept. From the moment he enters the Purple Pigeon Night Club on the Mexican side of the border in *The Girl of the Rio*, Carrillo shows a typical gangster's interest in money, sex, and violence. But he seeks these rewards of evil in ways that would shame a Cagney or an Edward G. Robinson. Cowardly, obnoxious, usually drunk, constantly surrounded by halfbreed trollops, Carrillo plays an oil-rich villain named Señor Tostado ("Toast"), who boasts he is the "best caballero" and "wealthiest caballero" in all of Mexico. His life's ambition is to marry a glamorous cantina dancer called "The Dove" (Dolores Del Río), who is already spoken for by an American gambler named Johnny Powell. Using his position as leader in the underworld, Carrillo frames Johnny for murder, then agrees to spare his life if Dolores will desert the gringo and marry him. Needless to say, Carrillo comes to the ill end he richly deserves.[19]

[18] I am indebted to Allen L. Woll, "Hollywood's Good Neighbor Policy: The Latin Image in American Film, 1939–1946," *Journal of Popular Film* 3 (Fall, 1974): 278–293, for information on Hollywood-Mexican relations and for some insight into the film *Juarez* as well.

[19] For a review of Carrillo's film career, see Frank J. Taylor, "Leo the Caballero," *Saturday Evening Post*, July 6, 1946, p. 26.

The formal objections of the Mexican government to *The Girl of the Rio* were based not on the Carrillo character alone, but on several other aspects of the film. The legal system of Mexico is made to appear as a corrupt market where favorable verdicts go to those who can pay the most. That this injustice was sometimes the case in the depression era made the image no less irritating to Mexican sensibilities. The minor Mexican characters in the movie are uniformly unattractive; purveyors of sex and liquor, corrupt politicos and policemen, obsequious waiters, and humble passers-by who doff sombreros or peek furtively around corners. Despite official Mexican protests, the film's popularity led to a sequel, *In Caliente*, which features the same assortment of cabaret dancers, corrupt gamblers, excitable domestics, and brown buffoons who speak broken English.[20]

The most ambitious border-gangster film of the 1930's, however, was *Bordertown*. This film combines a hard look at a Mexican vice center with a subtle variation on the silent-film theme of the "good" Mexican who rejects the milieu appropriate to his race and covets instead the respectable world of the Americans. Johnny Ramírez (Paul Muni), raised in the Mexican quarter of depression-wracked Los Angeles, for five years does manual labor by day and studies by night to graduate from the Pacific Night Law School, an organization dedicated to uplifting minorities through legal action. Johnny's ideal is Lincoln. He loves the United States; he has high ambitions to become a Supreme Court Justice. Anxious to do good and well simultaneously, winning entrance to the Anglo world by aiding his race, Johnny is brought down by a combination of amateurish practice of law and an explosive "Mexican" temper.

In his first case, taking a rich society lady to court for crashing her sports car into his client's vegetable truck, Johnny's sincere but clumsy attempt to "get justice" cannot match the polished techniques of the debutante's lawyer. The case is refused hearing on insufficient evidence. When the girl's lawyer

[20] Roeder, "Mexicans in the Movies," app., p. 30.

144

calls him a "cheap shyster," Johnny attacks him and is disbarred. Renouncing samaritanism, he travels south to Tijuana, rises rapidly in a cabaret as bouncer and submanager, then uses cash borrowed from his boss's wife to open a splashy new casino. Simultaneously, Johnny pursues the society woman he met in court; she sees him as a "pre-historic savage . . . , something out of *Carmen*," but is temporarily attracted to his dark handsomeness. But when Johnny goes so far as to propose marriage, the playgirl rebuffs him with a classic line: "Marriage isn't for us. . . . You belong to a different tribe, Savage." The act of rejection brings Johnny to full awareness of his "racial" limitations and his "place" as a Mexican. Selling the casino, he endows a law school for the poor with the proceeds and confesses his "sins" to a priest, who speaks of patience as one of the virtues of "our people." Taking the priest's advice, Johnny returns to his natural habitat—the slums of Los Angeles—there to live a humble life with his mother, "where I belong . . . with my people."[21]

Bordertown is a disturbing film. Either its beginning or its finish is a lie. For most of the film we see a hero victimized by a corrupt system. The ending, however, changes tone abruptly. It seems to ascribe Johnny's fate to a racially determined fall from grace, arguing that the "American" traits of ambition, honesty, and fortitude he displayed through most of the film were really borrowed, and the barrio is where he belongs. Yet for all its faults, *Bordertown* at least offers a complex character who happens to be Mexican—a far cry from the run-of-the-mill Hollywood *cholo*.

The vices and weaknesses of the movie Mexican during this period are further highlighted by the large number of films featuring Saxon heroes as samaritan crusaders who perform good deeds on behalf of downtrodden Mexicans. The samaritan is, of course, a standard character in western fiction. But

---

[21] Johnny Ramírez's "typically Mexican" excess of emotion is all the more notable in light of the film's sequel, *They Drive by Night*, which stars George Raft as a cool and competent American gangster who succeeds in precisely the same role that brought Johnny's ruin in *Bordertown*.

the border samaritan is particularly attractive, at least to Anglo
viewers. He retains the superlative strength, courage, and
common sense bequeathed him by his dime-novel predecessors, but rejects their earlier callous conduct towards Mexicans.
Thus, the emphasis is switched from the hero as deadly and
brutal greaser fighter to the hero as deadly and devoted defender of Mexican rights. The common denominator of these
films involves helping people who cannot help themselves. If
the rescued or protected Mexicans prove ungrateful, the samaritans either turn the other cheek or abandon all pretensions
to saintliness and dish out summary Beadle-type vengeance.[22]
Usually, however, they can expect to receive fulsome thanks
from hat-doffing male Mexicans and a shower of kisses and
flowers from curtsying females. Their acts of charity range
from saving innocent Mexicans from lynching (*A Mexican's
Gratitude*) to forcing a cruel Mexican land baron to restore
water rights to the poor peasants he rules with an iron fist
(*Land Baron of San Tee*). Saxon samaritans may break up
gangs of rustlers who are impoverishing defenseless Mexicans
(*On the Rio Grande, Señor Daredevil, Border G-Man, Durango Valley Raiders*), or they may side with dispossessed Spanish dons against land-hungry gringos (*Rose of the Rancho,
California Frontier, Fighting Gringo, In Old Caliente*). Occasionally they may even help the Catholic church. In *Margarita
and the Mission Funds*, a Saxon adventurer, commissioned by
the governor of the recently acquired U.S. territory of California to collect taxes from the old Spanish churches, falls in love
with a mission girl named Margarita and captures a bandido
who tries to rob one of the churches. When the clergy objects
to the levy imposed by his government, the samaritan tax col-

[22] In *A Western Child's Heroism*, for example, a wounded Mexican rustler, nursed and protected by an American miner's family, tries to rob the
miner and kill his family but is thwarted by the miner's young son. In *Captured by the Mexicans* a bandido named Mexican Pete, dying of thirst on the
desert, is rescued by an American couple going west and shows his gratitude
by returning with a band of friends and kidnapping the couple. Roeder, "Mexicans in the Movies," app., pp. 16, 19.

Cinematic Degradation of the Mexican

lector pays the tax out of his own pocket and becomes a member of the Church himself.[23]

The most persistent of the Saxon samaritans are the famous grade B cowboy stars of the 1930's. Their good deeds are not confined to aiding Mexicans. Serial heroes of the caliber of Tom Mix, Hopalong Cassidy, Gene Autry, Roy Rogers, and Tex Ritter succor the sick and defend the defenseless wherever they may roam. Yet the acts of such Anglo folk heroes strongly reinforce the cinematic spectrum of Mexican stereotypes. Hopalong Cassidy, for example, protects a Mexican community from bandidos in the film *In Old Mexico* and wins the heart of a lovely señorita before bidding her a chaste and affectionate farewell. Tex Ritter captures Mexican criminals in *Song of the Gringo*, then tracks munitions smugglers into Mexico in *Starlight over Texas*. Tim McCoy does what he can to improve international relations in *Two Gun Justice* by breaking up a bandido gang. Buck Jones gives aid and comfort to California landowners who are being driven off their property by gringo land grabbers in *California Frontier*. The Lone Ranger captures bandidos in several early Masked Rider movies, and Gene Autry combines two noble deeds in *South of the Border* by simultaneously rescuing a conservative "Latin" government from sabotage-minded rebels and encouraging a teenaged señorita to enter a convent.[24]

By the end of the 1930's, however, the cinematic Mexicans are beginning to help themselves. *Juarez* stars Paul Muni in a panegyric to the leader of the anti-Maximilian forces in the Mexico of the 1860's. It also stars Abraham Lincoln. His spirit haunts the film from start to finish. Juárez rarely appears in his office without a portrait of the Great Emancipator peering over his shoulder. When forced to flee before advancing French troops, he removes the picture of Lincoln from his office before gathering any of his official documents. It may

[23] Roeder, "Mexicans in the Movies," app., pp. 8, 14, 17, 20, 24, 26, 32–35.

[24] Ibid., app., pp. 32–34, 36.

147

be true that a famous character from American history helped the home audience identify with an alien figure about whom they knew nothing. Nevertheless, the constant comparison becomes oppressive. The film, moreover, looks not only backward to the era of Lincoln and Juárez, but also forward to the looming fascist menace in Europe. Juárez becomes the "defender of democratic principles," while Maximilian and Napoleon III represent "the dictators who seize power illegally." Indeed, the Mexican president's climactic speech could just as easily have been delivered in Washington, D.C., on the eve of the American entry into World War II: "By what right, señores, do the Great Powers of Europe invade the lands of simple people . . . kill all who do not make them welcome . . . destroy their fields . . . and take the fruit of their toil from those who survive? The world must know the fate of any usurper who sets his foot upon this soil."

While easy to ridicule in the context of 1979, *Juarez* is impressive in many respects. The film's cultural chauvinism reflects an American movie made for an American audience and must be measured against the "universal" intention of the message and the impressive research conducted in the Mexican archives. More than any American film before *Viva Zapata!* (1952), *Juarez* was based on sound documentation and a sympathetic regard for Mexican history and the Mexican people. It impressed the country it dealt with as well as the country for whose audience it was intended.[25]

Two other films, both released eight years after *Juarez*, also attempted to portray "Latin" characters as dignified human beings. John Huston's *Treasure of the Sierra Madre* features a Mexican outlaw, played by Alfonso Bedoya, who steals several scenes from Humphrey Bogart. Elevated to an existential hero

[25] A portion of the dialogue of *Juarez* was actually derived from Mexican congressional debates of the 1860's, and President Lázaro Cárdenas urged that *Juarez* be presented in the Palace of Fine Arts; it was the first motion picture so honored. When Benito Juárez (Muni) explained the difference between constitutional democracy and despotism, the premiere audience stopped the show with applause. Woll, "Hollywood's Good Neighbor Policy," pp. 283–285.

who faces death with honor, Bedoya shows qualities of courage, wit, and pride foreign to the stock Hollywood *bandido*. John Ford's *The Fugitive* is one of the few pro-Catholic Hollywood films made about Mexico. The movie begins with a careful statement that although it was filmed in Mexico, the locale is an imaginary small state somewhere in Latin America. The film's overtones and undertones, however, are alike Mexican. It is based on Graham Greene's novel *The Power and the Glory*, set in Mexico during the anticlerical reforms of the twenties and early thirties. And Henry Fonda's characterization of a whiskey priest who begets a bastard child and abandons his flock stands as a tragic embodiment of the tangle of good and evil in the human spirit. Exhausted by his flight from government troops, rotten with his own vices, the priest remains inspired by an inner fire. He is hounded both by the government and by the inner beast that tracks his errant soul down the labyrinthine ways of human fallibility. Safe in exile, the priest summons the courage to return to his native state, is betrayed by a seedy police informer, and goes willingly to his death.

One might argue that casting an American actor as the hero and a Mexican actor, Pedro Armendariz, as the fanatically antireligious lieutenant who pursues him upholds Hollywood's belief that Americans can play good Mexicans better than Mexicans can. On the other hand, the unorthodox subject matter probably demanded a box-office star of Fonda's stature to carry the message. Casting Ward Bond as an American bandit who dies in the priest's defense is a nice twist on the traditional juxtaposition of Saxon hero and greaser *bandido*. And Dolores Del Río as the woman who brings her illegitimate child to the priest for baptism and later imperils her own life in an attempt to lead the priest to safety is one of the finer portrayals of the sacrificial dark lady in American film. It may be true that the movie was tailored to the requirements of institutional Catholicism. Certainly the simple dichotomy of Good Church versus Bad State is as irritating as it is fictitious. The symbolism —the priest's shadow assuming the form of the crucifixion; the

149

cross glowing in the darkness like a neon-lighted trademark—
can often be clumsy. Yet *The Fugitive* remains the most sympathetic approach to Latin Catholicism in Hollywood's history.

With the notable exceptions of *Juarez* and *The Fugitive,*
the Mexican movies made by Hollywood between the first decade of the century and the end of World War II tend to repeat plots which had passed inspection in the earliest years of
the industry. Most of these movies lack serious dramatic intent.
Almost all feature bandidos bent on murder and rape, brown
versions of Mantan Morland, or light-skinned dark ladies who
are permitted to desert their race and declare allegiance to the
heroes and the United States which they represent. Generally
speaking, the treatment of the Mexican in the first half-century
of the Hollywood cinema is simply another example of the use
of fixed dramatic patterns that can be repeated indefinitely
with a reasonable expectation of profit. Greaser films follow
each other as musicals, gangsters, or westerns follow each other
in predictable turn.

Formal protests from the Mexican government in the late
twenties and early thirties culminated in some efforts at infor-
mal censorship and led to a temporary slowdown in Mexican
caricatures. Nevertheless, the bandidos and the dark ladies
were back in force behind the boulders and the barroom doors
by the late thirties. There they remained through the forties.
This does not mean that the position of the Mexican remained
entirely unchanged for half a century. For example, the Anglo
heroes of the silent films are far more self-righteous, self-as-
sured, and patronizing than their successors of the talkies. It is
also necessary to distinguish between the Mexican as character
and the Mexican as backdrop, as mere local color for films with .
Anglo themes and Anglo feature players. On the whole, however, aside from a few suicidal maniacs who try to be "good"
Mexicans but generally succumb to death or disappointment,
the mass of Mexican characters in the early cinema seems to
support the assumption that most members of their race are
evil or promiscuous, cowardly or inept. Given these fixed racial
traits, it seems axiomatic that individual or collective repent-

ance and atonement for all the Mexican "crimes" and "sins" committed against the American heroes and heroines is simply out of the question. Whether as villains or buffoons, halfbreed sluts or "white" dark ladies, celluloid Mexicans tend to be treated as a series of shadow figures: cutouts and puppets whose behavior is as wooden as it is unconvincing. By the end of the first half-century of Hollywood cinema, the artistic image of the Mexican was still one of the gullible greaser, capable at best of a primitive and unreliable allegiance to white folks —and for that very reason more to be ridiculed and reviled than admired, respected, or even feared.

Part III
REPENTANCE

WORLD WAR II brought an increased need for agricultural labor that in turn generated another flood of immigrants from Mexico to join their predecessors in the Southwest's barrios and *colonias*. Most were located in unincorporated areas adjacent to a town or city, but invariably on "the other side" of something: a railroad track, a bridge, a river, a highway. Site location was, and still is, determined by cheap rents, low land values, prejudice, proximity to employment, or the undesirability of the site itself—for poor drainage, lack of water, or distance from business establishments or from high-class Anglo residences. Physical isolation in turn contributed to social introversion and psychological alienation. An immigrant-aid structure established to serve the needs of newcomers from eastern and southern Europe too often failed to understand that some newly arrived Mexicans did not wish to stay permanently; or if they did, they did not wish to abandon their culture entirely. Geographic proximity to Mexico encouraged retention of previous cultural loyalties and led some American authorities to believe that these alien charges were backward, retarded, or both. The depressing social statistics on immigration and barrio conditions were frequently interpreted in terms of what they apparently revealed about the inadequacies of the Mexican character and temperament: lack of leadership, discipline, organization, cleanliness, thrift, and enterprise.

155

Aside from the debatable abstract question of how much assimilation of "alien" ethnic groups is necessary or desirable, Mexican Americans at mid-century found themselves damned by the Anglo community if they did not assimilate, yet also damned to an inferior position if they did. In the wake of World War II, an increasing number of Mexican Americans began rejecting the entire notion that "Americanization" was necessary to success. The evolution and adoption of the name Chicano reflects their new search for an ethnic identity and a cultural synthesis which would represent an alternative to the dominant Anglo society. The concept of Chicanismo is an assertion that a unique culture had long existed in the Southwest, a culture neither entirely American nor entirely Mexican, whose bearers identify themselves as *los Chicanos, la Raza de Bronce* (the Bronze Race) that inhabits Aztlán, the name for the Southwest that serves as a unifying force and symbol for many Chicanos.

Yet despite publicity, despite local victories, despite a new pantheon of heroes, Mexican Americans in the Southwest still find themselves labeled as "the invisible minority," "the forgotten people," or "the minority nobody knows." The average income of Mexican Americans as an ethnic group is lower, their unemployment rate is higher, their average education level is lower, and their plight is less recognized nationally than that of black Americans. To say that this is largely the result of Anglo prejudice, ignorance, and disinterest is a truism that has become a cliché in contemporary American culture. It is far less easy to say what might be done about it—or, more precisely, what Anglo-Americans are willing to do about it. Perhaps the most disturbing aspect of the problem is that many Anglos continue to misunderstand just who Chicanos are, what they want, and what they are about. At the risk of belaboring the thesis of this study, it seems clear that the main cause of the Anglo-American's misconception of the Mexican American is still what it was one hundred years ago: continued ignorance of or indifference to the enormous differences between the widely accepted Spanish heritage of the Southwest on the one hand and the mestizo, Indian, and Chicano heritages on the other. The "Spanish" legacy of the Southwest—carefully distinguished from the Mexican or Indian heritages—continues to be accepted as a colorful corollary of the dominant culture. The Mexican and Mexican-Indian cultures still constitute a neglected or denigrated subsidiary.

The growing visibility of the Mexican has combined with the growing ambivalence of the Anglo position to produce uncertain tones in what have been familiar themes. No longer is the Saxon the triumphant conqueror certain of his own righteousness. Chapter 7 introduces a job-lot collection of do-gooders, either guilt-ridden would-be uplifters of their erstwhile victims or seekers after the truths of a simpler place and time which they see embodied in Mexican or Mexican-American behavior patterns. And if the Mexican is still presented in terms of stereotypes, the stereotypes are increasingly complex. In chapter 8 the sluts and bandidos of an earlier era are joined by victims and avengers, natural men and men on the make. Low-cut rebozos and dirty charro suits are being exchanged for the rags of the slum dweller and the paisano or the gray flannel of the aspiring junior executive. The cinema continues to lag behind in its imagery, but chapter 9 shows an increasing attempt to take not only Mexicans, but Mexico itself, as more than a set of backdrops for blue-eyed supermen. The content of all three chapters is amorphous; their tone is ambiguous. But perhaps these qualities indicate the beginning of the end of the theme of this work: the seemingly ineradicable dichotomy between the ethnic communities.

CHAPTER SEVEN

THE AMERICAN AS SINNER-SAMARITAN

By THE MIDDLE of the twentieth century an increasing number of eastern writers, distressed by what they saw as an unholy alliance of Christianity, capitalism, and imperialism masquerading as civilization, began seeking antidotes to the ills of a sick and suicidal society. Some found a cure-all in the ancient and serene culture of the Hispanic Southwest. They sought to replace traditional ethnocentricities with a new generosity of feeling towards the victims of Anglo progress. Their focus, however, is not pro-Mexican as much as it is anti-American. If the Mexican is seen in a more favorable light than in his previous literary incarnations, he remains a background figure. The Anglo is still central to these modern works. Instead of the Saxon superman, he simply becomes the bad gringo or the conscience-stricken American.

The process began with fictional reinterpretations of the conquest itself. Usually works with this theme are set in lower Mexico instead of the Southwest. The American movement for independence in Texas remained in fiction a defensive struggle against a country that had abridged the rights of Americans it had invited there in the first place. The conquests of New Mexico and California could still be presented as essentially peaceful infiltrations of bankrupt and inefficient societies that had been long destined to become part of the United States. The Mexican War itself, however, was another story.

As early as 1888, in *A Fortune Hunter; or, The Old Stone Corral* by John Carteret, Lieutenant Bruce Walraven from New York willingly asks forgiveness of the Mexican heroine for invading her country.[1] John R. Musick's *Humbled Pride: A Story of the Mexican War* begins with an impassioned tirade: "In the light of reason, humanity and justice, is there anything save the admiration of strategy, might and bravery in the Mexican war, to delight the patriotic heart of the honest-thinking American, who wishes to deal as fairly by nations as by individuals? Was the Mexican war really more than a war of conquest—a gigantic robbery of a nation by a nation?" (p. 21).

Recent novelists have maintained this antiwar attitude. In *Folded Hills*, by Stewart Edward White, Andy Burnett, a Yankee trapper who married into California aristocracy in the 1830's, is genuinely torn between his native and adopted countries. When war breaks out, Burnett tries to serve as mediator, urging negotiation rather than confrontation. As an established great-house baron, Burnett admittedly stands to lose his huge tracts of land to Yankee interlopers, yet his disapproval of his former countrymen is founded on cultural animosity as well as economic self-interest. He regards Fremont's Bear-Flaggers as a rabble who boast that "Ammurica is the greatest kentry in God's universe!" and that "an Ammurican can lick any ten furriners—yes, and ary twenty of these yere yaller-bellies!" Burnett interprets Kit Carson as little better than a murderer and Fremont as a shifty-eyed rascal who forces the Californios into war. Burnett eventually accepts the Yankee invasion and retains his estate. He refuses, however, to fight on either side and makes it clear that his heart lies with the conquered.[2]

Modern authors make their sympathies known in ways

---

[1] John Carteret, *A Fortune Hunter; or, The Old Stone Corral*, pp. 21–26, 39–46.

[2] Stewart Edward White, *Folded Hills*, pp. 258 ff. In a previous novel, *Ranchero*, Burnett arrives in California and takes a "Castilian" wife.

other than their hero's ideological affiliation. While conquest
fiction is replete with scenes of battle between heroic Americans and cowardly Mexicans, there are few military encounters
in recent novels about the Mexican War. Nor are American
victories presented in the same moral light as those of San
Jacinto or Santa Fe. The Mexican enemy has gained in courage if not in competence. In Herbert Gorman's *The Wine of
San Lorenzo* the Mexicans fight gamely but are victims of poor
leadership and outmoded equipment. In Richard Wormser's
Battalion of Saints, which chronicles the trek of the Mormon
Battalion, the Mexican opposition is hampered by bureaucratic
ineptitude and inefficient supply lines, not lack of courage. In
Julia Davis' *Ride with the Eagle*, Doniphan's Missourians still
easily defeat the Mexicans at the battles of Brazito and Sacramento, but they concede that they are fighting an ill-trained
and poorly supplied army of demoralized peasants who are
armed with antiquated weapons and fear their commanders
more than the enemy. In *Two Roads to Guadalupe*, by Robert
Lewis Taylor, a few Mexicans choose to stand, fight, and die
alone as their compatriots flee the field at the battle of Sacramento.[3]

Among the more moderate fictional apologists for his native country's conduct in the Mexican War is Charles Livingston, protagonist of *The Wine of San Lorenzo*. A survivor of
the Alamo, he is adopted by Santa Anna, rechristened Juan
Diego, and determines to devote his life to fostering good will
between Mexico and the United States. He reasons that his
marriage to a Mexican aristocrat will stand as symbol of the
emerging ties between the United States and Mexico:

> That was it. He would labor all his life to wed the two Repub-
> lics, to make them husband and wife as Doña María Catalina

---

[3] Julia Davis, *Ride with the Eagle*, pp. 134–135, 163–166; Robert Lewis
Taylor, *Two Roads to Guadalupe*, p. 187. For another account of the Doniphan expedition which takes the more traditional approach to Missourian
"courage" and "Mexican "cowardice," see Ottamar Hamele, *When Destiny
Called: A Story of the Doniphan Expedition in the Mexican War.*

and he would be husband and wife. Each had so much to give the other and together they would be an insuperable couple. Mexico was feminine and the United States was masculine. The one was excitable, sensitive, quick to anger and quick to love, sometimes coy and always vivid with human vanities, suspicious, proud, displaying weaknesses, petulant, adorable; the other was harder-willed, egotistic, strong, possessive, sometimes bull-headed, generous, foresighted and smart. Together they would be perfect. . . . Their single names might be Mexico and the United States but their married name was America. [Pp. 218–219]

Just how and when this marriage will take place is not clear. The implication is that it will be put off for a long time. By the close of the novel Juan Diego himself deserts Mexico, reclaims his original name of Charles Livingston, and moves to Washington, D.C. Entering a business partnership with his wealthy father-in-law, Livingston forms a financial association familiar in conquest fiction, but one which leaves the international partnership question posed earlier in the novel very much in limbo.

Direct feelings of Anglo guilt for the conquest of the Southwest have been strongly focused on a highly unlikely figure: Billy the Kid. In film and print he is commonly portrayed as a white victim of the conquest's power structure who devotes at least part of his life to aiding its Mexican victims. The legend, of course, does not stand historical scrutiny. The Kid's actual association with Mexicans was largely confined to killing men and seducing women. In the folklore of the Southwest, however, "Billito" remains a bucktoothed Robin Hood who stole from the Anglo rich to give to the peon poor. He fights the Hispano's battles, shares their chili and women, doles out bags of silver to impoverished sheepherders, and fathers their illegitimate blonde children. In 1925, Harvey Fergusson claimed that the peons remained the Kid's friends to the last. The Kid could not have survived so long without them. They fed and hid him and gave him news of his enemies. He in turn gave

161

them money by the handful when he had it. "Like Robin Hood, he befriended the poor."[4] Walter Noble Burns, the Kid's most persistent Anglo legend maker, put the finishing touches on the cult when he "interviewed" a Mexican housewife in the 1920's: "Billee the Keed. Ah, you have heard of heem? He was one gran' boy, señor. All Mexican pepul his friend. You nevair hear a Mexican say cne word against Billee the Keed. Everybody love that boy. He was so kind-hearted, so generous, so brave. And so 'andsome. *Nombre de Dios!* Every leetle señorita was crazy about heem. . . . Poor Billee the Keed! He was a good boy—*muy valiente, muy caballero.*"

Movies also have sustained the legend of the Kid as friend of the oppressed Hispanos and foe of the Anglo cattle barons. Some are simplistic. *Billy the Kid* features the Kid as a philanthropist who shot Anglos only to avenge a wrong done to a friend, usually a Mexican friend. On the other hand, in Howard Hughes's notorious *The Outlaw,* the Kid spends most of his time courting a bosomy "halfbreed" señorita, played by Jane Russell, with little time left for deeds of samaritanism. In *Chisum* the Kid is a secondary character whose well-intentioned benevolence is thwarted by an impetuous violent streak repelling even his friend, cattle king John Chisum (John Wayne).

Two other movies attempt a more complex presentation of the Kid's fringe position in Anglo-American society as a major reason for his attempts to befriend Hispanos. The opening musical score of Arthur Penn's Freudian treatment of the Kid, *The Left-Handed Gun,* urges us to think tenderly of Paul Newman as a deprived teenager who tried to do what was right but went to his death because he was betrayed by both bad Anglos and ungrateful Mexicans. His closest protectors early in the film are two Hispanos, an old man named Saval

[4] Miguel Antonio Otero, *The Real Billy the Kid*; Harvey Fergusson, "Billy the Kid," *American Mercury* 5 (June, 1925): 224. Walter Noble Burns, *The Saga of Billy the Kid,* p. 19. Reasonably accurate portraits of the real Kid are such historical accounts of the Lincoln County War as Amelia Bean, *Time for Outrage*; Maurice Fulton, *History of the Lincoln County War*; and William A. Keleher, *Violence in Lincoln County.*

and Saval's lovely daughter, Celsa. The grateful Kid showers them with gifts and affection. Yet the Mexican recipients of Saxon generosity prove unappreciative. When the Kid, hunted by Sheriff Pat Garrett, asks once more for sanctuary in Saval's hut, Saval tells him that hiding a fugitive has brought his family nothing but grief and that he wants no more to do with him. Celsa, pregnant with the Kid's child and angry at what she perceives as his coldness and neglect, begs him to leave her alone. A shocked Kid backs out of the door and is gunned down by Garrett.

Mexican characters play similar pivotal roles in Sam Peckinpah's *Pat Garrett and Billy the Kid.* This time, however, the intentions of the Mexican characters are honorable and the Kid's role as sacrificing samaritan is more clearly defined. At the end of the movie the Kid (Kris Kristofferson) rides for Old Mexico to escape the pursuing Garrett (James Coburn). He happens upon a fatally beaten sheepherder, who with his dying breath tells the Kid how he was forced to watch his daughter gang-raped and murdered by men in the pay of cattle tycoon John Chisum. Forswearing sanctuary, the Kid returns to Fort Sumner to avenge his Mexican friends. Garrett, tracking the Kid to Sumner, courteously waits outside the bedroom where the Kid is spending his passion with his Mexican sweetheart, then shoots him down. The Kid, muttering "Jesus, Jesus," dies with arms outstretched in the posture of crucifixion.

The notion of the Anglo outlaw as a saintly samaritan takes a more positive turn in Eugene Manlove Rhodes's best-known short story, "Pasó por Aquí" (1926). The hero, Ross McEwen, is typical of Rhodes's dashing, irresponsible, and good-hearted bandit-cowboys. After robbing a bank, McEwen eludes a posse by scattering the money along his trail, simultaneously exposing the greed of the law and relieving himself of the overt stigma of criminality. He arrives at a tiny shack half-dead from fatigue and thirst. Yet when he hears a cough and enters the hut to find four Mexicans dying from diphtheria, McEwen does not hesitate to risk his freedom. With a cryptic "I am here to help you," he cleans phlegm-choked throats. He steals and butchers a neighboring rancher's beef to make bouillon. He sets soapweeds ablaze to attract attention. When Sheriff Pat Garrett (who historically was for a time sheriff of Doña Ana County, New Mexico) follows the smoke to the hut, he recognizes McEwen as the bank robber but conceals his own identity and sends for help. After all parties have recovered, McEwen bids farewell to the suitably worshipful Mexican family and rides with Garrett, whom he still does not recognize, to Tularosa. There he boards a train to start a new and honorable life in the East.

The story's point is made not by Garrett or McEwen, but by Monte Márquez, a Mexican card-sharp. When one of the Anglo nurses brought from town to care for the Mexican family questions the propriety of Garrett's conduct, Monte gives the story its title and delivers the most celebrated line in Rhodes's writing. "Thees redhead, he pass this way, Pasó por aquí . . . and he mek here good and not weeked. But, before that—I am not God!" Then, when asked about the possibility of someone informing on McEwen, a shocked Monte in five words sweeps the Mexican into full partnership with the Anglo in Rhodes's Code of Western Brotherhood. "We are all decent people."[5]

Outlaws of good will like Billy the Kid and Ross McEwen serve useful but limited roles as helpers of Mexicans in distress. They are, after all, men outside the law, lacking significant external resources to aid them in their good deeds. As outcasts, they seek the society of other outcasts. For all their good intentions, these outlaw-samaritans inevitably turn for succor to the people they seek to help more often than the Mexicans turn to them. It is therefore up to men and women who work within the system and are able to harness legal private and public resources to aid the oppressed Mexican on a systematic basis. Such samaritans have undertaken the task of lifting talented

[5] Eugene Manlove Rhodes, "Pasó por Aquí," in *The Best Novels and Stories of Eugene Manlove Rhodes*. The story takes its title from an inscription chiseled on a butte by conquistador Don Juan de Oñate: Pasó por Aquí, "Passed This Way."

Mexicans out of the muck and into the mainstream of Anglo-American society since Ethel Hueston published *Eve to the Rescue* in 1920. The eponymous heroine, mistress of a large California estate, undertakes to civilize a "high caste Mexican girl" named Marie as part of a national effort to eliminate the threat of bolshevism during the Red Scare of the twenties. Adopting Marie as her sister, Eve informs her that her regeneration will benefit her personally, but it will also enable her to act as agent in the Americanization of other members of her race who have been infected by communist notions of equality and revolution. At novel's end Marie offers the definitive clue to this version of samaritanism: "Talk is nothing. Social service is a game. But when one makes living so fine that everyone in the world wants to live that way—then it is Americanization."[6]

The samaritan theme recurs in *Border City* by Hart Stilwell, a novel set on the Texas side of the Rio Grande in the early 1940's. During his short-lived career as reporter for the *Border City News*, Dave Atwood takes on the town's leading business tycoon and political strongman, Jim Billings, raper of a teen-aged house servant named Consuelo Moreno. Though Atwood is soundly defeated by the Billings machine, he manages to expose Texan prejudice in the process. When a desk clerk refuses to permit Atwood and Consuelo to enter a swank hotel to attend "The Inter-American Ball Commemorating the Texas Good Neighbor Policy," on the grounds that admitting a Mexican girl would be pushing inter-Americanism too far, Atwood persists. Once inside the hall, he secures an interview with the governor of Texas:

> I've got no prejudice against the Mexican people—met a lot of fine people. You know it's surprising how many fair-skinned people you find there. Lots of them have light hair and blue eyes, too. Fairer than I am. Why, it's a pleasure to associate with people like that. Of course I don't want them bringing around any of those black, greasy pelados with sores on them. . . . and expecting me to associate with them. . . . We don't have

[6] Ethel Hueston, *Eve to the Rescue*, pp. 195–223, 274, 308, 322–327.

any race trouble and we don't want any. . . . We know how to get along with Mexicans here in Texas—hell, we've been doing it for over a hundred years.

That evening the governor gives a speech at the Good Will Banquet about "the new feeling of friendship existing between the two peoples" of the border, after which the Mexican and Texas delegates dine in separate rooms.[7]

The principal problem in most of the samaritan novels is that the heavy-handed treatment of the subject diminishes the credibility of both the crusading Saxons and the victimized Mexicans. These characters are symbols. They are meant to be taken very seriously indeed. Yet for all that, they tend to remain cardboard figures. Such a hero is Albert Hastings in *The Silk and the Husk* by Albert George Haskell. As a labor contractor for California's southern crop district during World War II, Hastings emerges as an archetypical gruff samaritan. En route to the crops with his dysentery-plagued migrants, he doses them with paregoric and bismuth and chides them when they drink and gamble too much. Once in California, he keeps large doses of penicillin on hand to ward off venereal disease, but charitably turns his head when a cavalcade of jalopies, rumble seats filled with hay and hookers, cruises into camp. When his charges threaten to stage a riot in the dining hall over some ill-cooked beans, Hastings perceives at once that it is not the beans that are bothering them. It is exclusion from the decision-making process about how the beans ought to be cooked. Calling for a "democratic election," he asks for a show of hands from those who wish the beans cooked differently, followed by a show of hands from those who wish them cooked as usual. All the migrants raise both hands both times, and the problem is solved. The implications Hastings' behavior offers about the unstable, childlike Mexican male scarcely require elaboration. Toward the end of the novel, however, his career as crusader takes a more constructive turn when he offers to finance the engineering education of a talented mi-

[7] Hart Stilwell, *Border City*, pp. 38–48, 72–79, 130–131, 272–275.

grant worker and sends a large relief check to locust-plagued villagers in central Mexico.[8]

Perhaps the most ambitious samaritan figure in all southwestern literature is Leslie Benedict of Edna Ferber's *Giant* (1952). Her career as reformer begins on her first day in Texas. Violating the convention that only Mexicans walk in Texas, Leslie strolls to the Mexican quarter of her husband's domain. She finds it a shambles, the shanties "flimsier, even, than the Negro cabins she had seen so familiarly in Virginia." There is no shade, no grass, no gardens, no "pleasant human hum of life." Climbing the steps of a tumbledown shack, Leslie sidesteps the rats and finds a sick mother unable to nurse her child. After changing the boy's diaper, she brings food from the Benedict big house and saves his life. Though her infuriated husband warns her that "messing around" with the Mexicans will damage his reputation, Leslie responds by bribing a local *coyote* (Mexican labor contractor) to take her to one of the dysentery- and tuberculosis-infected migrant camps nearby. There she finds another sick woman with a stillborn child, gives the woman some money, and, blind with tears, stumbles into an open latrine.

Leslie Benedict's personal excursions into the Mexican underworld come to a close very early in her married life. Her creator, however, consistently uses other characters and events to chastise the "Texicans" for their attitudes toward "the *cholo*, the Tex-Mex, the spik, the disinherited *Tejano*." In their zeal to produce beef and oil, the Texans dash madly back and forth between the nineteenth and twentieth centuries—between boots and saddles, steel and plastic. Meanwhile, the Mexicans coax flowers to sprout in the dry desert soil. One race rapes the land; the other makes love to it. In the neighboring town of Benedict, Anglos build New England–style front porches that are totally unusable in the hot Texas sun. They plant trees and shrubs which promptly perish: "We're the white Americans, we're the big men, we eat the beef and drink the bourbon, we

<hr>

[8] Albert George Haskell, *The Silk and the Husk*, pp. 10–11, 38–40, 62–66, 235.

don't take siestas, we don't feel the sun, the heat or the cold, the wind or the rain, we're Texans. So they drank gallons of coffee and stayed awake while the Mexican Americans quietly rested in the shade, their hats pulled down over their eyes."

Ferber's solution for the national disgrace of Texas racism is to combine the "higher" elements of the two races through intermarriage and then to put the younger generation to work as samaritans. Her instrument for effecting both solutions is the son, Jordan Benedict III. Jordy takes his degree in medicine from Columbia University. Returning to Texas, he practices medicine in the barrio, then commits race treason by marrying a "Mexican" girl who, for all Bick Benedict's reluctance to accept the color distinction, looks entirely "Spanish." Indeed, Jordy and the "camellia-white" Juana are so alike in coloring that Ferber seems to suggest it should not be too difficult for the new generation of liberated Texans like Jordy to mix with pale-skinned Mexicans like Juana.[9]

The pervasive theme in most of these works is the heroic attempt of evangelistic Anglos to uplift their privileged Mexican charges as quickly and as thoroughly as possible. A handful of fictional Americans, however, are portrayed as having lost all faith in their bigoted countrymen. Their response is to attempt reversal of the accepted acculturation process by undertaking to "Mexicanize" themselves. The results are usually unimpressive. In Paul Horgan's No Quarter Given, Edmund Abbey, unhappily married composer, and Maggie Michaelis, part-time actress and sculptress who becomes Edmund's lover, renounce the vulgarities of their American friends in Santa Fe and pointedly nickname themselves "the Mexicans." Though they profess some concern over the living conditions in the native quarter of town, Edmund and Maggie spend less time

---

[9] Edna Ferber, Giant, esp. pp. 60, 124–137, 189–195, 242–244. The filmed version of the novel (1956) makes much of a sequence at the roadside cafe in which Bick Benedict (Rock Hudson) challenges the proprietor's insult to his dark-skinned grandson and goes down to defeat in a Hollywood fistfight. But at least the restaurateur is impressed with Benedict's physical prowess. In the novel the incident takes less than two pages, Bick is not present, and Leslie herself, after being called a chola, decides against telling her husband of her humiliation (pp. 382–383).

in samaritan efforts than in self-oriented pursuit of the goal of becoming what they consider to be full-fledged Mexicans in spirit. When Edmund first confesses his love for Maggie, for example, he declares that his feelings are based on the release of primal emotions repressed by his Yankee upbringing. Maggie agrees: "We're all Mexicans. You and I and David [Edmund's son]. I suppose we all have the same simplicity." Actually, Edmund and Maggie find Mexican simplicity hard to come by. For the duration of the novel they search out this elusive "native" quality, finally finding it in the person of a toothless old woman, Concepción Fuentes, whom Maggie recruits to pose in her studio as the New Mexican symbol of the Natural Woman. While Maggie fashions her likeness in clay, Concepción chatters away about the simple pleasures of the uncluttered life. Watching the old woman closely, Maggie feels that she, too, is beginning to embrace the primitive. Edmund, peering from the far end of the studio, feels similar vibrations of primeval inspiration whch enable him to finish a musical composition that has been giving him trouble for months.[10]

The notion of Mexicanizing a select group of disillusioned Americans appears in even simpler-minded form in *The Devil's Pitchfork*, written in collaboration by Ruth Artist and Leora Peters. The heroine, Becky Lane, R.N., of Gopher, Wyoming, champions migrant laborers, calling them "my Mexicans," and insists that the Devil himself is responsible for their hard lot, because with his pitchfork he constantly prods bad Anglos into acts of discrimination. Declaring that her life's work is laid out for her in competing with the Devil for custody of the migrants' souls, Becky rejects a bigoted doctor who rants about the "damned black-skinned Greasers." She marries instead a young Mexico City football star of wealthy family whose skin is "rather like any white man's who had been in the sun a great deal."[11]

[10] Paul Horgan, *No Quarter Given*, pp. 70–77, 82, 156.
[11] Ruth Artist and Leora Peters, *The Devil's Pitchfork*, pp. 30–31, 117, 122, 292. The samaritan heroine of *Three Sides to the River*, by Estelle Curruth, also rejects American bigotry by marrying a light-skinned Mexican and dedicating herself to good works in the Little Mexico section of the border town of Chaparral, Texas.

The marriages of Jordy Benedict and Becky Lane lead into an increasingly important theme in twentieth-century southwestern literature. Particularly since the publication of *Giant* in 1952, novelists have begun abandoning the samaritan theme for a more complex examination of the Anglo's conflicting feelings of attraction for and aversion to the Mexican race. Dropping the element of guilt while retaining the anguish of conscience, these mid-century writers have penned a number of works closely resembling those written by race-tormented southerners. Sometimes the analogy is explicit. In an autobiographical novel entitled *Southwest*, published in the same year as *Giant*, John Houghton Allen tells us more than we want to know about his love-hate relationship with the Southwest in general and with Mexican women in particular. He links both attitudes to his southern heritage. Allen's feelings about race apparently reflect the double burden of guilt over southern mistreatment of the blacks and guilt over southwestern mistreatment of the Mexicans. But while the southern half of Allen's guilt is based exclusively on the legacy of slavery, the southwestern half involves a kind of geographic determinism. The "bilious" and "libidinous" landscape of the Southwest poses a grave psychic threat to American and Mexican alike. The elements themselves join to conspire against "reality": "The brush and the brutality and the bitter beauty . . . the pathetic things, the hateful things. . . . You drink the hot beer in the dark cantina, and when you go out to urinate you are blinded by the sun. . . . You put another nickel in the greasy juke box and play Mexican music so loud that you cannot think. . . . It is like a bad dream . . . and the gringos can't take it. . . . There is not a thing to do in this lonely land but drink and fornicate."

Allen's solution to the problem posed by the southwestern landscape is to view it through the bottom of a glass, aided when necessary by drugs, bullfights, or love songs. When he tries to see the Southwest soberly, he finds that physical horrors turn into psychic nightmares. "Don't ask me what makes the gringo go haywire on the Mexican border," Allen concludes, "all I can say is that something seems to get in the gringo's blood down here, strange and gorgeous and exotic like marihuana, and men do inexplicable things." All gringos who stay on the border too long become hybrid monsters who possess "the heart of a Mexican, and the head like a gringo." As these pseudogenetic freaks belonging to neither race, they are periodically seized by a devastating emotional disorder called *coraje*, a "disease" that attacks both Mexicanized Americans and Americanized Mexicans. As an illustration, Allen relates the antics of an Americanized carpenter and plumber named José. When the demands of his American-style job become unbearable, José gets drunk, commits sexual atrocities, and fails to show up for work. When he does show up, José works like a Mexican. Door handles go on backwards, windows are installed upside down, faucets leak more after he has tampered with them than before, and toilets over-flush. To avoid a similar loss of talent and character, Allen flees the Southwest for good. As parting advice, he recommends that all border Americans who wish to retain their sanity and their normal sexual habits had best do the same.[12]

Allen is not alone in his conscience-stricken approach to the border Southwest. Larry McMurtry has established a regional and national reputation as the author of fiction set in rural and small-town Texas. Though he sometimes champions downtrodden Mexicans, his novels more frequently feature young Americans who encounter psychological difficulties similar to Allen's when they venture too close to the border. In *The Last Picture Show*, the sensitive high school hero Sonny and his more callous friend Duane drive five hundred miles to the border town of Matamoros to "see some wickedness." Repelled by the sights and smells of what they take to be authentic Mexico, the boys nevertheless plunge into the experience to have something to brag about back home. Accosted at the first stop sign by a score of preadolescent pimps scrambling for the American trade ("Clean girls?" "Boy's Town?" "Dirty movie?"), the boys are led through a dark alley to a family dwelling where the

---

[12] John Houghton Allen, *Southwest*, pp. 9–15, 55–57, 81–83, 152–155, 160–161.

father of the house offers to show some border-style home movies. Pleading that they are unable to enjoy pornography within sight of sleeping children, Sonny and Duane are then taken
to a nearby shack where they view a film entitled "Man's Best
Friend," featuring a man and a woman having intercourse with
a German Shepherd. Moving on to the dimly lit "Cabaret Zee-
Zee" in the red-light section of Matamoros, Sonny selects a girl
still in her early teens, discovers that she is pregnant, vomits,
and drives home feeling simultaneously filthy and wise. Though
McMurtry does not push the point, the moral message is obvious. Who are the greater border sinners, the Mexican pimps
and prostitutes who populate the dens of iniquity in Tijuana
and Mexicali, Nogales and Ciudad Juárez, El Paso and Matamoros, or the American customers whom they serve and without whom they would not exist?[13]

The question of border depravity is posed more tragically
in a later McMurtry novel, *All My Friends Are Going to Be
Strangers*. This disturbing work of black humor either belongs
in the company of Ken Kesey's theatre of the absurd or stands
as the sole genuine tragic novel to emerge from the border
Southwest. Twenty-three-year-old novelist Danny Deck is en
route from California to Texas on a search for himself reminis-
cent of Sal Paradise's quest in *On the Road*.[14] He stops briefly
at his Uncle Laredo's ranch near the Texas border. Ninety-
year-old Uncle Laredo embodies the Anglo offal of the modern

---

[13]Larry McMurtry, *The Last Picture Show*, pp. 133–140. For data on
actual border conditions, see J. Allan Beegle, Harold F. Goldsmith, and
Charles P. Loomis, "Demographic Characteristics of the United States–
Mexican Border," *Rural Sociology* 25 (March, 1960); William V. D'Antonio
and William H. Form, *Influentials in Two Border Cities: A Study in Community Decision-Making* (Notre Dame, Ind.: University of Notre Dame Press,
1965); and Ellwyn R. Stoddard, *Comparative Structures and Attitudes along
the United States–Mexican Border* (El Paso, Texas: Conference on Urbani-
zation of the United States-Mexican Border, 1968).

[14] In Jack Kerouac's *On the Road* (New York: Viking, 1955), the wan-
dering antihero Sal has a meteoric affair with a Mexican American girl named
Terry, whom he picks up near Los Angeles and accompanies to the girl's
hometown near Sabinal, California. There, Sal adopts the casual attitude of
Terry and her brother, Freddy, passing the days and nights doing nothing.
Eventually, however, Sal grows restless and leaves Terry to continue his mad
driving across the country (pp. 84–102).

Southwest. By day he rides off into the far horizon, bound for nowhere to do nothing. By night he travels to a neighboring ranch to have dinner with his wife, who lives several miles away because she cannot stand to be closer to him. Everyone who comes in contact with this wicked old man is corrupted in one way or another. One of his Mexican employees, driven to insanity by systematic starvation and sadistic treatment, has intercourse within a matter of minutes with a posthole, a camel, and the gas tank of a pickup. His two companions, fearful for their own sanity, tired of eating upholstery from the seats of junked tractors and hay balers, flee the "crazy ranch," leaving their sex-crazed partner to try to cope with his employer alone.

Still seeking his bearings after his antic encounter with the New West, Danny drives to Reynosa, just across the river in romantic Old Mexico. He picks up a prostitute named Juanita and follows her to a crib outfitted with cheap furniture and photographs of the whore's children. Unlike Sonny of *The Last Picture Show*, however, Danny experiences the high point of his life with this updated dark lady—a final expression of self-worth which simultaneously shows the extent of his desperation: "She wasn't my friend, she didn't love me, she wasn't the whore-with-the-heart-of-gold pouring out sympathy. . . . In my whole life I had never felt so certain that I was more or less a good man. . . . I was right on an edge. I couldn't get lonelier and stranger than I was or I would never stand a chance of getting back where the normal people were. Juanita was my best hope."

The hope is not a realistic one. Danny's quest for "meaning" in Mexico skitters first into farce, then swerves toward madness, and finally plunges into tragedy. When Juanita rejects his offer to come to Texas because she can make more money whoring in Mexico, Danny races to the neighboring border town of Roma, Texas, where the film *Viva Zapata!* was made. With the help of whiskey and mushrooms, he hopes to find peace through spiritual communion with Zapata, his childhood idol. Instead, no sooner does Danny get to the point of envisioning Jean Peters walking to church for a rendezvous with Marlon Brando than the image blurs, fades, and turns into hallucinating nightmare. No longer able to carry "so many images of people who were lost to me," and believing that his life has been wasted in trying to write novels when he should have been traveling through Mexican towns "full of whores, people, and goats," Danny follows Ambrose Bierce into the middle of the Rio Grande in search of Zapata and the secret source of life. His last vision of what he calls the Country of his Soul—the "thin little strip between the country of the normal and the country of the strange"—is precisely that thin ribbon of water running between the United States and Mexico. The Rio Grande, fabled river of American and Mexican song and verse, becomes the symbolic boundary line between the ordinary and the extraordinary, the sane and the insane. With his aborted novel tucked under his arm, Danny wades halfway across the Rio Grande, sinks the manuscript, and drowns himself.[15]

The above plot summaries are extensive. They are also necessary to show that psychodramas of the Allen-McMurtry type fail to sustain their heavy burdens of guilt and emotional imbalance. Their implications are as obvious as they are simple. There is something "strange and gorgeous and exotic," as Allen puts it, about the Mexican border country, a feeling and a state of mind that both attracts and repels the gringo intruder. Life there is foreign, forbidding, decadent, and unclean. Americans who wish to practice normal behavior had better stay away. If, like Allen himself in *Southwest* or Sonny in *The Last Picture Show*, curious Americans visit the border briefly to see what Hell is like, they had best return to the antiseptic and rational United States thankfully and quickly. Otherwise, like Danny in *All My Friends Are Going to Be Strangers*, they might lose their ethnic, national, and emotional bearings and succumb quickly to exile or death.

Whether portraying their Anglo protagonists as guilt-ridden samaritans or as conscience-stricken victims of Mexican de-

[15] Larry McMurtry, *All My Friends Are Going to Be Strangers*, esp. pp. 152–179, 229–247.

pravity, the authors discussed in this chapter have two general tendencies in common. First, they attempt to reverse the position of the Saxon hero and heroine as members of a morally righteous master race. No matter how high-minded they may be, these new-model samaritan protagonists no longer take pride in the racial record of their countrymen. Consumed by guilt, submerged in moral ambiguity, they share the disillusionment of their creators. Second, the creators of sinner-samaritans focus on the Anglo side of the racial dilemma. Whether venting their anger on American bigots, making their heroes try to reverse the course of decades of prejudice, or allowing their characters to surrender to total despair, these writers almost invariably utilize Mexicans, individually and collectively, as living clubs with which to beat their own errant race. Whatever the vagaries of a given plot, the Mexican in sinner-samaritan fiction still serves rather as puppet than as protagonist. He is a brown symbol by which to measure the evils of a race as monstrous as it is masterful.

The principal weakness in the sinner-samaritan novels, whether the protagonists are preaching self-help sermons or sounding self-destructive notes of doom, is overkill. All too often the instruments used to dissect the anatomy of racism and moral perversion are so heavy and blunt, so burdened by clichés, so lacking in any form of artifice, that the moral point is buried beneath layers of blood, guilt, sexual depravity, or recrimination. With few exceptions the characters, brown and white alike, move woodenly through pages and situations. Their missions, their purpose, their achievements, and their failures are alike contrived. Their misfortunes and adventures evoke sympathy and empathy only to a limited point. The warm-hearted and pious samaritans exist too obviously to highlight the perfidy of the rest of their race. The sinners stand equally as symbols of Anglo degradation. And the guilt-stricken, irrational misfits of the Allen or McMurtry type are so consumed by self-indulgent remorse that they are incapable of constructive action. Indeed, the problem with such sinner-samaritans resembles that of the dark lady of chapter 3. It is not that they lack qualities of character, but that they have too many of them. Drifting back and forth from page to page between saintliness and sinfulness, samaritanism and selfishness, sanity and insanity; alternately compassionate and callous, helpful and harmful; they are in the last analysis cat's-paws in the hands of fumbling artists, soap opera figures who fail to transcend the symbolism they evoke and lose their credibility with their identity.

Obsessed with the American side of the battle between the brown and white races, the writers of sinner-samaritan fiction have leveled their heaviest verbal artillery against the massed ranks of Anglos, bad, good, and indifferent. Not all novelists, however, concentrate their fire on the small group of heroic samaritans or the mass of spineless sinners. Other writers, many of them already burdened by guilt for white mistreatment of the black and red races, discovered yet a third oppressed minority that deserved to be heard from directly rather than through the pious or haunted voices of the sinner-samaritans. The result was the creation of no fewer than four new Mexican stereotypes, each as radically different from the traditional bandido-buffoons and Castilian dark ladies as the American samaritans were from the old-time greaser fighters: the Mexican as victim, conformist, avenger, and clown. Their appearance will be discussed in chapter 8.

CHAPTER EIGHT

FOUR FACES OF THE MEXICAN
IN MODERN POPULAR FICTION

SINCE THE 1930's an increasing number of Anglo writers have presented the Mexican as noble savage, victimized by forces beyond his control, struggling to survive as a human being in a degraded and prejudiced America. These persecuted pawns of Anglo racism are a mixed bag, with little save their alienation in common. They assume no fewer than four distinct fictional forms. There are the harassed victims who retreat passively from the American enemy, only to be apprehended and sacrificed to American prejudice. There are the light-skinned, Americanized Mexicans who manage to "make it" in Anglo-American society. There are the dark avengers who set out to cripple and wound the American oppressor. And finally, there are the jolly loafers who accept their miserable lot with little bitterness or recrimination.

Most of these protagonists begin in segregated poverty in the backlands of rural America or the asphalt jungles of the modern urban Southwest. Sometimes they battle the hostile forces of the Great Depression. Occasionally they bear the brunt of wartime discrimination. Often they endure more covert postwar prejudice. Of the four types, the passive, dark-skinned victim invariably goes down to defeat or death. The aggressive, light-skinned Mexican, on the other hand, tries so hard to abandon his brown brothers and join the "white" race that he usually wins a permanent position within the ranks of the favored society. By contrast, the avenger, bent on punishing the white man for his sins, poses such a genuine threat to the dominant society that he must somehow be punished. His equally dark counterpart, the jolly loafer, is harmless—so harmless that he may be safely ignored or may be subjected to humorous, even affectionate, harassment.

In popular literature set in the modern Southwest, the Mexican as passive victim is usually portrayed as helplessly caught between the appeals and standards of Mexican and American ways of life. His most common response to Anglo-American oppression is, strictly speaking, no response at all. He submits and suffers. In Richard Summers' *Dark Madonna,* a novel set in a Tucson barrio in the 1930's, the heroine, Lupe Salcido, is raped at the age of fifteen by an Anglo sheriff. Her father, a debt-ridden moonshiner, supplies the crooked American lawmen who then turn him in. Lupe's mother spends so much money on witch-repelling candles that the family is reduced to eating dog meat. One light-skinned brother, product of an extramarital affair, stabs his wife with an ice pick, shoots a deputy, and deserts his family to become a hack artist in Mexico. Another sibling is a marijuana addict, so burdened by "Mexican" visions brought on by puffing the weed that he kills a man guilty of seducing his brother's wife and in turn is shot and killed by the sheriff. The final message in *Dark Madonna* is that the modern Mexican, however much he may be a figure of tragedy and a prisoner of American perversity, is quite helpless to change his lot, much less to reverse the downward course of his race. At the end of the novel, Lupe, left with a bastard child, no man, and a destitute family, plans to become a prostitute.[1]

The theme of Mexican helplessness in the face of Anglo dominance is reiterated in several novels set in depression California. In *Tumbleweeds,* by Marta Roberts, Pedro García, a farmer imported from Mexico to work in the San Bernardino switchyards, loses his job at the start of the depression. His

---

[1] Richard Summers, *Dark Madonna,* pp. 30–36, 77–81, 101–111, 189–192, 227–228, 260–288.

wife Concha crowds six children into a one-room shed and takes a job as housekeeper for a wealthy bigot named Wilhelmina Robertson, who raves about lazy Mexicans while demanding that Concha put in an eleven-hour workday for three dollars a week. When Concha fails to "keep up to the work schedule I've outlined for you," Wilhelmina fires her and, in a parting sermon, urges her not to "go and have another baby which seems to be a habit of you people when you're not employed." Pedro for his part takes to gin and bread lines.[2]

South of the Angels, by Jessamyn West, carries the problem of Mexican helplessness even further. Pete Ramos' great-grandfather owned thousands of acres stretching from the mountains to the sea. Now Pete works as a hired hand for an American rancher near Los Angeles and watches the land of his fathers being bulldozed into suburban homes and ten-acre citrus farms. When his friend Julián Ortiz is seduced by an Anglo slut named Medora Cudlip and then beaten senseless by Medora's redneck father, Pete comes to Julián's aid. He is promptly killed by Cudlip, who in turn pleads that he was protecting his daughter from "rape" and is freed by the California courts.

Probably the most familiar novel with a California setting presenting the Mexican as victim is Don Mankiewicz's *Trial*. Teenaged Angel Chávez is accused of raping and killing a white girl who actually died of a rheumatic heart. An Anglo samaritan, David Blake, professor of criminal law, tries to defend Angel but is caught between two equally vicious forces. On one side is a racist mob which chants "Hang Angel Chávez to a sour apple tree" and packs the jury to assure a guilty verdict. On the other is the Communist party, which publicly raises funds for Angel's defense and privately plans to sacrifice him as an illustration of American racism. At novel's end Blake, the voice of liberal reason, loses to both right and left. Angel is hanged by the "fascist" state. The Communists siphon $100,-000 raised for Angel's "defense" into the party war chest and hold a rally "honoring the memory of Angel Chávez" where

---

[2] Marta Roberts, *Tumbleweeds*, pp. 23–38, 48.

"authentic Mexican frijoles and tamales" are served. Angel's well-meaning but simple mother delivers a party-produced hack speech about "my-country-making-war-on-her-dark-skin-peoples." As in most novels of the brown victim genre, white bigotry triumphs over any ideology, even communism.[3]

New Mexico also provides a setting for fiction juxtaposing American oppression and Hispano submission. Edwin Corle's *Burro Alley*, a series of short stories set in Santa Fe at the peak of the depression, presents two Hispano men as symbols of their victimized race. Floriano haunts a roadhouse patronized by Anglos, coaxing the last drops of liquor from bottles tossed into the alley until he collapses in his own vomit and is carted home in a wheelbarrow by his mother and sister. Another degraded Hispano, pointedly named Amador, searches out lonely Anglo women and, true to his name, falls in love with them for one evening each at a high price. During the day he joins the rest of the town's Hispano underworld in restless sleep, tossing and turning while awaiting the next night's orgy. Curtis Martin's *The Hills of Home* is another collection of short stories focusing on the plight of the mid-century New Mexican Hispano. In "Blood," Juan Chávez, a former high school athlete now reduced to menial labor, is snubbed by his former sweetheart, a wealthy sophisticate whose views about skin color have pointedly changed since graduation. Another high school prodigy, Alfred García, takes a hard-earned degree in chemistry at New Mexico State University only to be refused appropriate employment on the grounds of race. Drawing a bitter distinction between the lot of the Hispano in the Southwest and that of the black in the South, García tells a friend that being a greaser is worse than being a nigger because blacks "are treated for what they are, while I am treated for something that I am not." The Hispano's unique burden in the United States, in other words, is to look almost white but to be treated as a non-white.[4]

[3] The film version of *Trial* starred Glenn Ford as David Blake and featured justice triumphant.

[4] Curtis Martin, *The Hills of Home*, pp. 85–104.

Two novels by Joseph O'Kane Foster, *In the Night Did I Sing* and *Stephana*, incorporate a somewhat more sophisticated version of Hispano society, presenting both successful *vendidos* who sell out to the Anglo oppressors and honorable Hispanos who do not. In the first novel, Ferdinando, veteran of three years in the American army, grows rich by running a hotel for gringos and uses the proceeds to launch a corrupt political career in Santa Fe. In a subplot, an elderly champion of the traditional ways loses his ranch to a tyrannical store owner who mortgages the homes of his fellow Hispanos and hands them over to foreclosing Anglo-Americans. The light-skinned heroine of the second novel, Stephana Díaz, is burdened by a family that is completely unable to adapt to Anglo ways. Her mother insists on living as an imitation great-house lady. Her father spends his days beating his wife, sipping wine, and watching the sand dunes spill into his drought-stricken alfalfa fields. Stephana's fourteen-year-old sister is a *pachuca* whose suicidal battles with the hated gringos mark her for prison or an early death. Her younger brother suffers from feelings of intellectual inferiority. Stephana herself is forced to endure persecution in high school, where she is charged with being a nymphomaniac and is referred to in the plural as "you people."

In spite of all this, Stephana remains determined to take the "wonderful, impossible way toward the Gringos" but has trouble finding a male member of her race who is willing to take the plunge with her. In a final attempt to enliven her boyfriend Gabriel, she wakens him at noon, earlier than usual, and asks: "Don't you want to be anything—get anywhere?" Gabriel replies, "Nowhere," and predicts that in her eagerness to join the Anglo establishment, Stephana will be a pushover for weak or immoral gringos. His prophecy proves correct. At the age of fifteen she is seduced by a high school teacher who urges her to take pride in her Hispano heritage and then flees home to Boston. To support her penniless father and mother, Stephana changes her surname to Du Bois and lands a managerial job in a bank, crossing the color line successfully until she is unmasked by a jealous female employee. She is rescued from demotion and disgrace by a rich easterner who removes her from prejudiced New Mexico to settle in the relatively tolerant East.[5]

Despite the soap-opera elements of her life story, Stephana Díaz introduced the second type of Mexican protagonist in modern fiction: the "superior," light-skinned mestizo who actively engages the Anglo-American on the latter's own terms. Generally, however, this new protagonist is a male, a "manly" Mexican who possesses a particular gift or skill—good looks, physical prowess, managerial capacity. Indeed, he is often not even *visibly* a Mexican. The shock and pathos that readers are expected to feel in the presence of the "white" Mexican is inspired by the fact that he appears to be doomed unfairly to the same outcast position as his darker brother. His skin gives him a status approximating that of an illegitimate half-brother, semirespectable but uncertain. And like many another literary bastard, the aspiring Mexican tries harder. Far from being physically degenerate, mentally undeveloped, or morally bankrupt, a fit subject alternately for uplift or rejection, the manly Mexican is a sympathetic character. He boasts the finest qualities that can be ascribed to him by writers of the master race. With luck and good management he may actually cross the ethnic barrier into the Anglo promised land.

One of the earliest of such transfers occurs in Hamlin Garland's "Delmar of Pima" (1902). The eponymous hero is a tall, blue-eyed Arizona sheriff who is "half-Spanish" but whose Spanish half emerges only in his facility with "the Mexican

---

[5] *The Life and Death of Little Jo,* by Robert Bright, contains the same pessimistic outlook for the poverty-stricken rural Hispano. Rafael, owner of a monopolistic company store in a small mountain village north of Santa Fe during the war, is a *vendido,* a sellout who kowtows to his Anglo-American customers and, as financial *patrón* of his people, holds most of the villagers' lives in fief through mortgages on their property. Lacking a son, Rafael tries to pressure Little Jo Sandovilla, the novel's young Hispanic hero, into becoming his adopted son with the idea of marrying the boy to his daughter and installing the two as heirs to his tiny mercantile kingdom. In the end Little Jo renounces Rafael's commercial bid for his soul and leaves town, but in doing so he falls prey to a more devastating enemy. Joining the U.S. Army, Little Jo loses his life on Bataan in the Philippines fighting an unknown enemy on behalf of a cause he neither understands nor accepts.

dialect." Otherwise he wears a white hat, drinks lemonade, and in general displays the modesty, courage, and high moral sense characteristic of pulp-fiction lawmen. While Sheriff Delmar suffers the discrimination endured by darker Mexicans, he clearly does not deserve the ethnic slurs heaped upon him by bigoted Anglo-Arizonans. His behavior, however, might justify them in plot terms. Delmar is a sheriff with a difference. He aligns himself with the poor Mexican sheepherders of his country against the rich American cattlemen and wins a decisive victory by arming the heretofore cowardly Mexicans. The story, however, offers no indication that Delmar's helpers are capable of any action beyond blindly following a "Mexican" who is really an Anglo in everything but name. Nor does Delmar emerge as a permanent leader of the Hispano community. Instead, by story's end he is well on the way to being accepted as part of the Arizona establishment, having earned his place by his intelligence and courage.[6]

Like Delmar, Dionisio Molina, the half-Mexican, half-American hero of Claud Garner's *The Wetback*, bears no visible physical or psychological marks of inferiority. Six feet tall, red-haired, and fair-skinned, he swims the Rio Grande illegally and joins a Mexican labor gang in Texas, grubbing mesquite by day and teaching himself to read English by night. Four pillars of a Texas border community—a banker, a merchant, a tractor dealer, and a priest—attest to the boy's un-Mexican qualities of courage, resourcefulness, and honesty. Dionisio eventually becomes a member in good standing of Texas society. Yet the novel's essential point is that his extraordinary feats of courage and endurance are not to be confused with the behavior of most members of his race. Since border Mexicans as a group are "fellows of low habits and evil tongues," Dionisio Molina is bound to remain the exception, a Mexican whose "American genes" enable him to prevail over his background.[7]

---

[6] Hamlin Garland, "Delmar of Pima," *McClure's Magazine*, 1902, reprinted in *The Chicano: From Caricature to Self-Portrait*, ed. Edward Simmen, pp. 72–88.

[7] Claud Garner, *The Wetback*, pp. 23–44, 131–159, 178, 216.

Another example of complete assimilation occurs in A. A. Gallen's *Wetback*. Joe De Soto grows to manhood in the Imperial Valley in the 1930's believing that he is a "full-blooded Mexican." Nonetheless, Joe manages to do all the right things. Whether butting heads on the playing field or running for class president, he easily bests his Anglo classmates. He wins a football scholarship that takes him to the Rose Bowl. He marries his all-white high school sweetheart. He serves a stint against Hitler. Then he takes a law degree and returns to the valley to break singlehandedly the combined power of the Ku Klux Klan and the American Citrus Growers' Association, led by a villainous former classmate who smokes cigarettes, drinks beer, brutally beats his migrant workers, talks a pregnant girl into hanging herself, and receives his comeuppance only when he is "bitten by a poisonous reptile." While the reader is still wondering why the snake did not die instead, Joe's real mother appears. She turns out to be a prosperous white woman who had a brief affair with a wetback, and she informs Joe that she abandoned him at birth for his own good, to see if he could make it as a "Mexican." Joe's reaction is implausibly positive. Exclaiming, "Gee, it's great to be an American," he offers a New Deal view of the solution to the racial problem which may sound naive in the 1970's but is presented without irony: "So long as we have constitutional government based on the sacred principles of our Constitution and the Bill of Rights we shall lick every injustice that may come up. But if we allow ourselves to be torn apart by internal jealousy and demagogues and disregard the sacred principles of the greatest document ever written, we shall sink into darkness and carry the world along with us. . . ."[8]

Particularly when summarized for analytical purposes, such works tend to evoke amusement or anger. But the reader who is willing to suppress his giggles at pretentious plots and stilted prose will note significant similarities between the light-skinned "Mexican" of the Joe De Soto type—who often turns out to be

[8] A. A. Gallen, *Wetback*, pp. 78–82, 236–243.

half-Mexican and half-American—and the off-white "Castilian" heroes and heroines of the old days. Times and costumes change, but plots, settings, and ethnic lines remain much the same. There is really little new about these updated, pale, and proper "Americanized" Mexicans who win their way into the mainstream of Anglo-American society. They are only claiming their rightful heritage.

Such is not the case with the third type of modern Mexican protagonist, who is radically different from both the dark victim and the light victor. He is the dark avenger who seeks vengeance on the white race for its multiple racial sins, past and present. This awesome character is altogether new in southwestern literature, a product of the shifting racial values and fears of our own time. Yet he has not proved to be a popular protagonist, especially among Anglo-American writers and their readers. The reason is not particularly subtle. Few Anglos can or wish to identify personally with dark-hued mestizos who pose threats a little too close and a little too real for comfort. The result is that these brown avengers, whether sinister and self-serving or altruistic and self-righteous, sooner or later fail in their quest. At the very least, they fall short of their aim of turning selected targets within Anglo society on their ears. Jack London's short story "The Mexican" (1911), features a mestizo avenger in southwestern literature who actually wins his fight against the gringo enemy. London's hero is a man of power and menace. Felipe Rivera journeys north to California to join the resistance against dictator Porfirio Díaz. He becomes a boxer to raise money, though he despises prize fighting as "the hated game of the hated gringo." After several small-time fights in Los Angeles, Felipe takes on a top-rated American pugilist and, spurred by the "resplendent and glorious vision of the red revolution sweeping across his land," defeats the champ. But instead of joining the gringo enemy in the style of the light-skinned Mexicans discussed earlier in this chapter, Felipe promptly turns the gate receipts over to the movement. Despite the story's dated Marxist rhetoric, it replaces the loquacious, hot-tempered, cowardly halfbreed of the contemporary pulps with a quiet, courageous mestizo who combines admirable principles with impressive force of body and spirit. It is one of few works to do so.[9]

Forty-two years after London's alienated boxer, Irving Shulman offered another brown challenger in *The Square Trap*, derived from the movie, *The Ring*. This time, however, the prospective avenger goes down to double defeat. Tomás Cantanios enters the ring as the way out of the Los Angeles barrio of the 1940's and into the glittering world of the gringo. Fighting under the Anglicized name of Tommy Kansas, he uses the proceeds of a few victorious fights to buy fancy cars, flashy clothes, and a blonde mistress. The gringo's respect, however, is not for sale so cheaply. Cantanios' victory over his Anglo-American foes proves far more short-lived than that of London's fearsome fighter. Accidentally over-matched, Cantanios is badly beaten and falls overnight to a used-up pug who predictably descends into the lower ranks of his oppressed race.

An even more disastrous fall attends the threat posed by one of John Steinbeck's earliest Mexican characters, Pepe Torres of "Flight" (1938). Pepe is not sufficiently intelligent to pose an actual threat to Anglo society. He would in fact be just another passive Mexican hanger-on were it not for the fact that he is able to flick a switchblade knife into a corral post with blinding speed—a gift that leads to his death. When his widowed mother tells him that at the age of nineteen it is finally time for him to be trusted to ride into Monterey alone for the family's monthly supplies, Pepe wanders into a saloon. Acting virtually by reflex, he knifes a man who insults him. Then his instincts take complete control. Pepe is transformed from a feeble-minded teenager into a cunning escapee who strikes out for the mountains, communicating along the way with other wild animals like himself. Finally trapped by pursuing vigilantes, he chooses death by standing high on a rock and exposing himself to gunfire from below.[10]

In certain respects Pepe Torres is more Steinbeck than

[9] Jack London, "The Mexican," in *The Night-Born*, pp. 260–290.
[10] John Steinbeck, "Flight," in *The Long Valley*, pp. 45–72.

186

Mexican. The destruction of the individual by a brutal group is a recurring theme in Steinbeck's fiction. Many of Steinbeck's Anglo protagonists, like Lenny in *Of Mice and Men*, are also so primal, such creatures of instinct, that they never quite become human. Pepe's fate, however, is typical of that meted out to Mexicans who challenge the Anglo establishment for any reason. If not broken by fist or gun, they are victims of their own greed. Jesús Martínez, of R. L. Hardman's *No Other Harvest*, is a labor contractor and foreman for the McPhail cotton dynasty in the San Joaquin Valley in the 1950's. He is determined to avenge himself on his oppressors. He clears a handsome personal profit by cheating both his Mexican laborers and his Anglo employers. He pockets social security and insurance payments. He short-weighs cotton. He houses workers in filthy shacks on property he owns himself. Martínez places migrant children in the fields at the age of six, seduces migrant daughters to keep their fathers in line, and chooses his workers, "like another man might select breeding stock," on the basis of their degree of desperation. When the McPhail empire passes to heirs who threaten to eliminate migrant labor by introducing mechanical cotton pickers, Martínez skillfully plays the members of the family against each other, finally winning the right to handle the McPhail cotton as he sees fit. Yet at the moment of his greatest triumph, Martínez is the agent of his own fall. After seducing yet another migrant worker's daughter, in an orgy of victory celebration he suddenly loses his awesome sexual powers. Convinced that he has also lost the hormonal source of his *macho* mastery over his Anglo-American employers, Martínez commits suicide.

First impressions might suggest that Martínez's behavior is at best implausible. His own emphasis on his sexual powers and their role in his overall success, however, is typical of the mestizo avengers of modern formula fiction. In this respect the avengers strongly resemble the black characters of Twain, Faulkner, Styron, and other southern novelists who vent generations of humiliation on the bodies of white women. This pronounced sexuality is a sharp contrast to the chaste behavior of the light-skinned Americanized Mexican. It is, moreover, generally presented in an extremely unsympathetic fashion. Frank Waters' *The Yogi of Cockroach Court*, set in a border town on the Gulf of California in the 1940's, features a host of beggars, drunks, lesbians, pimps, and prostitutes whose degree of depravity seems closely linked to the color of their skin. One of the main characters, Barby, a "quivering, fear-struck little bastard" with the "broad, brutal face of a halfbreed," grows to manhood as a gangster, bootlegger, pimp, rapist, and womanbeater. Like his light-skinned fictional brethren, his real ambition is to cross into the promised land to the north. When he does so, he is promptly humiliated by an Anglo citrus rancher who caps a brutal verbal assault by questioning his manhood and sexual prowess. Driven back into Mexico and inferiority, Barby returns to theft and pimping, bolstering his shaky ego by insisting that he never really wanted to be an American after all.

The novel's other main character, Barby's mestiza girl friend Guadalupe, is more successful at entering the American establishment. Attaching herself to a California lesbian who acts as her "agent," she rises rapidly from a hustler working sleazy bars on the Mexican side of the border to a "Spanish" Flamenco dancer and high-priced prostitute in a swank American club. Her past more or less behind her, she expands her horizons beyond border riffraff to take in—literally—several of California's top businessmen and politicians. Since she does not pose the same type of sexual threat to Anglo readers as dark-skinned male rapists and seducers, she does not need to be eliminated or humiliated in the manner of Barby and other brown menaces. Nevertheless, Lupe's unsavory qualities of character are typical of those ascribed to brown avengers in southwestern fiction: they are presented as part of her racial heritage.[11]

11 Frank Waters, *The Yogi of Cockroach Court*, pp. 1–26, 40–41, 271. Much the same caricature occurs in Waters' *People of the Valley*, a rambling novel about an eighty-year-old mestiza witch woman named María del Valle who fights unsuccessfully to prevent the Roosevelt administration from building a flood-prevention dam above a remote Hispano village in New Mexico. Ex-

Waters seems convinced that the wickedness of Lupe, Barby, and other mestizo characters in the novel is based largely
on unfortunate racial blends. The "vicious" faces of the *leperos*
of the border, "yellow and cunning, with sly eyes and thin
lips," together with "the *cholos*, broad-cheeked and brutal,"
the *coyotes*, "stained dark red beneath the brown," and the
criollos, "sharp-featured with purplish lips," add up to an enormous degree of racial "pollution." Indeed, the most serious
handicap that Waters' border Mexicans face is not poverty,
squalor, or vice, but the physical decay caused by racial contamination that in turn creates poverty, squalor, and vice. In
the process of racial mingling the "favorable" ingredients are
leached out, leaving a polychromatic residue of "breeds" who
are physically degenerate, mentally obtuse, and morally perverted. Since their defects are congenital, any attempt to improve their lot will merely give them more latitude to destroy
themselves. Reform efforts are doomed to failure. The tragic
dimension of border life is undermined in Waters' fiction by
a cast of characters so grotesque that they fail to command
our compassion. In the end we are left not so much with a
sense of dismay over their lot as with feelings of distaste and
even disgust—emotions typical of those generated by most
works featuring would-be brown avengers of either sex.

By far the most common treatment of the modern Mexican
in English-language popular fiction is as an attractive counterpoint to an increasingly busy, increasingly conformist, American society. This Mexican comes in three forms. He may be a
modern equivalent of Rousseau's natural man. He may be an
individual who deliberately challenges Anglo pieties. Or he
may be a funny savage, more or less unconsciously trying to
avoid being trapped in a decadent world. All three types are
best illustrated in the writings of John Steinbeck. Fully half of
his works incorporate Mexicans or "paisanos." Three focus on

---

cept for María, the villagers are a weak and spineless lot, mere "satellites
swarming around a common sun" (María herself)—groveling subjects of a
harsh dictator who, once she is dead, will have to be replaced by someone
equally dictatorial to make their decisions for them.

native-born Mexicans living in Mexico: *The Forgotten Village,*
The Pearl, and the film script for *Viva Zapata!* Seven more—
The Pastures of Heaven, To a God Unknown, Tortilla Flat,
The Long Valley, The Wayward Bus, Sweet Thursday, and a
short section in *Travels with Charley*—deal with Americans of
Mexican descent living in California.

These works introduce approximately sixty Mexicans, including at least three major protagonists who elude facile typecasting: Emiliano Zapata, the renegade rebel in Steinbeck's
film script for *Viva Zapata!,* Juan Chicoy in *The Wayward Bus,*
and Joseph and Mary Rivas in *Sweet Thursday.* Zapata will be
discussed in the next chapter. Chicoy is a variant of the natural
man, a mestizo who also operates a service station and restau-
rant in a one-street town in northern California. He combines
"Mexican" *machismo,* piety, and humanity with "American"
energy, efficiency, and mechanical ability. He is dark-skinned
but is as much a member of the Anglo establishment as most
of the light-skinned Mexicans who "make it." Chicoy, however,
chooses instead to remain on the fringe of Anglo-American
society. He wears his color as a badge of pride. In an unusual
reversal of roles, he even becomes something of a brown samaritan to his flood-marooned Anglo passengers, protecting
them from harm while Steinbeck dissects their degenerate
minds and wicked souls. Yet Chicoy is more than a symbol of
compassion and courage. He is also a man of zest and humor,
capable of romping in the hay with a flirtatious passenger and
toying with the idea of ditching both the flood-stranded passengers and his shrewish Anglo wife. Chicoy's "fallibility" is
matched by a strong element of dignity and a large sense of
social responsibility. In short, he is a thoroughly human character who runs a gamut of emotions far wider than that allowed most fictional Mexicans.

No less than Chicoy, Joseph and Mary Rivas defies typecasting. A middle-aged survivor of a tough *pachuco* gang, he
operates a grocery store in Monterey and hires himself out as
a *coyote,* a part-time labor contractor of migrant field hands
from Mexico. Like Juan Chicoy, he is an enterprising business-

man. Unlike Chicoy, he is utterly unburdened by the Anglo sense of sin and corruption. Ever on the lookout for "a profession illegal enough to satisfy him morally, and yet safe enough not to outrage his instinctive knowledge of the law of averages," Joseph and Mary sees nothing wrong with resorting to a little chicanery to help his business. He puts a good deal of style into his corruption, however, and Steinbeck admires him for it. By novel's end he has joined the half-dozen friendly geniuses of immorality featured in Steinbeck's late writing: the "moral" men who cheat from principle rather than necessity.[12]

Steinbeck experimented with all three of the types of Mexican clown: the updated natural man (Juan Chicoy), the admirably "immoral" Mexican (Joseph and Mary Rivas), and the Mexican as a funny savage. The final character is usually presented as a cheerful loafer who suffers not at all from American oppression. Indeed, he seems to be funny *because* he is a Mexican and therefore possesses inherently amusing racial characteristics. This figure is close enough to the traditional brown buffoon to prove enduringly popular in comic books, westerns, and advertising. On the other hand, the Frito Bandido has found few equivalents in more serious contemporary popular literature, which tends to stress the Mexican as victim, achiever, or avenger. Once again, Steinbeck is the exception that proves the rule. Specifically, *Tortilla Flat* stands as the clearest example in American literature of the Mexican as jolly savage. For better or worse, this is the book that is most often cited as the prototypical Anglo novel about the Mexican American. That it has spawned relatively few imitators enchances its isolated position while highlighting the fact that the novel contains characters varying little from most negative Mexican stereotypes.[13]

[12] Cf. Alfred Kazin, *On Native Grounds: An Interpretation of Modern Prose Literature*, p. 309. I am indebted to Kazin, and especially to R. W. B. Lewis' fine essay, "John Steinbeck: The Fitful Daemon," in *The Young Rebel in American Literature*, ed. Carl Bode, pp. 121–141.

[13] Alan Moody's *Sleep in the Sun*, set in a coastal valley in southern California in the 1940's bears many similarities to *Tortilla Flat*. The main characters are a husband-and-wife comedy team, José and Mama Chula Mercado, who spend their days sleeping and palming the chores off on one

Published in 1935 when Steinbeck was thirty-three, the book was an instant popular and critical success, initially praised for both its parody of Malory's *Morte d'Arthur* and its presentation of paisano life in California. Steinbeck's characterization of the paisano universe was tied to his profound disenchantment with the machine-mad, corrupt Anglo world. The paisanos of *Tortilla Flat*, literally marooned on their flat, metaphorically inhabit a last piece of the garden before the Fall. Steinbeck's paisanos do not have a complete monopoly on such garden spots. The kindly whores and goodhearted bums who inhabit the boiler factories and flophouses of *Cannery Row* and *Sweet Thursday* are the Anglo counterparts to the paisanos of *Tortilla Flat*. Danny and his friends, like Mack and the boys, are nature's noblemen, the true "Virtues" and "Graces," as Steinbeck has called them, the surviving "Beauties" and "Saints" of a rapacious world. *Tortilla Flat* is a Mexicanized *Cannery Row*; Danny is Mack in brownface.

The necessary mood of reverence for nature is established in the opening pages of the novel. Squatting precariously on the steep slopes of a piny hillside overlooking the bay, the paisano quarter of Monterey has a charm wholly unlike the somber barrio settings in most depression novels with Mexican themes. Far enough removed from the town to discourage work, the flat is close enough to permit its inhabitants to steal the staples of life—a little food, a good deal of wine—without exerting themselves. Except for periodic forays into taverns, whorehouses, and cheap restaurants, these children of nature stay clear of the contaminating influences of the American flatlands below. Like Joseph and Mary Rivas, they are unburdened by moral scruples. Unlike Joseph and Mary, however, they are also unburdened by the problems of getting and spending that lay waste the souls of Americanized Mexicans and Anglos alike. Innocent of ambition or work, the paisanos

---

another. At the end of the novel, when the American authorities build a schoolhouse to educate the illiterate children of this paisano paradise, the Mercados and their neighbors band together and burn the building to the ground.

blend smoothly with their habitat. No electric lights mar the landscape. The rickety houses take on the tint of sea and fog. Paisanos bring flowers to the saints and stir up the hearth for dinnertime chili. American businessmen trudge wearily homeward or roar through Monterey's streets in high-powered cars on their way to gin fizzes at the Hotel Del Monte. Meanwhile, their women meet for tea and gossip and decide that their outdated information about vice and prostitution in the paisano sector of Monterey warrants another fact-finding trip to inspect the enticing dens of iniquity.[14]

Steinbeck's moral dichotomy between Anglo and paisano is badly overworked.[15] His paisanos are far from being paragons of virtue. The one reliable currency of Tortilla Flat, wine, is the weak foundation for a very shaky framework of social intercourse. The thirst of the main characters—Danny, Pilón, Pablo, Jesús María Corcoran, and Big Joe Portagee—is a ceaseless "raging fire." When they lower themselves to the level of the flatlanders, they do so to obtain wine. When they climb back up to their lofty perch, they return bearing wine. This single commodity of trade and barter controls the actions and dictates the fates of all the novel's characters. When they run out of wine, they daydream about turning the morning dew into diamonds which could be bartered for wine or condensing the rain clouds into wine showers that could be siphoned into huge storage tanks.[16]

If the Mexicans of *Tortilla Flat* drink enough to kill most people, unlike the besotted wretches we examined in the novels of the victim genre, they suffer neither physical ill effects nor psychological traumas. These children of nature also share their women with a degree of generosity that simply is not a part of Mexican or Mexican American culture. Indeed, sex runs

[14] John Steinbeck, *Tortilla Flat*, pp. 11–13, 65–68.
[15] Charles R. Metzer, "Steinbeck's Mexican-Americans," in *Steinbeck: The Man and His Work*, ed. Richard Astro and Tetsumaro Hayashi, pp. 141–155, points out that Steinbeck's interest in paisano characters focuses on two virtues as he sees them: (1) the paisanos' superior capacity to "merge successfully with their habitat," and (2) their "strong but different philosophic-moral system."
[16] Steinbeck, *Tortilla Flat*, pp. 14–15, 48–56, 122–123, 142–143.

a dead heat with wine as the principal topic of conversation and quest in the flat. While sunning themselves on the porch, Danny and the boys exchange anecdotes about the exploits of a woman of loose virtue who is famed throughout the quarter for filling the coffers of the church each Sunday with cash earned in sin.[17] To gain the affections of still another paisana of easy virtue, Delores Engracia ("Sweets") Ramírez, on a regular basis, Danny buys her a vacuum cleaner. Since there is no electricity in Tortilla Flat, this product of Anglo industry is useless except as a giant status symbol. Simulating an engine with her throaty voice, Sweets therefore runs the "sweeping machine" in front of the window in full view of her envious friends. When Danny tires of Sweets, he simply steals the vacuum cleaner, sells it to a tavern keeper, and turns his erstwhile love over to his comrades.

Such activities centered on theft, drink, and women-sharing inevitably expose Steinbeck to the charge of racism. The accusation partly misses the point. After all, Steinbeck had only to remind critics—as he did in a preface to later editions—that the novel, being a parody of Arthurian romance, did not necessarily represent paisano life as fact. One could extend this line of argument by suggesting that the paisano's sharing of women reflected the binding loyalty of male brotherhood in Malory's *Morte d'Arthur* which supersedes the link between a man and a woman. The absence of wives, children, and old people in *Tortilla Flat* could be excused by their corresponding absence in Malorian romance. Finally, the Arthurian bond of brotherhood might explain the novel's peculiar ending, in which Danny, driven to despair over the burdens of property ownership acquired through inheriting two houses from his grandfather, roars through the countryside stealing, wenching, and landing in jail as in the days before he became a propertied American. To bring him out of his depression, Danny's friends throw the wildest party in the history of the flat. Rising to the occasion, Danny puts the finishing touches on the Arthurian theme of hail-fellow bravado by outdrinking, outfight-

[17] Ibid., pp. 19–37, 54–55, 68–69, 78–80, 222–224.

ing, and outfornicating all rivals, finally dying a hero's death by charging, dead drunk, into a deep ravine used as a latrine.[18]

As the passing of King Arthur brought the breakup of the Round Table, Danny's death spells the abrupt end of the fellowship. Yet the manner of this death also tips *Tortilla Flat* over the edge of comedy into burlesque and reminds us of Steinbeck's frequent mixing of themes and symbols. Alternately tender and tasteless, subtle and simple, comical and crude, the novel is handicapped by a baffling mixture of moods and motifs which collide rather than meet. The mock-heroic elements conflict with the theme of paradise lost, and we are left uncertain as to which is more important. More significantly for the purposes of the present work, Steinbeck's treatment of the paisanos arouses suspicion of ethnically based distortions. Steinbeck's Anglo misfits are usually genuine freaks—idiots, cripples, and outcasts teetering on the edge of their own race. Danny and his companions, on the other hand, *are* their race as Steinbeck permits us to see it.[19] The other paisanos we meet in *Tortilla Flat* are, if anything, more outlandish than Danny and his close friends. There is not a rational, sober, industrious, or loyally married one in the lot. The characters suffer no feelings of doubt, deprivation, or despair. They maintain no significant family ties. Steinbeck's paisanos never work or try to work. They are rarely unhappy or discontent, nor are they dangerously at odds with the Anglo order. They get drunk

[18] Joseph Fontenrose, *John Steinbeck: An Introduction and Interpretation*, pp. 35–41; and Arthur F. Kinney, "The Arthurian Cycle in *Tortilla Flat*," *Modern Fiction Studies* 60 (Spring 1965): 11–20, explore the relationship between Steinbeck's paisanos and Arthur's knights. Howard Levant, "*Tortilla Flat*: The Shape of John Steinbeck's Career," *PMLA* 85 (October, 1970): 1087–1095, denies the relevance of the parallels to Malory. Stanley Alexander, "The Conflict of Form in *Tortilla Flat*," *American Literature* 40 (March, 1968): 58–66, also explores the relationship between Steinbeck's paisanos and Arthur's knights.

[19] To suggest, as does James Gray in *John Steinbeck*, p. 34, that Danny and his friends are the forerunners of the hippies of the 1960's is to ignore the sharp social and racial differences between Steinbeck's poverty-stricken paisanos and the young and essentially middle-class dropouts of the later era. Eleanor Clark, "Infantilism and Steinbeck," *The Nation* 164 (March 29, 1947): 370, charged that Steinbeck was guilty of "various falsifications of the 'lower depths' of this country."

enough to cause *delirium tremens*, but they do not suffer from alcoholism.[20] Even lust, when practiced by these uninhibited children of nature, becomes virtue; the characters rarely quarrel over anything except wine. Nowhere in the literature of the Southwest do we find such praise of poverty.

Whether the novel is taken as a charming fairy tale peopled by lovable eccentrics or interpreted as an accurate description of the paisanos themselves may depend largely on the reader's ability to divorce the book from his own time and attitudes.[21] Yet there is reason to believe that Steinbeck himself eventually saw the gap between the picturesque grotesques of *Tortilla Flat* and the paisano as he encountered him on his return to Monterey a quarter-century later. Entering a bar he used to frequent in the paisano sector of Monterey, Steinbeck initially believes he has stumbled upon a remnant of the enchanted world he presented in *Tortilla Flat*. Greeted with tears and *abrazos* by the paisanos, he slips at once into the extravagant vernacular of *Tortilla Flat*, relating in a somewhat self-mocking manner how much the bartender, Johnny García, has missed him over the years. Johnny, fat and tearful, declares that he has kept a certain barstool well-oiled and dusted for the happy day when "Juanito" might return to his people:

> "Juanito," he said, "Come home! Come back to your friends. We love you. We need you. This is your seat, *compadre*, do not leave it vacant. . . ."
> "*Cuñado mío,*" I said sadly, "I live in New York now. . . . Time has settled some of our problems."
> "Silence," he said. "I will not hear it. It is not true. You still

[20] In "The Challenge of John Steinbeck," *North American Review* 243 (Summer, 1937): 355–361, Edmund D. Richards approved the drunken conduct of Steinbeck's paisanos as commendably masculine and "passionate." For a general essay on the subject, see William Madsen, "The Alcoholic Agringado," *American Anthropologist* 46 (April, 1964): 355–361.

[21] According to Harry Thornton Moore, *The Novels of John Steinbeck: A First Critical Study*, Steinbeck learned most of his paisano lore not from "the paisanos themselves" but from Susan Gregory, a resident of Monterey to whom *Tortilla Flat* is dedicated. Webster Street, "John Steinbeck: A Reminiscence," in *Steinbeck: The Man and His Work*, ed. Astro and Hayashi, p. 38, asserts that the chief of police of Monterey, Monty Hellam, probably told Steinbeck "the actual activities of these people."

love wine, you still love girls. What has changed? I know you. *No me cagas, niño."*

"*Te cago nunca.* There was a great man named Thomas Wolfe and he wrote a book called *You Can't Go Home Again.* And that is true."

After a long and sodden discussion of the way everything in Monterey has decayed since he left, including by implication Johnny and Johnny's bar, Steinbeck suddenly realizes that he has also called attention to the distance that separates John Steinbeck, celebrated author and Pulitzer Prize winner, from Johnny García, illiterate paisano bartender. Johnny reacts at once. Pretending to select a heavy wine bottle to toast his old comrade, he says, "I guess you don't like us anymore. I guess maybe you're too good for us," and gets ready to brain Steinbeck. Steinbeck makes the door in two leaps and passes out of paisano life forever.

What is significant about the incident is that Steinbeck expresses no surprise at this sudden treachery. He seems to imply that these people can still be loads of fun, but they now suffer feelings of inferiority and insecurity that he did not observe in Danny and his friends a quarter-century earlier. The paisanos of the 1960's may still lie grandly, still drink heavily, and still use polite rhetoric to cover their deceitful actions. But they seem less happy than they were in the depression-wracked thirties. Indeed, they seem no longer pleased at all with the distance between their way of life and that of the successful gringos, whom Danny and his friends neither admired nor envied. Johnny García and his kind had changed a good deal in twenty-five years.[22]

What was more likely is that Steinbeck had changed. During the 1930's his uneasiness at the fragmentation of modern American life, his disgust with materialism and individualism, his sympathy for the primitive and the passionate, led him to seek "natural" characters who might offer attractive alternatives to the compulsive ambitions that he felt were corroding the Anglo soul. When he did not find them, he created them.

[22] John Steinbeck, *Travels with Charley*, pp. 178 ff.

It is therefore hardly surprising to find that many of Steinbeck's Mexicans are lost in the message they embody. Yet although Steinbeck produced his share of clowns and dimwits, nowhere in his writing do we find a single passive brown victim, a single light-skinned conformist, or a single dark avenger. This incorrigible generalizer also created a few Mexican characters who transcend stereotyping of any sort. Juan Chicoy, Joseph and Mary Rivas, and, as we will see, Emiliano Zapata are personalities in their own right, defying typecasting. Steinbeck's Mexican protagonists succeed or fail as characters to the extent that they are freed from their creator's coercion. Given Steinbeck's general tendency to allegorize, categorize, and typify, that any of them are so freed is significant.

Anglo novelists are also beginning to venture beyond the Mexican as a figure of burlesque to the Mexican as a figure of humor. Instead of the Merry Mexican, the buffoon providing contrast to or relief from Anglo sobriety, the reader finds brown comedic characters in works whose mood and setting differ strikingly from the victim-avenger-conformist genres. Frank O'Rourke's *The Springtime Fancy* juxtaposes Rosa Sánchez and her illegitimate baby with a crowd of reporters, outsiders in the New Mexican community on which they descend to investigate poverty. Inevitably they interpret Rosa's desire to live her own life as a manifestation of coercion by the Anglo establishment and launch an investigation enabling O'Rourke to caricature media do-gooders and would-be opinion makers. James Lehrer's *Viva Max!* is similar in tone. Its title hero begins as a greaser buffoon leading a comic-opera army to recapture the Alamo. The work rapidly evolves into a satire on Texas and United States bureaucrats who seek a solution to the problem first by force and then by compromise, with the President of the United States unveiling a replica of the Alamo in Mexico City as delighted crowds cry "Viva Max!"

Neither of these works is particularly subtle in its characterizations or its patterns of interaction. It is reasonable to interpret both as simple farces using Mexican characters as a starting point for caricaturing Anglo society. In the 1970's

Richard Bradford and John Nichols have been far more successful in creating Mexicans who are humorous characters rather than funny Mexicans. Nichols' *The Milagro Beanfield War* is not, however, a humorous novel, and its characterizations are more appropriately discussed in the Afterword. On the other hand, Bradford's *So Far from Heaven* is an ambitious send-up of contemporary New Mexican society. The Anglo hero, David Reed, a refugee from the mad getting and spending of Houston, is consistently upstaged by two Hispanos. Descendant of one of the state's oldest *rico* families, Juan de la Cruz Tafoya y Evans is similar in ancestry and status to the mass of *ricos*, dons, and grandees we encountered in conquest and great-house fiction. His activities and behavior, however, are markedly different from his ancestors in pride and privilege. Well-educated, level-headed, and humorous, Cruz reads Eric Hoffer while riding the range, supports a community school, and permits a group of hippies to stake out a brave new world on his property. His daughter Guadalupe holds a Phi Beta Kappa key from Bryn Mawr, an M.A. in Victorian literature from Berkeley, and a postgraduate degree in police-baiting. If she writes propaganda for the Compañía de Tierra y Libertad, an organization of Chicano farm workers closely modeled on that of Reies Tijerina, her approach is always tongue-in-cheek. When a spokesman for the *compañía* rhapsodizes about returning the land to the landless, Lupe presents an alternative image of the future Chicano utopia: "All the women are wearing *rebozos*; all the men are wearing big straw hats. Every few minutes somebody leads a burro through the plaza, for color. It would be sort of like Williamsburg with tacos."

No less than his daughter, Cruz is a New Mexican original. When the hippies seeking the Secret of the Great All on his property are stricken with the clap, Cruz pointedly reminds the head guru that his ambition to found an organic paradise has thus far given rise to a few straggling cornstalks, a vividly painted geoplastic dome, and gonorrhea. When the guru declares he has heard that Chicanos are soliciting volunteers to help "burn some of the Texas types out" and "give the land back to the people, you know?" Cruz replies that he cannot think of anything the Chicanos need "more than you and your little band of honest dirt farmers." He then urges the guru to lead his tribe into battle promptly, before they pass venereal disease on to his sheep. As a farewell present in lieu of unpaid rent, the counterculture leaves two kilos of marijuana, ten pounds of soya flour, and an unclaimed baby. A more deliberate reversal of the stereotyped contrast between the stable Saxon and the irrational Mexican can hardly be imagined.

The novel's end fails to sustain its satiric pace. David Reed marries blonde and rich Lupe and settles down to manage the ancestral fief—a resolution apparently a concession to the plot requirements of a popular novel. Yet at its best *So Far from Heaven* is a work of warmth and humor. Its Hispano characters are neither victims nor conformists, avengers nor clowns, heroes nor antiheroes. One might argue that the privileged status enjoyed by the Tafoyas permit them such tokens of elite status as telling Texan jokes that reverse traditional gringo-greaser witticisms. The same status also allows a degree of detached liberalism that may not be available to most modern Chicanos. Yet in the process of inverting some of the conventional fictional attitudes about *ricos* and gringos alike, Bradford delivers a broadside at traditional racial relations in the Southwest that is as good-humored as it is well-aimed.

Like their predecessors, the mass of works discussed in this chapter deal in stereotypes—different stereotypes, to be sure, but stereotypes nevertheless. The authors as a rule are so concerned with making social and moral points that they sacrifice most of their characters on the altar of symbolism. The Mexican victims remain blurred and indistinct, figures who are more frequently commented upon by a narrator or talked about as offstage abstractions than allowed to act as human beings. The light-skinned conformists who finally enter mainstream Anglo society are already so "Americanized" in complexion and attitudes that they seem mere reflections of the white establishment figures who function as their tutors, sponsors, and benefactors. Although these Mexicans on the make may provide some vicarious comfort both to their creators and to those who read of their achievements, they are hardly representative of their race, even in fiction. Most perplexing of all, the small number of brown avengers who appear in these novels are usually so repulsive in person and conduct that they can act only as temporary troublemakers whose victories are as morally questionable as their defeats are predictable. Rarely is the brown avenger a high-minded individual who sets out to reform society constructively. When he does, he is so crippled by activist clichés, whether of the 1930's or the 1960's, or so disfigured by saintliness that his superhuman deeds of altruism distort the justice of the cause he expounds.

Of the four faces of the modern Mexican, the clown is the least revealing of all. The very complexity of the comic mode—embracing humor, burlesque, satire, and parody—suggests that the public posture of the clown can rarely be equated with either his or his creator's innermost feelings. The function of the clown, after all, is to wear a mask, or a series of masks, that often camouflage the artist's intent. The rogues in *Tortilla Flat* are a classic illustration. Humor is by nature notoriously irreverent and unpredictable; it can embody the creator's attitudes but it does not automatically, or even customarily, do so. Given the elusive and unreliable nature of all stereotypes, however simple they appear on the surface, we must be cautious in drawing conclusions about what the four stereotypes examined in this chapter tell us about the Anglo-American's perceptions of the Mexican. What can be said with reasonable accuracy is that almost all brown characters in modern southwestern fiction—heroes or victims, seducers or mockers, clowns or conformists—are defined primarily by their actual and potential oppressors. Aside from Richard Bradford's free-wheeling Hispanos, independent-acting Mexicans in Anglo literature are few and far between. As a group they remain prisoners and puppets just as surely, if much more subtly, as the dime-novel greaser.

CHAPTER NINE

THE MEXICAN IN THE MOVIES, 1946–1976

THIS CHAPTER is the tip of an iceberg. Unlike the previous chapter on film, which contained summaries of a large number of movies no longer available for mass viewing, this one focuses on a smaller number of films representing only a fraction of the "Mexican movies" released by Hollywood in the past thirty years. This procedural framework was adopted for two reasons. It has the advantage of presenting movies which are at least vaguely familiar to many readers. It also permits a more detailed treatment of those films embodying an overt, sustained form of Anglo-Mexican interaction. I have chosen to omit the movies which use Mexicans essentially as local color. While this does mean sacrificing some interesting characterizations, one bandit lurking behind a rock, one peon dozing under a cactus, or one brown barmaid serving tequila while promising additional delights is too much like another to deserve consideration in detail. One film of this kind does, however, deserve special mention. *The Alamo* pays solid respect to the Mexican army as fighting men. While it portrays Santa Anna as swarthy and pompous, he is also shown as a general chivalrous enough to offer surrender terms to the garrison, to allow it to evacuate noncombatants in the midst of the siege, and finally to remove his hat and order his trumpeters to salute the widow of a Texan officer as she leaves the destroyed fort. It is a far cry from his literary image.

As might be expected, a large number of recent films feature the same three major stereotypes we encountered in the early movies: the dark lady, the bandido, and the clown. Only the brown avenger has been borrowed from print. Few directors have responded to fiction's recent interest in passive victims or Americanized conformists. The most plausible explanations are that one is too hopeless a case to excite audience interest while the other, since he is little more than a white man in brownface, does not promise audience appeal if given a separate screen identity. Of the four types mentioned above, the dark lady frequently serves as a temporary bedmate for fast-moving outlaws. In *Rancho Notorious*, Arthur Kennedy cavorts with Marlene Dietrich, one of the cinema's least credible examples of the stereotype, who runs a fancy "men's club" on the border and caters to degenerates who pause for relaxation between their brushes with the law. In *Showdown*, train robber Billy Massey (Dean Martin) cuts his lead over a pursuing sheriff by dallying at a shack which contains yet another of those incredibly clean and impeccably coiffed brown women who turn up, husbandless and eager, in the remotest corners of the cinematic Southwest. Remorse of any kind is rare among seducers and deserters of such dark ladies. More common is the callous behavior of California frontiersman Zandy Adams (Gene Hackman) in *Zandy's Bride*, who feels no pangs of conscience when he rejects a Mexican woman in favor of a mail-order bride (Liv Ullman) from Minneapolis whose main qualification is her ability to give him white children.[1]

When the dark lady of the modern movie is assigned a meatier role, it is frequently that of mistress to a white gunman. The gunman's peripheral position as a marked man, an

---

[1] Occasionally the dark lady keeps her man, especially, curiously enough, in the grade B westerns. In *Branded* Alan Ladd stars as a tight-lipped bad-good man named Choya who makes a one-man invasion of Mexico and, undeterred by an entire bandit army, rescues a rancher's lovely daughter (Mona Freeman) from the clutches of a fiendish bandido (Joseph Calleia) and marries her. More or less the same thing happens in *The Burning Hills*, in which Tab Hunter skirmishes with a bandido (Celleia again) and marries a señorita named María (Natalie Wood).

outsider even in the Anglo community, ensures that his affair
will be a fleeting one. It also makes his dallying with dark
ladies somewhat more tolerable to the ticket-buying public.
John Ford's classic film *My Darling Clementine*, based on the
Earp-Clanton feud in Tombstone, Arizona, offers a good example of such a relationship. The strumpet in question, "Chihuahua" (Linda Darnell), is a semiplatonic sex object for Doc
Holliday (Victor Mature), a tubercular and whiskey-wracked
exile from the East who is doomed to a fringe position even in
Tombstone because he is a poet. When the real heroine, Clementine (Cathy Downes), Doc's pale and proper former fiancée
from Boston, arrives in Tombstone to reclaim him, Doc rejects
her for her own good, arguing that he is a man of broken
health and morals. Yet even after Clementine is appropriated
by Wyatt Earp (Henry Fonda), Chihuahua must lose. Believing that Doc has abandoned her, she petulantly beds a teenaged badman, Billy Clanton (John Ireland), and pays fatally
for her promiscuity—the victim of Billy Clanton's jealous bullet
and Doc's bungling surgery.[2]

High Noon, a western best known for its depiction of a
lawman's position as outsider in the western community, is
also memorable for its highly original treatment of a Mexican
woman. Katy Jurado as Helen Ramírez is a creature of courage
and compassion. She repeats Chihuahua's role as rejected para-
mour, but with a measure of dignity and delicacy not usually
characteristic of the Hollywood dark lady. The affluent owner
of a store and saloon, Helen is an unmarried outcast who supports herself in high style while flaunting the mores of the
community. As former mistress to both murderer Frank Miller
and Marshal Will Kane (Gary Cooper), who sent Miller to
prison several years before, she is the character who knows
both hero and villain most intimately. Yet unlike other brown
mistresses of print and film who flit from man to man with few

[2] In this chapter I have used the names of historical characters (such
as Doc Holliday) when that name is common knowledge. On the other hand,
I use the name of the actor playing the character (John Wayne, Clint Eastwood) if his personality or reputation prevails over the character he plays in
a given film.

ethical reservations, Helen Ramírez uses her central position to act as Will Kane's mouthpiece. She is the one person in town who understands why he must face Miller and his henchmen alone and who expresses this understanding in a way impossible for Kane to do. If Kane were still her man, Helen declares, she would get a gun and fight too—a degree of romantic commitment not reached by Kane's Quaker bride Amy until she literally has one foot on board the train that would take her away from her husband. It is Helen Ramírez who points out the film's moral: the respectable citizens who advocate law and order and make bold promises of support in the abstract refuse to back the man they hired to do their unpleasant work for them. Helen epitomizes the viewer's combined distaste for the hypocritical townsfolk and admiration for Kane's lone stand against evil when she tells Amy: "When he dies, this town dies, too."[3]

No other Mexican woman in modern movies holds the key moral position of Helen Ramírez. Her closest competitor may be Claire Quintana (Lena Horne), mistress to aging Marshal Frank Patch (Richard Widmark) in *Death of a Gunfighter*. Like Will Kane in *High Noon*, Frank Patch has brought law, order, and progress to a Kansas town that now sees him as an embarrassing aberration. Unlike Kane, however, Patch is unable to adjust even marginally to changing times. At the turn of the century, while the town's pin-striped businessmen drive one-cylinder automobiles down the paved main street, the shabbily dressed Patch trots his horse down the same thoroughfare. More to the point, while Will Kane rejected his dark mistress to wed a prim and proper blonde, Frank Patch continues to board at a sleazy hotel with an outcast Mexican woman whom he refuses either to reject or to wed. That the affair is the talk of the town bothers him not at all. Indeed, the point

[3] An interesting reversal of the dark lady as fallen woman is the white lady who turns to dark decadence. Adelaide Greevy (Rita Hayworth) of *They Came to Cordura* is a scandal-tarnished harridan who takes up ranching in northern Mexico. Adelaide, correctly accused by the U.S. Army of giving highly personal aid and comfort to the Villistas, is linked in dress, speech, and morals far more closely to the stereotyped dark lady than to the usual Saxon heroine.

of this movie is that the Protestant pillars of the community are bothered less by Patch's old-fashioned approach to law and order than by his keeping a brown mistress. In a final, shocking scene that carries the theme of public ingratitude much farther than *High Noon*, Patch is gunned down by dapper bankers and bespectacled shopkeepers whose peaceful way of life has been made possible by Patch's years of sacrifice. And after a last-minute wedding ceremony, Claire Quintana, like her sisters in sin Chihuahua and Helen Ramírez, is left without a man.

My Darling Clementine, High Noon, and *Death of a Gunfighter* are examples of movies that employ death or desertion to end the unions between American gunmen-heroes and Mexican mistresses. Those films permitting white male-brown female relationships to continue beyond the last reel frequently do so in a conspicuously vague fashion. In *Vera Cruz,* set in Maximilian's Mexico shortly after the American Civil War, hero Ben Trane (Gary Cooper), former slaveowner and Confederate officer, develops an attraction for a Juarista dark lady named Nina (Sarieta Montiel). Yet most of the movie's key sexual situations are assigned to a French countess (Denise Darcel). Nina, moreover, courts Cooper with such aggressiveness and Cooper surrenders with such resignation that the viewer is left doubtful about the nature and durability of the union. A similar ill-defined relationship between an American gunman and a Mexican dark lady appears in *Bandolero!* set in South Texas and northern Mexico in the 1860's. Heroine Maria Stoner (Raquel Welch) is kidnapped during a bank robbery by a band of desperadoes led by Dee Bishop (Dean Martin). When Bishop's gang is in turn attacked by a band of *bandoleros*—a mongrel mixture of Indian and Mexican bandits with a consistent cinematic reputation for unrelieved wickedness— Dee rescues Maria from imminent rape at the hands of the leader but is killed in the process. Shrieking curses, Maria guns down the greaser murderer and rides off instead with the homely but steady Texas lawman (George Kennedy) who has been chasing Bishop. Yet there is little indication that Maria's affection for him is anything but sisterly and no guarantee that it will last beyond the ride back to Texas.[4] Like her literary predecessors in conquest fiction, the dark lady of today's cinema should apparently become involved with a Saxon only if she is prepared to lose him somehow.

Of the three major categories of Mexican males in recent American movies—avengers, bandidos, and clowns—the avengers are few in numbers but strong in character and heroism. The most striking difference between these characters and their novelistic counterparts is that the movie avengers are both manly and moral. Unlike the degenerates of printed fiction who exploit the white race primarily for reasons of personal gain, the cinematic avengers rise in righteous wrath against the Saxon oppressors. Whether or not they survive their tribulations, there is no question in the minds of the script writers or directors that these brown heroes ought to win. They are invariably presented as right, and their Anglo-American oppressors are just as invariably shown as wrong. This sharp role reversal may explain why there are so few Mexican avengers in the modern western. In *The Ox-Bow Incident*, Anthony Quinn plays a character simply called "The Mexican" who is charged, along with two Anglos, with murdering a Nevada cowboy in the 1880's. He is the one member of the trio who tries to escape. Wounded in the leg in the attempt, he extracts the bullet with a borrowed knife, then defiantly hurls the blade at the feet of his captors. Objecting to being hanged in the company of a pleading greenhorn and a cowardly old man, he confesses his sins to the single Mexican member of the lynch mob and dies with dignity.

"The Mexican" threatens, however mildly, to overturn the

[4] Rarely does a "white" woman court or flirt with a brown man. In *The Furies*, Barbara Stanwyck, daughter of a New Mexico cattle baron, does ease her ill-defined sexual frustrations (having to do with a father complex) by clandestine visits to the shack of a Mexican squatter (Gilbert Roland) until he is hanged by her father for horse stealing. Barbara Stanwyck, however, has a hard-earned cinematic reputation as a maverick, and Gilbert Roland (who also played the Cisco Kid) has an equally hard-earned reputation as a "Latin" lover. Moreover, the match does not last.

traditional cinema stereotype of male "greasers" as cowardly and inept. This may help explain why he had so few successors in movies produced during the forties and fifties. What, after all, was a director to do with a Mexican avenger? Should he be pitted against cowardly cowboys? Or if that implied too many contradictions in terms, should the manly Mexican be presented as a caballero aligned with courageous cowboys against bandidos of his own race? Even more perplexing, did casting a Mexican as a true hero make him eligible to court the Saxon heroine as well? Did success on the battlefield automatically open the door to the bedroom? The most usual answer to these upsetting questions was to avoid them entirely. Almost a quarter of a century passed before manly Mexicans who were not caballeros of the Zorro–Cisco Kid variety began to appear on the Mexican screen. When they did, they played unorthodox roles in unorthodox movies. Paul Newman's characterization of a Mexican accused of murder and rape in *The Outrage* is a case in point. A remake of Akira Kurosawa's *Rashomon*, the movie was among the first attempts to transplant a Japanese samurai story to the American Southwest. Here the results are undistinguished. If nothing else, Newman's all but unintelligible "Mexican" accent precludes the possibility of understanding his point of view, because few viewers can fully understand him. Yet while this greasy, hissing Mexican is hanged for allegedly seducing a white woman (Claire Bloom) and murdering her husband (Laurence Harvey), Newman's character is at least a potential brown avenger. He makes no secret of the fact that were he to be freed, he would wreak revenge on his oppressors—an implied threat to Anglo society that was not tolerated even in the early 1960's. His fate sustains the suspicion that the true cultural offender is not the brown avenger, but the bigoted jury which acts as the instrument of an avenging justice which ought itself to be punished.

An alternate depiction of the manly Mexican who, however passively he may behave, nonetheless poses an implied threat to Anglo dominance appears in *Death of a Gunfighter*. Lou Trinidad (John Saxon) is a Mexican sheriff who knows his place and adopts the degree of public servility necessary to retain his job. Summoned by the irate businessmen of Cottonwood Springs to replace the anachronistic Patch, Trinidad publicly tolerates the epithets of "Greaseball" and "Mex" dished out by the businessmen and privately kicks one of the name-callers in the crotch. His position between the two warring factions—the modern-minded businessmen and the oldtimer Patch—is more marked because he is presented as the film's lone man of reason who is able to cut through the weak arguments of both sides. Twice Trinidad tells the bankers and store owners that they want to rid themselves of the aging marshal because "Frank Patch is your conscience, and you fellows are afraid." Twice he tells Patch that his unwillingness to compromise and to accommodate himself to changing times makes him partly responsible for the feud with the townsmen. And when Trinidad learns that the townspeople plan to kill Patch, he urges the marshal to flee. Patch refuses and is murdered. Trinidad, the realist, the survivor in a world whose racism is beyond his power to change, takes his fury out on one of Patch's tormentors and leaves town, still a bitter compromiser who must continue to practice two codes of behavior —public servility and private manliness.[5]

Few roles imitate Lou Trinidad's position in the middle, a brave but cautious loner poised between the Anglo establishment and the mass of passive and repressed Mexicans. Most avenging Mexicans are depicted as superstuds bent on castrating the white man, symbolically or literally, for his racist sins. It is a role made familiar by such black actors as Richard Roundtree and such "black" films as *Superfly*. The Mexican avenger is the heroic man of color battling racist America as

---

[5] Lou Trinidad's role in the film is all the more impressive when compared to the weak-kneed greaser in the novel on which the movie is based, *Death of a Gunfighter*, by Lewis B. Patten. In the novel, Trinidad speaks weakly, sweats profusely, and looks like "a cornered rabbit." When Patch calls him a "damned little greaser rat" and boots him in the rear, Trinidad, afraid to draw, shuffles away, "his head hanging, digging at his eyes with his knuckles." Far from kicking anyone in the crotch and leaving with some measure of dignity, Trinidad joins the townsmen in murdering Patch.

embodied in bad sheriffs, evil gringo gunmen, and greedy cattle barons. Pierre Cordona (Jorge Rivero) in *Rio Lobo* is such a man—a Latin colossus who helps John Wayne bring Arizona landgrabbers to justice with a dazzling combination of skill with a gun and command of Oriental martial arts. Bob Valdez (Burt Lancaster), the Mexican-American deputy sheriff of *Valdez is Coming*, is even more formidable. Introduced as a hat-doffing servant of Anglo law, a man who knows his place, Valdez's similarity to Lou Trinidad quickly vanishes. Declaring a one-man war against a brutal cattle baron named Tanner who rules his domain with cavalier disregard for the law, Valdez raids Tanner's ranch headquarters, kidnaps his Anglo mistress (Susan Clark), and flees into the mountains. Pursued by Tanner and his men, Valdez picks them off at a thousand yards with a buffalo gun, wins the heart of the baron's lady, and emerges with both a moral and physical triumph over his cowardly adversary.

Another saga of brown revenge, *Mr. Majestyk*, carries the heroism of the super-Mex to absurd lengths. Ambitiously advertised as a hymn to the heroic migrant farm workers, the movie is nothing of the sort. The hero, half-Mexican, half-Slavic farmer Vincent Majestyk (Charles Bronson), a decorated veteran of Vietnam, tries to keep the Mafia out of his melon patch by hiring Mexican migrants instead of the American winos who are thrust upon him by eastern labor racketeers. When the Mafia machineguns his stored crop of melons, Majestyk turns on the goons. For sheer incredibility, his deeds of derring-do outstrip anything in the genre. After single-handedly exterminating the entire gang of Italian mobsters responsible for gunning his melons, he drives off into the sunset with Nancy Chávez (Linda Cristal), a Chicana field worker whose jeans have remained spotless after weeks of working crops.

The relatively small number of brown avengers suggests that although they may provide inspiration to critics of assimilation and accommodation, they have not proved very popular among rank-and-file Anglo moviegoers. Their cause may be just. Their methods may be as pure as possible, given the immoral enemy they are facing. They are still doomed to failure or disappointment. Neither their courage nor their short-term victories have won much acceptance in the cinematic social order of Anglo-America. Much more appreciated is the brown clown. Sometimes his role is no different from that of his cinematic ancestor. In John Wayne's *The Train Robbers*, for example, Wayne seeks escape from gringo gunmen. He commandeers a Mexican train, shoves a six-gun in the face of the portly engineer, and yells, "Vámonos!" The engineer, determined to defend job and country, replies, "No! No!" Wayne fires a warning shot; the engineer, jowls aquiver, declares, "Sí! Sí!" and Wayne crashes the train through the pursuing Americans.

But this one-dimensional character has increasingly given way to the Mexican as sympathetic sidekick. He is still a clown, but comedy relief is only one of his functions. The kindly sheepherder in *The Sheepman*, who plays the guitar for Glenn Ford and tells inane jokes, also dies bravely in a one-man fight with the vicious gringo cowboys who raid Ford's sheep. *Rio Bravo* features a Mexican who emerges as hero as well as buffoon. Early in the movie, John Wayne's morose serenity is relieved from time to time by the antics of a comedy couple named Carlos and Consuela Remonte. Passing from one marital crisis to another, they exchange uncomplimentary epithets intended to conceal their great devotion to each other. If Consuela is angry, Carlos sets things right by giving her a fancy red petticoat which he models before Wayne, pirouetting about in a scene that makes even Wayne laugh. "If you wish to know about women," the homely, diminutive Mexican tells the towering symbol of Anglo manhood, "come to me, Carlos Remonte." Yet it is Carlos who teams with Wayne, Walter Brennan, Dean Martin, and Ricky Nelson to best the bad guys late in the film—firing wildly from behind a corner, but making enough noise to simulate a large force of townspeople. Above all, he is *there*. An undersized hotel keeper from whom, according to the conventions of the cinematic western, neither skill nor courage can reasonably be expected nevertheless picks up his Winchester to join with and fight against professional gunmen. It is a pardonable exaggeration to suggest that Carlos Remonte may indeed be the manliest Mexican of them all.

Neither the dark avenger nor the brown buffoon can compete in numbers with one of Hollywood's favorite box office villains, the bandido. He comes in several categories. The first and most obvious is the target, who when he stands against the Saxon hero is killed as peremptorily as any dime-novel greaser. The two Mexicans who question John Wayne's right to claim the entire Rio Grande watershed as his private cattle preserve in *Red River*, for example, are summarily dispatched by Wayne's quick draw. Nor has the target become any handier with his fists over the decades. In dozens of saloon brawls staged in border westerns with such varied themes as *Vera Cruz*, *Rio Lobo*, *Lonely Are the Brave*, and *Cowboy*, one or two Anglo heroes send superior numbers of greaser barflies bleeding into the street.

Since the 1950's, however, two somewhat more sophisticated versions of the Mexican villain have developed: the bad bandido and his not-so-bad counterpart. For a script writer in search of a villain and possessing some imagination, these characters have certain significant advantages over both Anglos and redskins. They can be presented with all the trappings of a culture familiar enough to permit a reasonable degree of identification for an Anglo audience, yet at the same time they can be sufficiently different to inspire the kind of fear that comes in those nightmares where the known distorts into menace. It is, on the other hand, extremely difficult to depict an Indian villain except as a totally alien menace unless the film is given a weighty anthropological dimension—in which case it may well sink under the burden. And Anglo antagonists have been characterized so often in so many ways that originality is becoming increasingly difficult. The bandido, therefore, fills an important niche in the modern western cinema.

This fact is reflected in casting patterns. The all-bad bandido is sometimes played by an Anglo and sometimes by a Latin who has made a respectable career out of playing roles as Indians and bandidos: Rodolfo Acosta, Joseph Calleia, Ted de Corsica, Emilio Fernández, and, much less often, Gilbert Roland and Anthony Quinn. Their roles, however, seldom reflect the quality of the players. The all-bad bandido follows a predictable pattern of villainy examined in a previous chapter. One example should suffice to make the point that these modern figures differ from their celluloid ancestors only in the amount of sex, sadism, and slaughter they can actually practice on the screen. Anthony Quinn as José Esqueda in *Ride Vaquero!* is essentially a repeat of the bandidos of the 1930's and 1940's. The only difference is that he acts and talks in an explicit fashion that would be the envy of his earlier cousins in sin. They were confined to incomplete curses delivered in hissing accents pregnant with promises of off-screen violence and unnamed villainy. Esqueda is a roistering cutthroat and braggart who uses brandy as a gargle, cavorts with "gorls," curses as strongly as mid-century censorship standards will permit, and connives to keep God-fearing gringo settlers out of post–Civil War Texas by killing the men and raping the women. When a wealthy cattleman named King Cameron (Howard Keel) presumes to contest Esqueda's tyranny, Esqueda corners him in a saloon, floors him with a bullet, and systematically maims the cattleman for life in a sadistic shooting that would have remained on the cutting room floor in an earlier era. The close of the movie provides still another contrast with earlier films. In a climactic duel between Esqueda and a gringo gunman named Rio (Robert Taylor), a longstanding argument about which is the faster draw is resolved when they come out even—and very dead. In other words, José Esqueda is presented as genuinely dangerous.

Such a significant departure from the largely incompetent and ineffectual bandidos of the 1920's and 1930's is increasingly common in modern westerns. Nevertheless, the bad bandido usually continues to receive his comeuppance in the last reel. *Joe Kidd*, set in the 1880's, introduces Clint Eastwood in jail for urinating on the courthouse steps of a small New Mexican town. In the opening scene, Eastwood throws a pot of boiling stew in the face of a sneering bandido who shares his cell. Slow to learn, the greaser abuses Eastwood again and receives the pot itself, which dents the pot but leaves the greaser's features unchanged. For the balance of the movie Eastwood wages a one-man war against the white establishment and its brown challengers alike. For our purposes the key sequence occurs when Eastwood pursues the local bandit chief Luis Chama (John Saxon) into the mountains. In front of Chama's entire gang the Anglo gets the drop on the bandido and accuses him of preaching democratic revolution while practicing mere self-interested banditry. Chama cheerfully agrees, going so far as to tell his dark lady mistress, Helen Sánchez, that he enlisted her in the rebel cause "only for cold nights, and when there's nothing else to do." At film's end Eastwood turns Chama over to the Anglo authorities, wishes him luck at the bar of American justice, and rides out of town with Helen, who declares that she has had her fill of bandit revolutionaries.

There is little intellectual profit in lingering on the obvious similarities between the modern bad bandido and his earlier cousins in sin and slaughter. Far more interesting are the handful of half-good bandidos who play morally ambiguous roles that add a pleasant note of uncertainty to heretofore predictable patterns of villainy. It is not difficult to trace the origins of the good-bad bandido to the current crop of Anglo-Saxon good-bad men who are such a feature of mid-century westerns. He is, indeed, frequently played by an American actor in brownface. Jack Palance, John Saxon, and Eli Wallach in particular have spent a respectable part of their careers playing bandidos with a difference.

If his status is derivative, the good-bad bandido is nevertheless rapidly closing the once unbridgeable gap between the heroic Saxon and the wicked greaser. If by time-honored requirements of plot the Saxon usually prevails in the fadeout, it is hard to tell which character actually most deserves his fate. In the course of the action itself, one of two moral turnabouts is liable to take place. Either the formerly good Saxon lowers himself to the half-immoral level of the half-good ban-

214

dido, or the formerly all-bad bandido raises himself to the quasi-moral level of the Saxon good-bad man. Either way, the result is a blurring of the formerly sharp lines of moral demarcation between the two races. One of the best examples of this process occurs in *The Good, the Bad, and the Ugly*, which features Clint Eastwood as an unprincipled fortune hunter who teams with all-bad Anglo Lee Van Cleef and greaser bandido Tuco the Terrible (Eli Wallach) to steal a fortune in gold. Eastwood wins the prize, but by skill at conniving and profound greed rather than superior morality. To determine which of the three former partners will gain all the gold, Eastwood proposes that they stand in a circle, equidistant from each other, and shoot it out. The idea is that each opponent will be able to fire only in one direction at a time, with victory going to the fastest gun. Eastwood, however, has already surreptitiously emptied Tuco's weapon. After disposing of Van Cleef, he gets the drop on Tuco, still futilely snapping his trigger, strings him up for a slow hanging, and rides off with the treasure. Eastwood does courteously turn in the saddle at the last minute and shoot the rope that is strangling Tuco. His overall behavior nevertheless underlines the point that he is no better or worse than his brown rival. And in this way *The Good, the Bad, and the Ugly* is typical of the new amoral western. Quick thinking, quick acting, and technical skills alone determine victory. Moral sense is absent or attenuated in brown and white alike.

In at least a few recent westerns the reverse equation holds true. The Saxon heroes retain their concept of morality, and they are joined by brown men. This uplifting experience, however contrived it may seem, reaches its fullest potential in what might be called the team-samaritan movies widely produced in the 1960's and 1970's. This variant of the traditional western is interesting in itself and, since it plays a crucial part in the Hollywood concept of the Mexican, deserves extended explanation. Most of these team movies feature an international or interracial cast which forms a network of relationships that replaces the lone samaritan heroes of old, who worked at most with one or two partners. Members of the team are portrayed as experienced fighters, erstwhile loners now contributing their skills to a collective. This emphasis on the group is not entirely in keeping with the individualist philosophy of the Lone Ranger or Gary Cooper. The results, however, are impressive. The typical team is formed to foil one of two favorite negative forces in the modern cinema: Nazis if the setting is Europe, or bandidos if the backdrop is Mexico and the border Southwest. Unlike the cinematic Indians, whose villages apparently can always be penetrated by a lone hero, these adversaries offer the kind of complex social and military structure that requires a team to defeat it.

Whether battling Hitler's Germany or Villa's Mexico, the team is composed of men with special gifts contributing to the fulfillment of a specific mission. Depending on plot requirements, it includes a demolitions expert, an edged-weapons specialist, a linguist, a strategist, a mechanic, a gunman at home with revolvers or rifles, howitzers or Gatling guns. The emphasis is on technical skill and professional competence. The degree and quality of individual characterization depend on the size of the company. The team usually numbers four or more. The smaller the membership, the more necessary it becomes for each protagonist to be somewhat complex. The larger the company, the more vaguely the characters are liable to be sketched. What makes the team-samaritan genre informative for our purposes is that most of these movies boast at least one "minority" member. He provides ethnic variation in a genre where characters can be difficult to tell apart. He can also function as a symbol of brotherhood and unity.

The Mexican in war films generally plays a background role. In *Bataan*, Desi Arnaz is cast as Félix Ramírez, a "jitterbug kid" from California who dies of malaria before performing any significantly heroic actions. Similarly, Luis Jiménez of *The Dirty Dozen* has no chance to distinguish himself from the anonymous mass of the "dozen" before his death. *Midway* includes a light-skinned Hispano fighter pilot nicknamed Chili Bean by the rest of his flight. In the context of the U.S. Navy in 1942, neither the character nor the cognomen is inappropriate, and the character is shown as being at least as skillful as his Anglo comrades. He remains, however, as undeveloped as the other Mexican characters in films with a World War II setting. When such films wish to make eloquent moral statements they create Jews, Nisei, or, increasingly, blacks, to make them—still another indication of that localization which is so characteristic of the Mexican in American popular culture.

As might be expected, however, the Mexican comes into his own as a member of the team western. A good illustration of his role can be found in *The Magnificent Seven*. This film, one of the first and best of the team-samaritan movies, deserves special attention both because it offers an unusually well-defined set of characterizations and because it plays upon the eccentric personality of the good-bad bandido far more than do most of its many imitators. The plot focuses on seven gunmen who, in the name of compassion, justice, and twenty dollars, ride south to rescue a Mexican village from a plundering bandido. The team, led by Yul Brynner, includes a half-Irish, half-Mexican gunfighter named Bernardo O'Reilly (Charles Bronson) and a young Mexican dirt farmer attempting to conceal his identity (played by Germany's Horst Buchholz). When the marauding bandit Calvera (Eli Wallach) attempts to replenish his supplies in the usual fashion, he finds a village in rebellion. Although he manages to escape and even to capture the seven temporarily, Calvera makes the fatal mistake of freeing the gringos. His assumption that the hired gunmen will renege on their contract proves unfounded, and he is eventually defeated and killed by the seven in alliance with the villagers.

A man of humor and some pretensions as a homespun philosopher, Calvera is no ordinary bad bandido. He poses as the village's patron saint, even if they worship him at the risk of prompt death for heresy. Although he misjudges the seven's commitment to the villagers, he has his own code of professional ethics, which includes caring for his men and protecting the villagers from other marauders. His death also makes the movie's moral: the human sheep he has sheared for so long are honorable and courageous men when put to the test under anything like fair conditions. The point is made positively by O'Reilly. In the course of the film he becomes the Seven's moral mouthpiece, lecturing the children of the village on the follies of life by the gun and reminding them that their fathers are the salt of the earth.

What might seem mere preaching is elevated to something higher in one of the film's final scenes. Fatally wounded, O'Reilly looks about him at the villagers wielding machetes, axes, and furniture against the bad men of their own race. He gives the village children his last admonition: "See your fathers now!" He then asks, "What's my name?" "Bernardo! Bernardo!" cry the boys. "You're damn right!" answers O'Reilly, and he dies with a grin on his face. The seven were a necessary catalyst, but their example has borne fruit. In future the villagers will be able and willing to protect themselves. And in death, O'Reilly inverts a major traditional fictional stereotype by affirming his Mexican heritage.

For all the paternalism of *The Magnificent Seven*, it is one of a handful of team westerns in which one or more Mexican characters play roles of crucial moral significance. Such movies, however, are exceptions. Far more numerous are the westerns set south of the border during the decade of the Mexican Revolution of 1910–1920. For better or for worse, these are probably the most influential type of Mexican movies produced by Hollywood. As popular as they are pretentious, these works are notably different from their predecessors of the first two decades of the film industry. The revolutionary movies released between 1911 and 1934 rarely took ideological stands on the great struggle to the south, preferring instead to employ those stock themes of Saxon heroism and greaser villainy that had already proved their box-office value north of the border. On the other hand, the revolutionary westerns produced since the 1930's often attempt to combine entertainment with history, political science, and ethics.

Ideologically these movies come down heavily on the side

of the rebels. Yet Hollywood's conception of the conflict that overthrew Porfirio Díaz and ushered in a new era of relatively democratic elections and relatively progressive socioeconomic reforms is grounded in a curious contradiction. While applauding the principles of the revolution, most filmmakers disparage and denigrate the revolutionaries. The result is simultaneous repudiation of the conservative, government-backed military forces and the liberal, right-minded, but unpleasant rebels. Readers familiar with the overall history of Hollywood will not be surprised to find the industry rejecting the *federalistas* as both antidemocratic and uninteresting. Since the rebels are well outside the conservative establishment, however, we might expect them to be viewed both as acceptable alternatives to tyranny and as attractive figures in their own right. Movie addicts accustomed to Hollywood's favorable treatment of Yankee, Irish, French, and German revolutionaries might readily anticipate similar treatment of Mexican rebels. In terms of box-office appeals, one could say the ticket buyer has a right to expect the *federalistas* to be depicted as corrupt, pompous, and ugly and the rebels as correspondingly handsome, humble, and honest. Yet the rebels are almost invariably depicted as just as decadent as the establishment they challenge.

Part of the explanation for the peculiar combination of worthless rebels fighting in a worthwhile cause is that the Mexican unfortunates are forced to compete directly with Anglo soldiers of fortune. These men usually ride south of the border to aid the rebels, then learn that the rebels do not deserve their help and end as independent-minded men giving battle to or rejecting the positions of both the federalists and the rebels. The Anglo viewer can therefore assume a high-minded neutrality. He can watch each side kill the other without becoming involved. If he chooses a moral position, he must base it on immoral alternatives. He has the option of siding with unclean, sadistic, and moronic bandit-rebels who commit countless atrocities or with unclean, sadistic, and wrong-headed government forces who commit equivalent atrocities. In any case, Hollywood presents the revolution that changed the entire course of Latin American history as a contest between perverted opponents who operate in a moral vacuum.

This is not to argue that the historical revolution was free of immoral agents and actions. Needless slaughter, corruption and venality, petty bickering over direction and purpose—all are faithfully rendered on the Hollywood screen. Yet the revolution did also have direction and purpose. It did have some high-minded heroes who, with one or two exceptions, are conspicuously absent from the American screen. The treatment of Pancho Villa clearly illustrates this Hollywood consensus on the subject of the revolution and the revolutionists. The movie that sparked the genre was *Viva Villa!*—an overtly fictionalized account of Villa's life casting him as a cross between Robin Hood and the Marquis de Sade. Throughout the film Villa functions as a variant of the natural man who performs well enough in a state of savagery (the battlefield) but goes to pieces in civilization. After winning a few victories that would have been decisive had he followed them up, he vacations in El Paso, wenching with halfbreed "gorls" and killing a bank cashier who refuses to cash a check after closing hours. Later, as interim president of Mexico, he attempts to solve the state's economic problems by printing bales of paper money that fools no one. Toward the end of the film, on the way to buy some trinkets for his latest "bride," Villa is shot from ambush. Calling in his self-appointed American press agent, he demands that the newspaperman tell him what he ought to say on his deathbed as parting words to posterity. The educated American complies. Villa parrots a noble litany about robbing the rich to give to the poor and dies in self-conscious dignity.[6]

Subsequent Villista movies are even less distinguished. In *Villa!* Rodolfo Hoyos plays Villa as a surly and cruel buffoon who murders rich landowners, keeps the captured loot for himself, and accumulates a retinue of "wives" whom he treats

[6] When the movie premiered in Mexico City, protesters threw firecrackers into the crowded theatre and wounded three women. The Mexican government banned the film for several months until tensions eased. See Allen L. Woll, "Latin Images in American Films," *Journal of Mexican History* 4 (1974): 28–40.

as callously as he does his men. Sam Peckinpah's *Villa Rides* features Yul Brynner as a Villa who spends most of the movie adjusting a lop-sided wig and staring at the audience. His lieutenant Rodolfo Fierro (Charles Bronson) replaces Villa as the quintessential beastly rebel who shoots prisoners while he eats breakfast and who, when a *federalista* takes refuge in a well, tosses a stick of dynamite down the well and walks coldly away without waiting to see the results.

The undisputed master of the bandit-rebel genre, however, is Sergio Leone, godfather of the spaghetti western. In the first Leone feature, *A Fistful of Dollars*, Clint Eastwood "liberates" a Mexican town by helping two rival revolutionary factions, brutes all, destroy one another. In the sequel, *For a Few Dollars More*, he teams with Lee Van Cleef to gun down more or less effortlessly another gang of Mexican revolutionists. But Leone's master characterization of the Mexican revolution is a movie aptly titled, *Duck, You Sucker*, a film that carries all the distinctive Leone trademarks to extreme. It is a pastiche of bad dialogue, gaudy colors, and insulting caricatures. In the opening scene the "hero," a simple-minded Villista played by Rod Steiger, robs a stagecoach by posing as a dim-witted peon who is permitted to ride inside with the well-to-do passengers so they can poke fun at him. Leone uses the episode to poke some fun of his own at a carefully screened cross-section of the Mexican elite. A pallid bishop and a portly banker swill wine, gnaw chicken bones, and drool saliva down their fine clothes while exchanging anecdotes about the bad manners of the boorish lower classes. The bishop observes that "even the peasants—a bit of mustard please—have their rights" but that he must beg to be excused from associating with the swine outside the confession box. The bald and impotent banker raves enviously over the genitalia of the rebels. His wife, an unfulfilled nymphomaniac, sucks a cherry, exchanges hungry glances with Steiger, and eagerly listens to tales about peasant boys who sleep with their sisters and mothers. After robbing the coach, Steiger gratifies the woman in a nearby chicken coop, strips the bishop and the banker of money and clothes, marches them in humiliating nakedness past the female passengers, and sends the entire assemblage of nude *aristoi* careening down the hillside in a buckboard, which overturns at the bottom and dumps them into a patch of cactus.

What makes Leone's treatment of the revolution offensive is that the viewer has no moral guidelines by which to measure and judge the conflict. Both sides are repulsive. From start to finish the Steigeristas behave like normal cinematic Villistas. They are sadistic, filthy, promiscuous, and stupid. When the script calls for an itch, they go into spasms of scratching in private places. Instead of smoking, they chew cigars to shreds and swallow them in single gulps. Instead of planning raids, they rely on spontaneous inspiration. What makes the rapes and burnings, decapitations and detonations irritating is that they are obviously intended for laughs only. As in animated cartoons about the cat and mouse or the coyote and the road-runner, who are repeatedly "killed" only to rise again, we laugh on cue because we realize that the "corpses" will come back to life. Most disturbing of all, Leone offers no good Mexicans of any class, caste, or condition—no Villas or Zapatas, no Carranzas or Maderos—to offer some contrast to depraved autocrats and manic bandidos. The Mexico of *Duck, You Sucker* is an insane asylum inhabited by a race of lunatics. Yet this movie is also the crowning achievement of a genre as popular as it is pernicious. Faced with the challenge of making sense of a sprawling and complex series of events, most filmmakers revert to oversimplification or parody, embroidering the revolution's shortcomings while ignoring its achievements. Serious social commentary, particularly in a non-American setting, is generally considered bad box-office. A decision to address the philosophical issues of the revolution requires some commitment on the part of the filmmaker and some knowledge of Mexican history—attributes seemingly at odds with producing money-making hits.

Despite these handicaps, Hollywood has produced two or three respectable movies about the Mexican Revolution. *The Professionals*, a team western roughly similar in concept to

The Magnificent Seven, certainly makes no pretense to a comprehensive ideological survey of the revolution. Yet in sharp contrast to the novel on which it is based, *The Professionals* does portray the Villistas reasonably sympathetically. It also offers two Mexican characters who actually alter the moral conduct of the members of the team. The plot is unpretentious. Four seasoned adventurers—former Rough Rider Lee Marvin and demolitions expert Burt Lancaster (both disillusioned veterans of the Mexican Revolution) as well as packmaster Robert Ryan and black tracker and archer Woody Strode—are hired by a Texas tycoon to rescue his wife, a Mexican marquesa (Claudia Cardinale), from a Villista abductor named Jesús Raza (Jack Palance). Penetrating Raza's stronghold without serious mishap, the four execute their designated roles on cue. Marvin designs a plan of action. Strode sets off demolition charges with arrows loosed unerringly in total darkness. Ryan holds the horses. Lancaster, tossing the marquesa over a shoulder, lights sticks of dynamite with a cigar and blows a path to freedom. Against such overwhelming odds two hundred Villistas stand little chance. Yet after this predictable start, *The Professionals* veers in an unaccustomed direction. Initially the protagonists are bent on nothing more than collecting the tycoon's reward money for the return of his wife. But as the four flee north toward the border, dragging the reluctant marquesa, who actually loves Raza, Lancaster is forced to shoot a *soldadera* who used to be Lancaster's mistress in the days when he and Marvin also rode with Raza. As he cradles the dying woman in his arms, Lancaster experiences his first serious doubts about the validity of turning against his erstwhile comrades in arms. Raza for his part reverses his printed character and proves several cuts above the stock cinema bandido by pausing between exchanges of shots with Lancaster to comment on the course of all revolutions. He is not particularly profound in his description of rebellions as beginning as virgins ripe with love and ending as worn-out whores rotten with lust, but his sincerity impresses Lancaster sufficiently to persuade his fellow professionals to renounce the Texas tycoon's reward.

223

Together the four return the marquesa to Raza. Despite its streak of sentimentality, and for all Raza's dependence on the good will of the samaritan four to regain the marquesa, *The Professionals* is still one of the few "revolutionary" movies in which the bandit-rebel actually wins the heroine from a Saxon rival, fights courageously, and survives beyond the fadeout. In a real sense Raza is the film's victor.[7]

Despite its modest success as a character sketch of a Villista revolutionary, *The Professionals* makes no attempt to pass judgment on the revolution itself. The outstanding feature of *Viva Zapata!* is that it tries to do justice both to the larger issues of the revolution and to Emiliano Zapata as a person. John Steinbeck's original screenplay, Elia Kazan's masterful direction, and Marlon Brando's brilliant performance as Zapata mark this film as the most accomplished cinematic portrait of a Mexican revolutionary. It does not entirely succeed, but *Viva Zapata!* stands alone in the American cinema, a monument to what Hollywood can accomplish in social biography when the right script writer, the right director, and the right actor come together.[8]

One of the film's unique features is that there are no Anglo

---

[7] *The Professionals* was adapted loosely from Frank O'Rourke's *A Mule for the Marquesa*, discussed in chapter 4.

[8] I wish to thank Elia Kazan for providing me with a list of the sources Steinbeck used in researching his script (Elia Kazan to Arthur Pettit, December 1, 1961.) As part of my own research I used a copy of the original screenplay provided by the stenographic department at 20th Century Fox. Since then the screenplay has been published as *Viva Zapata! The Original Screenplay by John Steinbeck*, ed. Robert E. Morsberger. I am indebted to Professor Morsberger for helping me to obtain the screenplay before it was published and for his excellent essay, "Steinbeck's Zapata: Rebel versus Revolutionary," originally published in *Steinbeck: The Man and His Work*, ed. Richard Astro and Tetsumaro Hayashi, pp. 43–63. Morsberger's essay has decisively influenced my own views on Zapata. In an interview for *Saturday Review* (March, 1952, p. 6) Steinbeck said: "I interviewed every living person I could find in Mexico who had known or fought with Zapata." Actually he missed most of them. In my interviews with more than one hundred Zapatistas in Morelos and neighboring states in December, 1961, April, 1966, and April, 1969, I heard several complaints about the manner in which Steinbeck conducted his research. However, given the restrictions of time and Hollywood's tendency to stay close to urban centers while filming in Mexico, the miracle is that Steinbeck saw as many Zapatistas as he did.

characters in it at all. No fair-haired Saxons ride south of the border to elbow out the Mexican in love and war. Steinbeck and Kazan also pose moral questions that provide keys to the Mexican Revolution and the film's moral dimension. Was Zapata a natural revolutionary who hated the establishment and demanded radical reconstruction of his society? Or was he a reluctant rebel who flirted with the power structure and, once he entered the rebellion, exasperated his more doctrinaire comrades by his ambivalent stands on social and political issues?

Most of the film's conflicts focus on the fact that Zapata was in fact affected by a desire to conform to the ruling order. Its most distinguished achievement is the successful contrasting of Zapata the "common" rebel with the elitist forces of Mexico, represented by his wife and his father-in-law. This is done in scenes which are controversial but essential. They accurately show that Zapata had his elitist side and that he was indeed torn between respectability and rebellion. Throughout the film Zapata fluctuates between behavior tying him to the people he leads and behavior setting him apart from them. He speaks for the *campesinos* in the famous and fictitious audience with dictator Porfirio Díaz that opens the film, but he refuses leadership because he is courting a member of the establishment. He ropes a machine gun spitting death at farmers, but he waits too long to cut a policeman's rope dragging a farmer to death. He cuts down a soldier, but he hires himself to a wealthy planter. He lives in a hut after his marriage to a dowried woman and rejects President Madero's offer of a large ranch, but he dreams of retiring to the life of a substantial farmer. On a more personal level, too, Zapata's behavior fluctuates between polished mannerisms borrowed from the gentry and rustic patterns reflecting his village background. Brando's inspired impersonation, based on carefully studied photographs, constantly reminds the viewer that the historical Zapata was caught in an uncomfortable middle position as a man of the people who is not *quite* of the people but eventually fights for them.

More than any single feature of the film, its portrayal of Zapata's courtship and marriage accurately contrasts his dedication to the revolution with his desire to lift his own status—an "unsavory" side of Zapata that some historians have tried to ignore. For all the cinematic liberties taken with Zapata's relationship with Josefa Espejo and her father, who actually died before Zapata married his daughter, the film accurately reflects what little we know about the private side of Zapata's life. To contrast Zapata's concern for the common folk with his aristocratic leanings, Steinbeck and Kazan introduce three fictitious episodes which challenge the posthumous picture of Zapata as a common peasant. More than any other episodes, these were responsible for the film's banning in Mexico for several years. In the first, Zapata sees Josefa (Jean Peters) coming out of her father's house, follows her to the church, and proposes while Josefa is reciting her rosary. When Josefa predicts that the woman who marries Zapata will find herself "washing clothes in a ditch and patting tortillas like an Indian," Zapata loses his temper—not because Josefa has maligned the Indian, but because she has forgotten that he is descended from a distinguished family, the Salazars, and that "Zapatas were chieftains here when *your* grandfather lived in a cave!" In the second related scene, a rich sugar planter hires Zapata as chief horse buyer in his Mexico City stables. On an inspection tour of the stables, Zapata watches a starving boy devouring grain in the stalls. When the manager whips the boy, Zapata knocks the manager down. Chastised by his aristocratic employer, Zapata does not proclaim revolution. Instead, he accepts a cigar and apologizes to the man he struck.

These two fictitious episodes—Zapata's argument with Josefa over his ancestry offset by his anger over hungry children—effectively highlight his position between the common folk he often champions and the aristocracy he sometimes emulates. They also prepare us for the third scene, which decisively severs Zapata from the establishment. After declaring his intentions to marry Josefa and renounce revolution, Zapata encounters two *rurales* who have captured and trussed up an old farmer, significantly named Innocente, for slipping into a cornfield he once owned. When one of the policemen jerks Innocente off his feet, Zapata, who initially tried to reason with the *rurales*, cuts the rope dragging Innocente to death—too late to save the farmer but in time to bring Zapata into the revolution. Yet even after this incident Zapata tries to find a middle ground between respectability and rebellion. He rides to the Espejo house to ask for Josefa's hand. Mouthing his pre-rehearsed lines with obvious distaste, Zapata vows that he will someday be "a man of substance." Espejo accuses Zapata of precisely the qualities that the movie audience admires about him: "A fighter, a drinker, a brawler; these things you are." He then repeats his daughter's prediction that the woman who marries Zapata will wind up "squatting on the bare earth, patting tortillas like a common Indian." Yanking the merchant to his knees, Zapata tells him to find his daughter "a musty, moth-eaten man like yourself," a mousy man who will make her "queen of the warehouses and mistress of the receipt books!" The point of the retort is that Zapata's contempt for Espejo is based on his questioning Zapata's personal and family credentials. As a *charro*, a man on horseback poor in property but rich in breeding and natural endowments, Zapata considers himself several cuts above the tacky bourgeois dealer in goods—and so do we. Zapata's decisive emotional victory over Espejo provides an effective fictional resolution to a crucial historical question: Would Zapata the dispossessed mestizo, proud of his trace of Spanish blood and his landed past, desert the common people? Would he choose respectability over rebellion? The requirements of film forced Steinbeck and Kazan to answer this complex question in brief and simplistic terms. The fictitious confrontation between Zapata and Don Espejo proved to be a brilliant solution.

Viva Zapata! is equally successful in conveying Zapata's unbending commitment, once made, to the people he led. Obsessed with staying true to the goal of returning the land to the landless, Zapata was the sole leader of the revolution who did not betray a promise. Somehow the film had to telescope his ten-year tenacity into a few scenes of representative action and symbolic dialogue. With characteristic boldness, Steinbeck and

Kazan present two negative fictitious scenes which show that even Zapata was tempted by power. In one, Zapata's old friend Pablo Gómez, accused of deserting the revolution, makes a last speech insinuating that Zapata, too, is becoming corrupted by power and violence:

> PABLO: If we could begin to build—even while the burning goes on. If we could plant while we destroy. . . .
> SOUND *of executions offstage.*
> FERNANDO: interrupts "You deserted our cause!"
> PABLO: Our cause was land—not a thought, but corn-planted earth to feed the families. And Liberty—not a word, but a man sitting safely in front of his house in the evening. And Peace—not a dream, but a time of rest and kindness. The question beats in my head, Emiliano. Can a good thing come from a bad act? Can peace come from so much violence? (*He looks now directly into Emiliano's immobile eyes.*) And can a man whose thoughts are born in anger and hatred, can such a man lead to peace? And govern in peace? I don't know, Emiliano. You must have thought of it. Do you know? Do you know?[9]

Pablo's death at Zapata's hands eventually serves a higher purpose than his life. When Zapata takes temporary occupancy of the presidency, he once more steers close to corruption. And again it is a native of Morelos who recalls him to his sense of duty. A delegation from his home state arrives in the capital to complain that his brother Eufemio has seized hacienda lands for himself. Zapata hedges, using the tactics of evasion he has always despised in his enemies. In a dramatic re-enactment of his own confrontation with Porfirio Díaz at the start of the film, Zapata circles the name of an especially arrogant member of the delegation. Suddenly recalling the incident with Díaz, Zapata gathers his weapons and tells Fernando, his secretary, that there are some things he almost forgot. Now that he has remembered them he is going home:

> FERNANDO: So you're throwing it away. . . . I promise you you

[9] Steinbeck, *Viva Zapata!* pp. 85–87.

won't live long. . . . In the name of all we fought for, don't leave here!

EMILIANO: In the name of all I fought for, I'm going. . . .[10]

Rejecting nationalism for regionalism, law for land, courts for corn, Zapata returns home to prepare the farmers to continue the struggle. He tells them: "This land is yours. But you'll have to protect it. . . . Don't discount your enemies. They'll be back. But if your house is burned, build it again. If your corn is destroyed, replant. If your children die, bear more. . . . You've looked for leaders. For strong men without faults. There aren't any. . . . There's no leader but yourselves . . . a strong people is the only lasting strength."[11] Shortly before he rides to his death, Zapata gathers his followers around him and asks them what will become of them if "something happens" to him. The farmers' replies confirm Zapata in his belief that he has not misjudged them. "We'll get along," says Zapata's protégé, the young man whose belligerent remarks in the presidential palace recalled Zapata to his own commitment. "And someday we'll go down into the valleys again" and take back what is ours. And so they did.[12]

Viva Zapata! is not without its weaknesses. Steinbeck's presentation of Zapata as illiterate is both bad history and at odds with his commendable effort to show that Zapata was somewhat higher in station than many of the people he led. The distortion of chronology can also be disconcerting. The first third of the film takes up a few days, the middle third is spread over a few months, and the last third compresses five years into what seems a day or two. Zapata's long, lean years of bargaining with and fighting against five successive presidents who refused to adopt his plan for immediate and sweeping land reform are passed over lightly. More serious than the time distor-

[10] Ibid., pp. 99–102.
[11] Ibid., pp. 104–105.
[12] Ibid., p. 115. For the legends surrounding Zapata's death, and the manner in which he has been used by opposing factions in the post-revolutionary government, see Arthur G. Pettit, "Emiliano Zapata and the Mexican Agrarian Revolution," (M.A. thesis, San Diego State College, 1962), pp. 141–171; and John Womack, Jr., *Zapata and the Mexican Revolution*, pp. 379–385.

tions, however, is the fact that we do not learn much about the mass of farmers who fought for Zapata: who they were, how they lived, what they thought. Aside from one episode in which government troops machinegun a band of farmers trying to survey lands they claim, and the related scene in which Innocente is killed, we have only Zapata's word that his countrymen were brutally oppressed. Relatively little screen time is devoted to the hit-and-run "little war" that emerged from this oppression and was Zapatismo's military essence—sabotaging railroads, burning cane fields, raiding towns, disbanding whole armies at harvest time so peasant legions could bring in the crops. We learn about this process primarily through the lips of a complaining enemy officer.

There is corresponding neglect of the havoc wreaked by the revolution: no illustration of the fact that Morelos lost one-quarter of its entire population in a single year or that this once-rich state lay in ruins by the close of Zapata's career. Most disturbing of all, there is no consideration of Zapata's major accomplishment, land redistribution. In all the film there is not one scene depicting Zapata returning the land to the landless —not one scene showing the farmers plowing, planting, and harvesting the acres regained at such terrible cost. Such episodes would have been both accurate history and effective cinematic drama. They could readily have been included at the expense of some of the bedroom interaction between Zapata and Josefa. Instead, Steinbeck and Kazan omit to show Zapata putting philosophy into practice—doing what he promised to do and in fact did. The result is a combined philosophical and biographical error: the failure to match Zapata's creed to the man, thus failing to realize the full artistic and historical potential of Zapata himself as a character.[13]

[13] More than military strength, it was Zapata's land allotments that upset the rival factions of the revolution and lent national significance to his rebellion. His "Plan de Ayala," now enshrined in the National Museum in the capital, reads as a catalog of what Steinbeck and Kazan might have attempted in scenes employing an economic focus: severe limits on the size of individual agricultural holdings and direct expropriation of all land beyond those limits, a definition of village land as perpetually inalienable, the prohibition of agricultural syndicates and companies, and the use of municipal rather than state authorities for local jurisdiction.

Yet if we confine ourselves to the film's striking success as social biography, we can indeed learn something about how fiction can be used to present historical complexities. For all its limitations, *Viva Zapata!* is essentially faithful to the two central questions posed by Zapata and his career. The first—Would he forsake the people for personal power and profit?—is brilliantly resolved through his relationship with Josefa and her father. The second and far more disturbing question—Does a man who is in the right always do right?—is posed through Zapata's rejection of his friend Pablo Gómez and his renunciation of presidential power. No other film about the Mexican Revolution has raised these two questions so well. And no other film about the revolution has asked so bluntly whether violence ever leads to peace and whether the rebellion men like Zapata led could bring lasting change. For these achievements Steinbeck and Kazan deserve gratitude. In a medium that does not often distinguish itself in the field of social criticism, it is doubtful that such careful attention to the Mexican Revolution will happen again.

Only one film since *Viva Zapata!* has used the revolution as a backdrop for serious social commentary and moral instruction. Some readers will be offended to see Sam Peckinpah's *The Wild Bunch* discussed in the same context as Steinbeck's and Kazan's classic. As a result of the ongoing disagreement over whether this movie is among the best or the worst westerns ever made and the attention lavished on the film as a violent commentary on superannuated gunmen, the most distinctive feature of *The Wild Bunch* has been ignored. After the opening slaughter in the South Texas town of San Rafael, the entire film is set in Mexico. The rebellion that changed the course of Mexican history also controls the action and dictates the fate of each member of the Wild Bunch. Revolutionary Mexico serves as the vehicle for Peckinpah's moral pronouncements on sex, sadism, violence, law, crimes, and social orders —especially social orders. From the moment the Wild Bunch crosses the Rio Grande, Peckinpah takes special care to set up two rival Mexicos, each symbolized in three ways: by a single person, by a group of persons, and by a place. On the one hand there is the good, natural Mexico, represented by the Villista village, by the Villistas themselves, and especially by Angel (Jaime Sánchez), the Villista member of the Wild Bunch. And then there is evil, unnatural Mexico, represented by the sadistic federal officer Mapache (Emilio Fernández), by the Mapachistas, and by the squalid town of Agua Verde, Mapache's base.

Peckinpah's moral dichotomy is absolute. General Mapache is a nightmarish caricature of the greasy bandit we have met so many times in film and fiction. Strutting the streets of his town in medal-bedecked splendor, he spills tequila down his filthy uniform, squints drunkenly up skirts and down blouses, pocks the plaza with machinegun bullets, and drags the captured Angel through the streets behind his fire-engine-red automobile. Yet Mapache is more than simply a wicked man. He is the offal of the revolution, and he gathers similar scum about him. The two starched advisors of the Imperial German Empire, who hold their Aryan noses against Mapache's filth in an attempt to bring his troops into World War I, are even more sinister and cruel than the Mexicans they manipulate. The mass of Mapachistas, even if innocent before Mapache got hold of them, have been so debased by their leader's wickedness that they, too, are uniformly decadent and immoral. Carefully avoiding contact with the roving Villista enemy, the Mapachistas instead revel in unjustified celebrations: showering themselves with confetti, setting off skyrockets, shampooing each other with tequila, and lapping liquor up a whore's thighs as far as the film's R rating will allow. And like their leader, they are indiscriminately violent. These dregs of the revolution are forever killing one another, getting killed, watching others get killed, or celebrating killing. Therefore, in Peckinpah's way of viewing things, they themselves deserve to die.

The massacre that concludes the film has received an enormous amount of critical attention, ranging from nausea to unqualified praise. Yet most critics, in concentrating on the Wild Bunch's suicidal decision to avenge Mapache's murder of Angel, have neglected the fact that the slaughter also demonstrates Peckinpah's heartfelt conviction that the Mapachista scab on the revolution must be peeled off—violently and at once. It is indeed disturbing that the Bunch, in their zeal to take as many Mapachistas with them as possible, can make no distinction between those deserving death and those less deserving. Old men and innocent men, defenseless women and children alike fall before Anglo lead.

Yet for all the heavy price paid in blood to make a moral point, Peckinpah does make a compelling one. Mapache and his brainwashed followers are not to be taken as archetypal representatives of the Mexican race. There is another Mexico: the good, natural Mexico represented by Angel's native Villista village, by his fellow Villistas, and by Angel himself. Peckinpah makes the point with great care and affection. In contrast to Mapache's lively town perched in the middle of a dun-colored desert, Angel's serene village, cradled in a mountain valley, seems to sprout from Mother Earth herself. Flowers adorn the patios and plaza. Children play at the water's edge. Women pat tortillas and promenade in the plaza, their loosely flowing skirts offering a pleasing contrast to the tight, flashy dresses worn by Mapache's whores. There is no ear-splitting mariachi music, no drunken debauchery. The male villagers sit in the cool mountain sun that holds none of the desert's bite, whiling away the late afternoon hours quietly drinking pulque. These white-clad men of the mountains seem to rise out of the bowels of the earth in manly contrast to the glittering toy-soldier atmosphere of Mapache's filthy troops. They are Peckinpah's pure-minded men of the revolution—the guardian angels of Mexico dedicated to ridding the country of the Mapaches who have raped and gutted their *patria chica* for centuries.

Angel, the young Villista who joins the Wild Bunch to steal money for the rebel cause, is as pure-minded as his name implies. More than any Mexican character in a team western—surely more than his counterparts in *The Magnificent Seven* and *The Professionals*—he serves as the pivotal figure in the moral regeneration of the Saxon "heroes," in this case the errant Wild Bunch. His commitment to "my people, my village, Méjico" separates him from the Bunch, who are committed only to each other until Angel's execution takes them to their own deaths—if not for Angel's values, at least for his spirit. It is Angel who wins our sympathy early in the action by flinging the Bunch's racism in their faces, and it is Angel who shows the Bunch an alternative to Mapachismo by taking them to his native village. It is Angel who gives his fellow Villistas a case of ammunition, throwing Mapache into the fit of rage that leads to the film's violent climax. It is Angel who is the catalyst for both the physical destruction and the moral resurrection of the Wild Bunch. By awakening his fellow outlaws to the moral dimensions of the revolution, Angel serves as the spiritual center, the conscience, the moral burden, and, ultimately, the redeemer of the Bunch.

Together, Angel and the Villistas of his native village put the finishing touches on Peckinpah's carefully constructed double vision of Mexico: Mapache's Mexico and Angel's Mexico, the one of drunkenness, filth, "dirty" sex, and perverted violence, and the other of sobriety, cleanliness, open affections, and "clean" violence. To accuse Peckinpah of separating good Villistas too sharply from bad Mapachistas, good village Mexicans from bad town Mexicans, is to consider only half the point. The entire film is played out against the backdrop of civil war in which some of Mapache's reluctant revolutionaries were recruited from villages similar to Angel's. Yet they have become so corrupted by contact with Mapache that they, like their general, have betrayed the revolution and must pay the price.

In killing off the Mapachistas, Peckinpah argues that he is ridding Mexico of a blot on the revolution. It is what the Mapachistas stood for and what they wrought that was the great tragedy of the Mexican Revolution. What the Villistas stood for and what they tried to accomplish was for Peckinpah the unfulfilled promise of the revolution. His idea is oversimplified, but essentially he is right. His way of showing us he is right is to present two Mexicos and two types of Mexicans in conflict. The difference between the Mapachistas and the Villistas is less a matter of innate racial or personal depravity than of ideological affiliation and environmental circumstance. When in the clutches of a Mapache, Peckinpah's Mexicans are physically degenerate, mentally childish, and morally bankrupt. Freed of the Mapaches, they can be a people of courage, dignity, and compassion.

Peckinpah's vision of the two Mexicos is most graphically presented in the Wild Bunch's exit from Angel's village—an early scene repeated at the end of the movie. As the last shot of orphaned children, crippled men, and widowed women streaming out of Mapache's graveyard village fades off the screen and we prepare to leave the theatre, Peckinpah brings us back to a happier part of the story. Resurrecting the Wild Bunch, he places us in a theatre within a theatre, superimposing in the center of the dark screen a small, home-movie shot of the outlaws riding out of Angel's Elysian village. As the Bunch moves slowly down the flower-strewn lane beneath giant shade trees, their backs dappled by the sunlight filtering through the leaves, the entire village turns out to bid farewell. They doff hats, wave mantillas, toss flowers, shed tears. Depending on personal taste, the sendoff is either unbearably sentimental or profoundly moving. However, there can be no question about where the scene fits in Peckinpah's double vision of Mexico.[14]

Yet if we read *The Wild Bunch* as Peckinpah's personal statement about the revolution, then it is obvious that he is pessimistic about its ultimate outcome—far more so than Steinbeck and Kazan in *Viva Zapata!* For while the earlier film ends with a positive feeling about the Zapatistas inheriting a new

[14] For the fullest criticism of Peckinpah's work in general and *The Wild Bunch* in particular, see Stephen Farber, "Peckinpah's Return," *Film Quarterly* 23 (Fall, 1969): 2–11; Jim Kitses, *Horizons West: Anthony Mann, Budd Boetticher, Sam Peckinpah: Studies in Authorship within the Western*, pp. 139–173; Mark Crispin Miller, "In Defense of Sam Peckinpah," *Film Quarterly* 28 (Spring, 1975): 2–17; and Arthur G. Pettit, "Nightmare and Nostalgia: The Cinema West of Sam Peckinpah," *Western Humanities Review* 29 (Spring, 1975): 105–122.

Mexico, Peckinpah seems to be saying that the dilemma of revolutionary Mexico is that it is already in enemy hands— those of the Mapachistas, who embody all that is evil in the revolution. Despite the slaughter of Mapache and most of his immediate followers, Peckinpah is under no illusions that they will not be replaced and that the evil faction will prevail in the end. He makes his point bluntly in *Bring Me the Head of Alfredo Garcia*. The Anglo "hero," a broken-down piano player named Benny (Warren Oates), wears a motorcycle jacket with "Viva Zapata" stitched on the sleeve and spends most of the movie carrying on a crazy colloquy with a fly-infested head bouncing about on the front seat of his battered red convertible. Although as in *The Wild Bunch* there are bad town Mexicans and good country Mexicans, the viewers do not get to know either side well enough to appreciate Peckinpah's moral distinction. This ambiguity in turn reflects Peckinpah's growing awareness that his two Mexicos are not so far apart as he had hoped. The scenes of the pristine countryside are offset with airplanes, slums, and gangsters. When the good country Mexicans—the modern counterparts of Angel's Villista villagers—try to give battle to the big-city goons, they are gunned down at the edge of the highway that connects their once-isolated village to nearby Mexico City. It is difficult to imagine a sharper contrast between Angel's Elysian Mexico and its modern, nightmarish successor. Peckinpah's good country Mexicans have obviously lost the struggle and the spirit of the revolution to the bad city Mexicans. For him the great tragedy of the Mexican Revolution is not that it happened, but that forces of degeneration eventually successfully appropriated the movement as their own. In doing so they placed a curse upon the revolution and the country.

AFTERWORD   *by Dennis Showalter*

PROFESSOR PETTIT'S ILLNESS progressed too rapidly for him
to prepare even preliminary notes for a conclusion to this vol-
ume. My own contributions to its writing and editing, however,
have led me to some hypotheses which I believe reflect the
general nature of his thinking.

Above all, the stereotypes of the Mexican described here
are enduring. There are few essential differences between the
images of chapter 1 and those of chapter 8. Perhaps the best
illustrations of this point come from two areas not included in
the body of this study—music and television—and from a specific novel, *The Milagro Beanfield War*. One can hear the Castilian heroine apotheosized when Glenn Yarborough sings
"Spanish Is the Loving Tongue." The brown flirt made a fortune for Marty Robbins as "wicked Felina," whose wicked
ways eventually cost the narrator of "El Paso" his life. She
makes a slightly more humorous appearance inviting an inex-
perienced Anglo to "Come a Little Bit Closer," only to abandon him when "bad man José" enters the "little cafe on the
other side of the border." The country hit "Colorado Kool-Aid"
describes the fate of another Anglo who tries to prove his
machismo in a Texas bar by spitting beer into the ear of a
much smaller Mexican. The Mexican promptly whips out a
knife, cuts off his antagonist's ear, and hands it to him with
the polite suggestion that next time he feels so inclined, he

237

can expectorate in his own ear. The song is intended to be humorous. Its tone is sympathetic to the Mexican. Yet it also reinforces the image of the Southwest as an alien country populated by people whose mores differ from those of the rest of the United States—to say nothing of its contribution to the stereotype of the Mexican as being quick to use a knife to avenge insults. The same song with a Georgia setting would almost certainly have culminated in a fistfight, not a knifing. Larry Adams' warnings against the perils of the border are echoed by the lyricist who finds himself "Wasting Away in Margaritaville," nursing a tattoo and a thirst and knowing "it's my own damn fault." And Linda Ronstadt's "Carmelita" alludes to the dark side of barrio culture with its references to "mariachi static" on the radio of a heroin addict bewailing the simultaneous loss of his methadone allowance and Carmelita's welfare check.

Turning to television, we find a similar situation. The Mexican remains localized and stereotyped. During the 1950's the Cisco Kid and Zorro re-established their cinematic images in successful television series. Leo Carrillo moved from greaser gangster to just plain greaser as the Kid's swarthy, perspiring sidekick Pancho, whose heavily accented English conflicted sharply with Duncan Renaldo's slight inflections. A minor character in the long-running series "Rawhide" suffered the indignity of having his name spelled phonetically in the show's credits. "Hey Soos" was presumably regarded as less likely to offend Anglo viewers than "Jesús."

This pattern has not been altered significantly. The best illustration of the argument is not such series as "Chico and the Man" or "CHiPS," whose Chicano protagonists as played by Freddie Prinz or Erik Estrada have used ethnicity as little more than local color for comedy or dramatic situations with general appeal. It is rather the long-running television series "The High Chaparral." The series featured two regular stars, one occasional featured player, and a regular minor character cast as Mexicans. Far from it being regarded as racist, its cancellation brought heated protest from Chicanos. Yet it also managed to incorporate virtually every stereotype discussed in this book. Linda Cristal as Victoria Cannon was, most of the time, the quintessential Castilian heroine, the lady of the ranch, a woman of grace and refinement, a civilizing influence on her craggy husband John (Leif Erickson) and the rest of the rough-hewn Anglo cast. In many episodes she followed the pattern of Helen Ramírez of *High Noon* and acted as a conscience, a voice for moral action even when it seemed less than practical. And every now and then she imitated Lupe Vélez, losing her temper and hurling strings of gibberish epithets at men who came to dinner with dirty hands or who failed to fetch wood and water.

Her brother Manolo (Henry Darrow) was an equally classic example of the Mexican male uplifted by contact with hardworking, straight-talking Americans. His original life-style was that of the indolent, pleasure-seeking *rico*. Only when he came north with his sister did he develop the qualities of manliness and independence which made him one of the most consistently attractive characters in the series. To be sure, he could still neglect work to pursue a woman or a drink. He could find a dozen ways of getting into trouble. But these characteristics were required of him not as a Mexican but as a second lead. He shared them, moreover, with John Cannon's scapegoat brother Buck (Cameron Mitchell). Don Sebastián Montoya, father of the central Mexican characters, appeared too infrequently to have a firmly fixed personality. He nevertheless usually showed characteristics of deceit and dishonesty, sometimes presented seriously and at other times played for laughs. His life-style was that of the great-house grandee, the man of inherited wealth and privilege. And his consistent contempt for his self-made son-in-law was also a recognizable heritage of conquest fiction. Interestingly, the least stereotyped Mexican character in the series was also the least important. Pedro was a simple ranch hand, a Mexican, not a greaser, set apart from his Anglo comrades only by legitimate distinctions of dress and accent and accepted by them on terms of equality so complete as arguably to do violence to the facts of bunkhouse life in the 1880's.

An even better single example of the strength of the Mexi-

can stereotypes can be drawn from the "Sesame Street" sequence mentioned in the introduction. In one of the episodes,
Luis and María, who is cast as a Puerto Rican, illustrate the
number eight by eating red chili peppers. When Muppet Oscar
the Grouch insists on sharing despite their warnings, they feed
him peppers, counting as they go. With each one Oscar's eyes
roll and bulge, yet he insists on continuing. When he finishes
his eighth pepper, he disappears into his trash can. Seconds
later a loud scream and a puff of steam lift the lid from the
can. Luis and María, who have both consumed the same number of chili peppers with no visible effects, promptly burst into
laughter at Oscar's deserved discomfiture. The skit is innocuous
enough, the viewer might think; and certainly it is anything
but racist in intent. Indeed, the situation reflects a fact: the
ability to eat raw red chilis is acquired through practice. But
the vignette also illustrates the basic assumption underlying
Anglo-Mexican relations. There *is* a difference between the two
peoples—the kind of difference that enables Luis to devour
food that is too hot for even a Grouch to stomach.

First impressions of John Nichols' *The Milagro Beanfield
War* suggest that at least this novel offers an exception to the
thesis that Mexican stereotypes in English-language popular
culture remain relatively unchanged. Nichols' work incorporates quite likely the most sophisticated treatment of Mexican
Americans by a modern Anglo writer. To some extent his success reflects his choice of theme. The "war" of the title, inaugurated by the illegal irrigation of a long-neglected bean field,
is actually part of an enduring conflict pitting the little men
of a valley in northern New Mexico, most of whom happen to
be Chicanos, against the establishment, downstate ranchers
and land developers, the state police, and the U.S. Forest Service, most of whom happen to be Anglo. This situation encourages the substitution of economics for ethnicity as the source
of the novel's dramatic tension. It encourages regarding the
struggle in terms of locals versus outsiders, as opposed to
brown versus white—an interpretation reflecting Nichols' mastery of the Fleming Effect. His Milagro Valley is a plausible

literary creation, whatever its relationship to the historic and sociological structure of the region. The credibility of the setting is enhanced rather than challenged by the novel's use of humor. Much of the comedy in *The Milagro Beanfield War* is based on yarn-spinning—embroidering a true, or at least believable, story that has been frequently told. It is a technique familiar to the raconteur and his audience in any milieu, whether faculty club, officers' club, or small-town cafe.

Nichols also challenges stereotyping by his characterizations. The novel focuses on two men who also happen to be of Mexican descent. Joe Mondragón, owner and irrigator of the bean field, is a feisty individualist, a regular resident of the county jail, a man who can use pilfered parts to repair any kind of machine, a beer-drinker, a bronc-rider, and a lover. Bernabé Montoya, introduced as a bumbling sheriff, develops into the novel's voice of reason—the common-sense kind of reason required for survival in a harsh environment. Neither characterization is on a par with Hamlet or Augie March. Nevertheless, Mondragón and Montoya are usually allowed to function as personalities instead of embodied ethnic symbols. Nor does Nichols' humor depend on ethnicity. His Mexicans are not involved in funny situations because they are Mexican. If a VISTA volunteer constantly finds himself at odds with his new environment, it is not because he is a New York Jew. It is rather because he has not acculturated to a world that demands a set of coping mechanisms not part of his previous experience. Nichols also allows some of his Anglo characters to function as antagonists with a comprehensible and defensible perspective. If this perspective is not presented in a way likely to prove attractive to the reader, neither are its advocates one-dimensional melodramatic villains. The valley's land baron is a businessman essentially more concerned with avoiding expensive public trouble than with teaching the greasers a lesson. His wife is a gentle alcoholic. One of his foremen, Horsethief Shorty Wilson, is a native of New Jersey who has spent forty years successfully transforming himself into a cowboy. And from the governor's mansion downward almost every one is frightened of what *might* happen should Mondragón simply be brought to trial for violating the state water laws. It is a far cry from the Saxon arrogance of nineteenth-century conquest fiction.

This fear generates a decision to do nothing drastic. Instead, the establishment decides to outwait the situation, applying legal and extralegal pressure with the community to convince Mondragón to abandon his project while simultaneously seeking a reason unrelated to his bean field to jail him. As days pass and rumors fly, the valley polarizes. Men buy guns; petitions circulate; tensions heighten. Confrontations occur between Forest Service officers and men liberating an impounded cow, between enraged locals and a heroin addict serving the police by throwing rocks at children, between members of rival factions using the same public toilet, between patrons of the same small bar. While these clashes frequently embody a comic twist or a humorous resolution, the reader is never allowed to forget that the guns are loaded. Any blood spilled will be real.

As the pressure builds, it seems to force more and more of the old fictional stereotypes into the open. Charley Bloom is as guilt-ridden as any suffering samaritan featured above in chapter 7. An expatriate lawyer seeking the simple life, he is married to a Chicana who initially longs for the mainstream but ends by accepting her own roots. Ruby Archuleta begins the novel as a liberated mechanic and plumber. She ends it as a reincarnation of the Amazon bandida who with her son and her silent brown-avenger lover outstalk and outshoot the novel's Anglo superman, a state police agent who has been established to the point of satire as never making a mistake of any kind. The spirit of Pancho Villa is embodied in the old men whose years have not diminished their willingness to use the rifles they carry. Even Mondragón unburdens himself of his father's life story: a poor Hispano broken by Anglo sheep owners and lawyers, dying in a Colorado potato field. The novel's climax is a triumph of Chicanismo. Joe and his allies outface the state police, then stage a raucous celebration rivaling that of *Tortilla Flat*'s final pages. Ruby makes plans for a symbolic communal harvesting of Joe's beans, then makes gentle open-air love to her brown avenger. Bernabé successfully frustrates a drunken Anglo reacting to defeat with threats of mass murder. The next day may bring aching heads and second thoughts. *The Milagro Beanfield War* nevertheless ends in a victory, however temporary, for the righteous. It also ends in a victory, however partial, for ethnic stereotyping.

This is not to say that Nichols surrenders unconditionally. A strong case can be made that if some of his characters act more and more like Mexicans are supposed to act in English-language popular fiction, this is necessary for the novel's development. The conflict which is its central theme involves polarization. This polarization in turn, given Nichols' setting, tends eventually to involve white versus brown dichotomies. It seems reasonable nevertheless to conclude that if a work of the caliber of *The Milagro Beanfield War* employs and manipulates stereotypes to the extent it does, these stereotypes are likely to endure in the foreseeable future. In fact, the very credibility of the setting and characters of the story arguably legitimizes the stereotypes Nichols does incorporate far more than would a pulp western of the Fargo genre or similar fiction that is virtually impossible to take seriously in any sense.

It is easier to demonstrate the continued existence of those stereotypes than to explain that existence. In an era combining Chicano militancy and Anglo sensitivity, the Frito Bandido was removed from television commercials. Jack Albertson's ethnic insults were toned down sharply after the first few episodes of "Chico and the Man." And that is all. One possible explanation for this essentially cosmetic approach is sociological. It lies in the continued influence of Mexican popular culture in the Chicano community. Unlike the black or the Indian, who was constantly confronted with his image as Stepin Fetchit or murdering savage in works designed for a white audience, and who until recently had no significant alternative to these images, the Mexican American has had constant access to films and records, books, magazines, and radio programs from below the border. Without denying the increasing impact of English-language television since the mid-1950's, it is possible to argue that the Mexican did not have to expose himself as heavily as did blacks or Indians to his negative image in Anglo popular culture unless he chose to do so. This pattern was reinforced by the strong geographic concentration of Spanish-speaking consumers, making it profitable to import cultural material from Mexico to the southwestern United States or to imitate such material. The Anglo images could therefore be largely ignored or be contrasted with favorable images brought from below the border or generated within the Mexican American community itself.[1]

This relative absence of pressure for change is reinforced by another factor. In *The Structure of Scientific Revolutions*, Thomas Kuhn argues that academic interpretations change when social environments and new evidence combine to make existing theories intolerable or unfashionable. Jack Kirby's *Media-Made Dixie* suggests that familiarity also contributes to change: repetition and imitation breed boredom; new approaches are developed to stimulate a jaded market.[2] Neither of these points apply significantly to the place of the Mexican in the western. If conquest fiction appears to have declined substantially in American popular culture, the traditional western remains alive and well in film and print. A temporary eclipse on television appears in the process of ending. As these lines are written in the spring of 1979, the success of such mini-series as "The MacCahans" suggests that westerns may soon again reclaim a place in prime time. Given the strength—one might almost say the necessity—of the roles assigned to Mexicans in westerns set in the Southwest, their stereotyped images do not seem likely to disappear. Black and Native American heroes seem to offer quite enough novelty in a genre that re-

[1] See the brief discussions in Américo Paredes, *A Texas-Mexican Cancionero: Folksongs of the Lower Border*, pp. 15 ff.; and Cecil Robinson, *Mexico and the Hispanic Southwest in American Literature*, pp. 308 ff.

[2] Thomas Kuhn, *The Structure of Scientific Revolutions* (Chicago: University of Chicago Press, 1970); Jack Kirby, *Media-Made Dixie* (Baton Rouge: Louisiana State University Press, 1978), p. xvii.

mains as popular as it is stylized. And even here there are substantial differences between the image of the Indian, for example, in major westerns and the pulps sold in drugstores and supermarkets.

By whatever name he is called—Mexican, Chicano, or greaser—the Mexican American appears stuck. Even Luis Valdéz, founder of El Teatro Campesino, appears to have conceded the point. His "Zoot Suit" may be, as *Newsweek* describes it, an attempt to "move into the theatrical mainstream [and] bridge the gap between his brown people and the white majority." But Valdéz does these things by skillful use of many of the stereotypes discussed throughout this book: Anglo samaritans, brown avengers, white and off-white heroines. As in *The Milagro Beanfield War*, the play's central character, Henry Reyna, is a personality instead of an embodied ideological statement. Particularly for Anglo reviewers and audiences, however, Henry tends to be overshadowed by his supporting environment.[3] In short, the Mexican American's place in American popular culture appears assured, for at least the foreseeable future. It is hardly a flattering place. The best that is likely to happen is that the images will be softened or presented in a more sophisticated, less offensive manner. As a conclusion to a work of over two hundred pages, this may seem anticlimactic. Yet if this book has established anything, it is the strength of Mexican stereotypes in Anglo-American popular culture and the absence of significant external and internal challenges to these stereotypes. Like the dog in "Silver Blaze" who did nothing in the nighttime, those are the curious incidents.

[3] "Heartbeats from the Barrio," *Newsweek*, April 9, 1979. See also the much harsher "Threads Bare," *Time*, April 9, 1979. These reviews were cited because they were from the two major news/opinion magazines in the United States.

SELECT BIBLIOGRAPHY

I. RACE RELATIONS—GENERAL

Daniels, Roger, and Harry H. L. Kitano. *American Racism: Exploration of the Nature of Prejudice.* Englewood Cliffs, N.J.: Prentice-Hall, 1970.

Degler, Carl. *Neither Black nor White: Slavery and Race Relations in Brazil and the United States.* New York: Macmillan, 1971.

Frederickson, George M. *The Black Image in the White Mind: The Debate on Afro-American Character and Destiny, 1817–1914.* New York: Harper, 1971.

Friedman, Lawrence J. *The White Savage: Racial Fantasies in the Postbellum South.* Englewood Cliffs, N.J.: Prentice-Hall, 1970.

Jordan, Winthrop D. *White over Black: American Attitudes toward the Negro, 1550–1812.* Chapel Hill: University of North Carolina Press, 1968.

Kovel, Joel. *White Racism: A Psycho-History.* New York: Random House, 1970.

McKitrick, Eric L., ed. *Slavery Defended: The Views of the Old South.* Englewood Cliffs, N.J.: Prentice-Hall, 1963.

Morner, Magnus. *Race Mixture in the History of Latin America.* Boston: Little, Brown, 1967.

———, ed. *Race and Class in Latin America.* New York: Columbia University Press, 1970.

Myers, Gustavus. *History of Bigotry in the United States.* New York: Random House, 1943.

Oñís, José de. *The United States as Seen by Spanish American Writers, 1776–1890.* New York: Hispanic Institute in the United States, 1952.

246

Pearce, Roy Harvey. *The Savages of America: A Study of the Indian and the Idea of Civilization.* Baltimore: Johns Hopkins University Press, 1965.

Stanton, William. *The Leopard's Spots: Scientific Attitudes toward Race in America, 1815–1859.* Chicago: University of Chicago Press, 1970.

Thomas, John L., ed. *Slavery Attacked: The Abolitionist Crusade.* Englewood Cliffs, N.J.: Prentice-Hall, 1965.

II. POPULAR CULTURE/LITERARY CRITICISM

Admari, Ralph. "The House that Beadle Built, 1859–1869." *American Book Collector* 4 (November, 1933): 223–225.

Alexander, Stanley. "The Conflict of Form in *Tortilla Flat.*" *American Literature* 40 (March, 1968): 58–66.

Amis, Kingsley. *The James Bond Dossier.* London: Pan Books, 1965.

Astro, Richard, and Tetsumaro Hayashi, eds. *Steinbeck: The Man and His Work.* Corvallis: Oregon State University Press, 1971.

Balshofer, Fred, and Arthur C. Miller. *One Reel a Week.* Berkeley: University of California Press, 1967.

Bishop, W. H. "Story-Paper Literature." *Atlantic* 44 (September, 1879): 387.

Cawelti, John G. "The Concept of Formula in the Study of Popular Culture." *Journal of Popular Culture* 3 (1969): 381–390.

———. "Myth, Symbol, and Formula." *Journal of Popular Culture* 8 (1975): 1–8.

———. *The Six-Gun Mystique.* Bowling Green, Ohio: Bowling Green Popular Press, 1971.

Etulain, Richard W. "Recent Views of the American Literary West." *Journal of Popular Culture* 3 (1969): 144–153.

Farber, Stephen. "Peckinpah's Return." *Film Quarterly* 23 (Fall, 1969): 2–11.

Fontenrose, Joseph. *John Steinbeck: An Introduction and Interpretation.* New York: Barnes and Noble, 1963.

French, Philip. *Westerns.* New York: Viking Press, 1974.

French, Warren. "The Cowboy in the Dime Novel." *Texas Studies in English* 30 (1951): 219–234.

Gans, Herbert J. *Popular Culture and High Culture: An Analysis and Evaluation of Taste.* New York: Basic Books, 1974.

Gray, James. *John Steinbeck.* Pamphlets on American Writers, no. 94. Minneapolis: University of Minnesota Press, 1971.

Gruber, Frank. "The Basic Western Novel Plots." *Writer's Year Book,* 1955, pp. 49–53.

Hampton, Benjamin. *History of the American Film Industry from Its Beginnings to 1931.* New York: Dover Books, Covici, Freide, 1931.

Harvey, Charles M. "The Dime Novel in American Life." *Atlantic Monthly* 100 (July, 1907): 44.

Havig, Alan R. "American Historians and the Study of Popular Culture." *Journal of Popular Culture* 11 (1977).

Jacobs, Lewis. *The Rise of the American Film: A Critical History.* New York: Harcourt, Brace, 1939.

Jenks, George C. "Dime Novel Makers," *Bookman* 22 (October, 1904): 112.

Jennings, Francis. *The Invasion of America: Indians, Colonialism, and the Art of Conquest.* Chapel Hill: University of North Carolina Press, 1975.

Johannsen, Albert. *The House of Beadle and Adams and Its Dime and Nickel Novels: The Story of a Vanished Literature.* 2 vols. Norman: University of Oklahoma Press, 1950.

Kazin, Alfred. *On Native Grounds: An Interpretation of Modern American Prose Literature.* New York: Doubleday, 1956.

Kinney, Arthur F. "The Arthurian Cycle in *Tortilla Flat.*" *Modern Fiction Studies* 60 (Spring, 1965): 11–20

Kitses, Jim. *Horizons West: Anthony Mann, Budd Boetticher, Sam Peckinpah: Studies in Authorship within the Western.* Bloomington: Indiana University Press, 1969.

Lamb, Blaine P. "The Convenient Villain: The Early Cinema Views the Mexican-American." *Journal of the West* 14 (October, 1975): 75–81.

Lawrence, D. H. *Studies in Classic American Literature.* New York: Doubleday, 1923.

Levant, Howard. "*Tortilla Flat*: The Shape of John Steinbeck's Career." *PMLA* 85 (October, 1970): 1087–1095.

Lewis, R. W. B. "John Steinbeck: The Fitful Daemon." In *The Young Rebel in American Literature.* Ed. Carl Bode. London: William Heinemann Ltd., 1959.

Lohof, Bruce A. "Popular Culture: The *Journal* and the State of the Study." *Journal of Popular Culture* 6 (1972): 453–462.

Macdonald, Dwight. "A Theory of Mass Culture." In *Mass Culture: The Popular Arts in America.* Ed. Bernard Rosenberg and David M. White. Glencoe, Ill.: Free Press, 1957.

Madden, David. "The Necessity for an Aesthetics of Popular Culture." *Journal of Popular Culture* 7 (1973): 1–13.

Marx, Leo. *The Machine in the Garden: Technology and the Pastoral Ideal in America.* New York: Oxford University Press, 1964.

Mast, Gerald. *A Short History of the Movies.* New York: Pegasus Books, Bobbs-Merrill, 1971.

Miller, Mark Crispin. "In Defense of Sam Peckinpah." *Film Quarterly* 28 (Spring, 1975): 2–17.

Moore, Harry Thornton. *The Novels of John Steinbeck: A First Critical Study.* Chicago: Normandie House, 1939.

Morsberger, Robert E., ed. *Viva Zapata! The Original Screenplay by John Steinbeck.* New York: Viking, 1975.

Munden, Kenneth W., ed. *The American Film Institute Catalog of Motion Pictures Produced in the United States: Feature Films, 1921–1930.* New York: R. R. Bowker Company, 1971.

Niver, Kemp R., ed. *Motion Pictures from the Library of Congress Paper Print Collection, 1894–1912.* Berkeley: University of California Press, 1967.

North, Joseph H. *The Early Development of the Motion Picture, 1887–1909.* New York: Arno Press, 1973.

Nye, Russel B. *The Unembarrassed Muse: The Popular Arts in America.* New York: Dial Press, 1973.

Paredes, Américo. *A Texas-Mexican Cancionero: Folksongs of the Lower Border.* Urbana: University of Illinois Press. 1976.

————. *With His Pistol in His Hand.* Austin, University of Texas Press, 1958.

Pearson, Edmund. *Dime Novels; or, Following an Old Trail in Popular Literature.* Boston: Little, Brown, 1929.

Pettit, Arthur G. "Nightmare and Nostalgia: The Cinema West of Sam Peckinpah." *Western Humanities Review* 29 (Spring, 1975): 105–122.

Pilkington, William T. *Harvey Fergusson.* New York: Twayne, 1975.

————. "Introduction: A Fistful of Westerns." In *Western Movies.* Ed. William T. Pilkington and Don Graham. Albuquerque: University of New Mexico Press, 1979.

Ramsaye, Terry. *A Million and One Nights: A History of the Mo-*

tion Picture. New York: Simon and Schuster, 1926.

Robinson, Cecil. *Mexico and the Hispanic Southwest in American Literature.* Tucson: University of Arizona Press, 1978.

Robinson, Henry Norton. "Mr. Beadle's Books." *Bookman* 60 (March, 1929): 22.

Roeder, George H., Jr. "Mexicans in the Movies: The Image of Mexicans in American Films, 1894–1947." Unpublished manuscript, University of Wisconsin, 1971.

Richards, Edmund D. "The Challenge of John Steinbeck." *North American Review* 243 (Summer, 1937): 355–361.

Singleton, Gregory H. "Popular Culture or the Culture of the Populace?" *Journal of Popular Culture* 11 (1977): 254–266.

Slide, Anthony. *Early American Cinema.* New York: A. S. Barnes, 1970.

Slotkin, Richard. *Regeneration Through Violence: The Mythology of the American Frontier, 1600–1860.* Middletown, Conn.: Wesleyan University Press, 1973.

Smith, Henry Nash. "Can 'American Studies' Develop a Method?" *American Quarterly* 9 (1957): 197–208.

————. *Virgin Land: The American West as Symbol and Myth.* Cambridge: Harvard University Press, 1971.

Sonnichsen, C. L. *From Hopalong to Hud: Thoughts on Western Fiction.* College Station: Texas A&M University Press, 1978.

Woll, Allen L. "Hollywood's Good Neighbor Policy: The Latin Image in American Film, 1939–1946." *Journal of Popular Film* 3 (Fall, 1974): 278–293.

————. "Latin Images in American Films." *Journal of Mexican History* 4 (1974): 28–40.

Wright, Will. *Six Guns and Society.* Berkeley: University of California Press, 1975.

III. The West as History

Audubon, John W. *Audubon's Western Journals, 1849–1850: Being the MS Record of a Trip from New York to Texas and an Overland Journey Through Mexico and Arizona to the Gold-Fields of California.* Cleveland: A. H. Clark, 1906.

Bancroft, Hubert Howe. *California Pastoral, 1769–1848.* San Francisco: The History Company, 1889.

————. *History of Arizona and New Mexico, 1530–1888.* San Francisco: The History Company, 1889.

Bandelier, Adolph A. *A History of the Southwest*. Vol. I. Ed. Ernest J. Burrus, S.J. St. Louis: Jesuit Historical Institute, 1969.

Bannon, John Francis. *The Spanish Borderlands Frontier, 1513–1821*. New York: Rinehart, 1970.

Barker, Eugene C. *Mexico and Texas, 1821–1835*. Dallas: F. L. Turner Co., 1928.

Barr, Alwyn. *Reconstruction to Reform: Texas Politics, 1876–1906*. Austin: University of Texas Press, 1971.

Bartlett, John Russell. *Personal Narrative of Explorations and Incidents in Texas, New Mexico, California, Sonora, and Chihuahua*. 2 vols. New York: Appleton, 1854.

Bean, Amelia. *Time for Outrage*. New York: Doubleday, 1967.

Beegle, J. Allan, Harold F. Goldsmith, and Charles P. Loomis, "Demographic Characteristics of the United States–Mexican Border." *Rural Sociology* 25 (March, 1960).

Bolton, Herbert J. *The Spanish Borderlands*. New Haven: Yale University Press, 1921.

Brack, Gene M. "Mexican Opinion, American Racism, and the War of 1846." *Western Historical Quarterly* 1 (April, 1970): 161–174.

Brayer, Herbert O. *William Blackmore: The Spanish-Mexican Land Grants of New Mexico and Colorado, 1863–1878*. 2 vols. Denver: Bradford-Robinson, 1949.

Brewerton, George D. *Overland with Kit Carson*. New York: Coward-McCann, 1930.

Browne, J. Ross. *Adventures in the Apache Country: A Tour Through Arizona and Sonora. . . .* New York: Harper, 1869.

————. *Crusoe's Island . . . with Sketches of Adventure in California and Washoe*. New York: Harper, 1864.

Burns, Walter Noble. *The Saga of Billy the Kid*. Garden City, N.Y.: Doubleday, 1926.

Chapman, Charles E. *A History of California: The Spanish Period*. New York: Macmillan, 1921.

Chidsey, Donald Barr. *The War with Mexico*. New York: Crown, 1968.

Cleland, Robert Glass. *This Reckless Breed of Men: The Trappers and Fur Traders of the Southwest*. New York: Knopf, 1950.

Connelly, William Elsey, *Doniphan's Expedition and the Conquest of New Mexico and California*. Ed. John Taylor Hughes. Topeka, Kans.: privately published, 1907.

Connor, Seymour. "Attitudes and Opinions about the Mexican War, 1846–1970." *Journal of the West* 11 (April, 1972): 361–366.

————, and Jimmy M. Skaggs. *Broadcloth and Britches: The Santa Fe Trade*. College Station: Texas A&M University Press, 1977.

Cooke, Philip St. George. *The Conquest of New Mexico and California in 1846–1848*. Chicago: Rio Grande Press, 1964.

Corle, Edwin. *The Royal Highway (El Camino Real)*. Indianapolis: Bobbs-Merrill, 1949.

Del Río, Angel. *The Clash and Attraction of Two Cultures: The Hispanic and Anglo-Saxon Worlds in America*. Tr. and ed. James F. Shearer. Baton Rouge: Louisiana State University Press, 1965.

Denis, Alberta Johnson. *Spanish Alta California*. New York: Macmillan, 1927.

DeVoto, Bernard. *The Year of Decision: 1846*. Boston: Houghton Mifflin, 1942.

Dufour, Charles. *The Mexican War: A Compact History, 1846–1848*. New York: Hawthorn Books, 1868.

Evans, George W. B. *Mexican Gold Trail: The Journey of a 49er*. Ed. Glenn S. Dumke. San Marino, Cal.: Huntington Library, 1945.

Fehrenbacher, Don E. *The Era of Expansion, 1800–1848*. New York: John Wiley and Sons, 1969.

Fergusson, Harvey. "Billy the Kid," *American Mercury* 5 (June, 1925): 224.

————. *Rio Grande*. New York. Knopf, 1933.

Ferris, Robert G., ed. *The American West: An Appraisal*. Santa Fe: Museum of New Mexico, 1963.

Flint, Timothy, ed. *The Personal Narrative of James O. Pattie of Kentucky*. Chicago: Lakeside Press, 1930.

Ford, Tirey Lafayette. *Dawn and the Dons: The Romance of Monterey*. San Francisco: A. M. Robertson, 1926.

Fulton, Maurice. *History of the Lincoln County War*. Ed. Robert N. Mullin. Tucson: University of Arizona Press, 1968.

Garrard, L. H. *Wah-To-Yah and the Taos Trail*. New York: A. S. Barnes, 1850.

Goetzmann, William H. *When the Eagle Screamed: The Romantic Horizon in American Diplomacy, 1800–1860*. New York: John Wiley and Sons, 1969.

Gregg, Josiah. *Commerce of the Prairies; or, The Journal of a Santa Fe Trader.* 2 vols. Philadelphia: J. W. Moore, 1851.

Hanke, Lewis. *The Spanish Struggle for Justice in the Conquest of America.* Boston: Little, Brown, 1965.

Harstad, Peter, and Richard W. Resh. "The Causes of the Mexican War: A Note on Changing Interpretations." *Arizona and the West* 6 (Winter, 1964): 289–302.

Horgan, Paul. *Great River: The Rio Grande in North American History.* 2 vols. New York: Rinehart, 1954.

Hutchinson, Cecil Alan. *Frontier Settlements in Mexican California: The Hijar-Padres Colony and Its Origins, 1769–1835.* New Haven: Yale University Press, 1969.

Jackson, Joseph Henry. *Bad Company: The Story of California's Legendary and Actual Stage-robbers, Bandits, Highwaymen and Outlaws from the Fifties to Eighties.* New York: Harcourt, Brace, 1949.

Keleher, William. *Violence in Lincoln County.* Albuquerque: University of New Mexico Press, 1957.

Kendall, George Wilkins. *Narrative of the Texan Santa Fe Expedition.* New York: Harper, 1844.

Kenny, William Robert. "Mexican-American Conflict on the Mining Frontier, 1848–1852." *Journal of the West* 6 (October, 1967).

Lacy, James M. "New Mexican Women in Early American Writings." *New Mexico Historical Review* 34 (January, 1959).

Lavendar, David. *Climax at Buena Vista: The American Campaigns in Northeastern Mexico, 1846–47.* Philadelphia: J. B. Lippincott, 1966.

Lowrie, Samuel H. *Culture and Conflict in Texas.* New York: Columbia University Press, 1932.

Madsen, William. "The Alcoholic Agringado." *American Anthropologist* 46 (April, 1964): 355–361.

Merk, Frederick. *Manifest Destiny and Mission in American History.* New York: Random House, 1966.

———. *The Monroe Doctrine and American Expansion, 1845–49.* New York: Knopf, 1966.

Moorhead, Max L. *New Mexico's Royal Road: Trade and Travel on the Chihuahua Trail.* Norman: University of Oklahoma Press, 1958.

Morefield, Richard. "The Mexican Adaptation in American California." M.A. thesis, University of California, Berkeley, 1955.

Nevins, Allan, ed. *Polk: The Diary of a President, 1845–1849: Covering the Mexican War, the Acquisition of Oregon, and the Conquest of California and the Southwest*. London: Longman, Green, 1929.

Otero, Miguel Antonio. *The Real Billy the Kid*. New York: R. R. Wilson, 1936.

Parkman, Francis. *The Oregon Trail*. Ed. E. N. Feltskog. Madison: University of Wisconsin Press, 1969.

Pettit, Arthur G. "Emiliano Zapata and the Mexican Agrarian Revolution." M.A. thesis, San Diego State College, 1962.

Pitt, Leonard. *The Decline of the Californios: A Social History of the Spanish-Speaking Californians, 1846–1890*. Berkeley: University of California Press, 1966.

Price, Glenn W. *Origins of the War with Mexico: The Polk-Stockton Intrigue*. Austin: University of Texas Press, 1967.

Quaife, Milo M., ed. *The Diary of James K. Polk*. Vol. I. New York: A. C. McClurg, 1910.

Robinson, W. W. *Land in California: The Story of Mission Lands, Ranchos, Squatters, Mining Claims, Railroad Grants, Land Scrip, Homesteads*. Berkeley: University of California Press, 1948.

Rosenbaum, R. J. "Mexicano vs. Americano: A Study of Hispano-American Resistance to Anglo-American Control in New Mexican Territory, 1870–1900." Ph.D. diss., University of Texas at Austin, 1972.

Ruiz, Ramón E., ed. *The Mexican War: Was it Manifest Destiny?* New York: Rinehart, 1963.

Russell, Carl P. *Firearms, Traps and Tools of the Mountain Men*. New York: Knopf, 1967.

Secrest, William B. *Joaquín: Bloody Bandit of the Mother Lode: The Story of Joaquín Murrieta*. Fresno, Cal.: Sage-West Publishers, 1971.

Sellers, Charles G. *James K. Polk, Continentalist: 1843–1864*. Princeton: Princeton University Press, 1966.

Simmons, Ozzie G. "Anglo-Americans and Mexican-Americans in South Texas: A Study in Dominant Subordinate Group Relations." Ph.D. diss., Harvard University, 1952.

Singletary, Otis A. *The Mexican War*. Chicago: University of Chicago Press, 1960.

Smith, Justin H. *The War with Mexico*. 2 vols. New York: Macmillan, 1919.

Trulio, Beverly. "Anglo-American Attitudes toward New Mexican Women." *Journal of the West* 12 (April, 1973): 229–239.

Vásquez de Knauth, Josefina. *Mexicanos y norteamericanos ante la guerra del 47*. México, D.F.: Secretaría de Educación Pública, 1972.

Vigness, David. *Revolutionary Decades, 1810–1836*. Austin: Steck-Vaughn, 1965.

Weber, David J. "Spanish Fur Trade from New Mexico, 1540–1821." *The Americas* 24 (October, 1967): 122–136.

————. *The Taos Trappers: The Fur Trade in the Far Southwest, 1540–1846*. Norman: University of Oklahoma Press, 1971.

Weinberg, Albert K. *Manifest Destiny*. Baltimore: Johns Hopkins University Press, 1935.

Westphall, Victor. *The Public Domain in New Mexico, 1854–1891*. Albuquerque: University of New Mexico Press, 1965.

Womack, John. *Zapata and the Mexican Revolution*. New York: Knopf, 1968.

Zavala, Silvio. "The Frontiers of Hispanic America." In *The Frontier in Perspective*. Ed. Walker D. Wyman and Clifton B. Kroeber. Madison: University of Wisconsin Press, 1965.

IV. Fiction

Aiken, Albert W. *The Fresh on the Rio Grande; or, The Red Riders of Rayon: A Story of the Texan Frontier*. Beadle's Dime Library, no. 461. August 24, 1887.

Allen, John Houghton. *Southwest*. Philadelphia: J. B. Lippincott, 1952.

Alsbury, Edward Plummer. *Guy Raymond: A Story of the Texas Revolution*. Houston: State Printing Co., 1908.

An Old Scout. *Young Wild West and the Greaser Giant; or, "Mexican Mike's" Mistake*. Wild West Weekly, no. 894. December 5, 1919.

————. *Young Wild West's Scrimmage in Mexico; or, Arietta and the Vaquero Dandy*. Wild West Weekly, no. 1006. March 23, 1923.

Andrews, Myrtle. *Red Chili*. Santa Fe: The Rydal Press, 1941.

Anthony, Wilder. *Star of the Hills*. New York: Macaulay, 1927.

Arnold, Elliott. *The Time of the Gringo*. New York: Knopf, 1953.

Artist, Ruth, and Leora Peters. *The Devil's Pitchfork*. Philadelphia: Dorrance and Company, 1951.

Atherton, Gertrude. *The Splendid Idle Forties*. New York: Macmillan, 1902.

Badger, Joseph E. *The Gold-Lace Sport; or, The Texas Samson's Wide Swath*. Beadle's Dime Library, no. 981. August 11, 1897.

————. *The Rustler Detective: or, The Bounding Buck from Buffalo Wallow*. Beadle's Dime Library, no. 450. June 8, 1887.

Barr, Amelia. *Remember: The Alamo*. New York: Dodd, Mead, 1888.

Barrett, Monte. *Sun in Their Eyes*. Indianapolis: Bobbs-Merrill, 1944.

————. *Tempered Blade*. New York: Bobbs-Merrill, 1946.

Barrington, G. W. *Back from Goliad*. Dallas: South-West Press, 1935.

Bartlett, Lanier, and Sylvia Bartlett. *Adios*. New York: William Morrow, 1929.

Bennett, Robert Ames. *A Volunteer with Pike: The True Narrative of One Dr. John Robinson and of His Love for the Fair Señorita Vallois*. Chicago: A. C. McClurg, 1909.

Benteen, John. *Apache Raiders*. Fargo Series, no. 6. New York: Belmont/Tower Books, 1973.

————. *Bandolero*. Fargo Series, no. 14. New York: Belmont/Tower Books, 1973.

Birney, Hoffman. *Eagle in the Sun*. New York: G. P. Putnam, 1935.

Bohan, Elizabeth B. *Un Americano: A Story of the Mission Days of California*. Los Angeles: Los Angeles Printing Company, 1895.

Bradford, Richard. *So Far From Heaven*. New York: J. B. Lippincott, 1973.

Brand, Max. *Border Guns*. New York: Warner Paperback Library, 1928.

————. *Flaming Irons*. New York: Dodd, Mead, 1945.

————. *Silvertip*. New York: Dodd, Mead, 1933.

Bright, Robert. *The Life and Death of Little Jo*. New York: Doubleday, 1944.

Briscoe, Birdsall. *Spurs from San Isidro: A Novel of the Southwest*. New York: E. P. Dutton, 1951.

256

Brown, Dee. *Wave High the Banner: A Novel Based on the Life of Davy Crockett.* Philadelphia: Macrae-Smith, 1942.

Brown, John Earl. *Yesteryears of Texas.* San Antonio: Naylor, 1936.

Buffalo Bill among the Cheyenne; or, The Rescue of Paquita. The Buffalo Bill Stories, no. 407. February 27, 1909.

Buffalo Bill and the Affair of Honor; or, Pawnee Bill's Mexican Comrades. The Buffalo Bill Stories, no. 562. February 17, 1911.

Buffalo Bill and Billy the Kid; or, The Desperadoes of Apacheland. The Buffalo Bill Stories, no. 268. June 30, 1906.

Buntline, Ned. *The B'hoys of New York: A Sequel to the Mysteries and Miseries of New York.* New York: Dick and Fitzgerald, 1850.

———. *The Ice-King; or, The Fate of the Lost Steamer.* Boston: George H. Williams, 1848.

———. *The Last Days of Callao.* Boston: Star Spangled Banner, 1847.

———. *Magdalena, the Beautiful Mexican Maid: A Story of Buena Vista.* New York: Williams Bros., 1864.

———. *Matanzas; or, A Brother's Revenge.* Boston: George H. Williams, 1848.

Burnett, W. R. *Adobe Walls: A Novel of the Last Apache Rising.* New York: Knopf, 1953.

Burns, Walter Noble. *The Robin Hood of El Dorado.* New York: Howard McCann, 1932.

Burr, Anna Robeson. *The Golden Quicksand: A Novel of Santa Fe.* New York: Appleton Century, 1936.

Carhart, Arthur Hawthorne. *Drum Up the Dawn.* New York: Dodd, Mead, 1937.

Carteret, John. *A Fortune Hunter; or, The Old Stone Corral.* Privately published, 1888.

Clemens, Jeremiah. *Bernard Lile: An Historical Romance.* Philadelphia: J. B. Lippincott, 1856.

———. *Mustang Grey: A Romance.* Philadelphia: J. B. Lippincott, 1858.

Cody, William F. *Wild Bill, the Wild West Duelist; or, The Girl Mascot of Moonlight Mine: A Romance of the Outlaw Owls of the Rockies.* Beadle's Dime Library no. 807. April 11, 1894.

Cole, Willis Vernon. *The Star of the Alamo.* New York: The Writers Guild, 1926.

Coolidge, Dane. *Gringo Gold: A Story of Joaquín Murrieta the Bandit.* New York: Morrow, 1939.

——. *Jess Roundtree, Texas Ranger.* New York: Dutton, 1933.

——. *Yaqui Drums.* New York: Dodd, Mead, 1940.

Corle, Edwin. *Burro Alley.* New York: Random House, 1938.

Crane, Stephen. *The Work of Stephen Crane.* 12 vols. Ed. Wilson Follett. New York: Knopf, 1925.

Crownfield, Gertrude. *Lone Star Rising.* New York: Thomas Y. Crowell, 1941.

Cull, John Augustine. *The Bride of Mission San José: A Tale of Early California.* New York: The Abingdon Press, 1920.

Culp, John H. *The Men of González.* New York: W. Sloane, 1960.

Curruth, Estelle. *Three Sides to the River.* San Antonio: Naylor, 1963.

Daggett, Mary Stewart. *Mariposilla: A Novel.* New York: Rand McNally, 1895.

Dake, Laura M. *A Man o' Wax.* San Francisco: Whitaker and Ray, 1902.

Davis, J. Frank. *The Road to San Jacinto.* New York: Bobbs-Merrill, 1936.

Davis, Julia. *Ride with the Eagle.* New York: Harcourt, Brace, 1962.

Dodge, Louis. *The American.* New York: Julian Meissner, 1934.

Drago, Harry S. *Rio Rita.* New York: A. L. Burt, 1929.

Driscoll, Clara. *In the Shadow of the Alamo.* New York: G. P. Putnam's Sons, 1906.

Duganne, A. J. H. *The Peon Prince; or, The Yankee Knight-Errant: A Tale of Modern Mexico.* The Dime Novels, no. 25. New York: Beadle and Adams, June 15, 1861.

——. *Putnam Pomfret's Word; or, A Vermonter's Adventures in Mexico on the Breaking Out of the Last War.* The Dime Novels, no. 30. New York: Beadle and Adams, 1861.

Dumont, Frank. *Evil Eye, King of Cattle Thieves; or, The Vultures of the Rio Grande.* Beadle's Half-Dime Library, no. 185. February 8, 1881.

Ferber, Edna. *Giant.* New York: Houghton Mifflin, 1952.

Fergusson, Harvey. *The Blood of the Conquerors.* New York: Knopf, 1922.

——. *The Conquest of Don Pedro.* New York: Morrow, 1954.

——. *Grant of Kingdom.* New York: Morrow, 1950.

——. *In Those Days.* New York: Knopf, 1929.

————. *Rio Grande.* New York: Knopf, 1933.

————. *Wolf Song.* New York: Knopf, 1927.

Foreman, Leonard London. *The Road to San Jacinto.* New York: E. P. Dutton, 1943.

Foster, Joseph O'Kane. *In the Night Did I Sing.* New York: Charles Scribner's, 1942.

————. *Stephana.* New York: Duell, Sloan, and Pearce, 1959.

Frazee, Steve. *The Alamo.* New York: Hearst, 1960.

Gallen, A. A. *Wetback.* Boston: Bruce Humphries Publishers, 1961.

Ganilh, Anthony. *Mexico versus Texas.* Philadelphia: M. Siegfried, 1838.

Garland, Hamlin. "Delmar of Pima," in *The Chicano: From Caricature to Self-Portrait.* Ed. Edward Simmen. New York: New American Library, 1971.

Garner, Claud. *The Wetback.* New York: Coward-McCann, 1947.

Gillespie, Foy. *The Defenders.* New York: Cosmopolitan, 1912.

Gorman, Herbert. *The Wine of San Lorenzo.* New York: Farrar and Rinehart, 1945.

Grant, Blanche C. *Dona Lona: A Story of Old Taos and Santa Fe.* New York: Wilfred Fund, 1941.

Gregory, Jackson. *Mysterious Rancho.* New York: Dodd, Mead, 1938.

————. *Riders Across the Border.* New York: Dodd, Mead. 1932.

Grey, Zane. *Desert Gold.* New York: Grosset and Dunlap, 1913.

————. *Majesty's Rancho.* New York: Harper, 1938.

————. *Stairs of Sand.* Roslyn, N.Y.: Walter J. Black, 1927.

————. *Wanderer of the Wasteland.* New York: Grosset and Dunlap, 1920.

Hamele, Ottamar. *When Destiny Called: A Story of the Doniphan Expedition in the Mexican War.* San Antonio: Naylor, 1948.

Hall, Sam S. *The Black Bravo; or, The Tonkaway's Triumph: A Romance of the Frio Ranch.* Beadle's Dime Library, no. 186. May 17, 1882.

————. *Dandy Dave and His Horse White Stocking; or, Ducats or Death: A Story of Texan Treachery and Texan Honor.* Beadle's Dime Library, no. 287. April 23, 1884.

————. *Desperate Duke, the Guadaloupe "Galoot"; or, The Angel of the Alamo City.* Beadle's Dime Library, no. 221. January 17, 1883.

————. *Diamond Dick, the Dandy from Denver: A True Story of the Mines of Mexico.* Beadle's Dime Library, No. 199. August 16, 1882.

————. *Double Dan, the Dastard; or, The Pirates of the Pecos.* Beadle's Dime Library, no. 256. 1883.

————. *Little Lariat; or, Pecan Pete's Big Rampage.* Beadle's Half-Dime Library, no. 404. April 21, 1886.

————. *Little Lone Star; or, The Belle of the Cibolo.* Beadle's Half-Dime Library, no. 455. April 13, 1886.

————. *The Merciless Marauders; or, Chaparral Carl's Revenge.* Beadle's Dime Library, no. 282, 1884.

————. *The Rough Riders; or, Sharp-Eye, the Seminole Scourge: A Tale of the Chaparral.* Beadle's Dime Library, no. 250. August 8, 1883.

————. *The Serpent of El Paso; or, Frontier Frank, the Scout of the Rio Grande.* Beadle's Dime Library, no. 217. December 20, 1882.

————. *Wild Will, the Mad Ranchero; or, The Terrible Texans: A Romance of Kit Carson, Jr., and Big Foot Wallace's Long Trail.* Beadle's Dime Library, no. 90. March 24, 1880.

Hamill, Katherine Bernie. *Flower of Monterey: A Romance of the Californias.* Boston: L. C. Page and Co., 1921.

Hammett, Samuel A. *Piney Woods Tavern; or, Sam Slick in Texas.* Philadelphia: T. B. Peterson, 1858.

Hardin, John W. *The Comancheros.* Sundance Series, no. 11. New York: Leisure Books, 1973.

————. *Sierra Silver.* New York: Belmont/Tower Books, 1973.

Hardman, R. L., *No Other Harvest.* New York: Doubleday, 1962.

Haskell, Albert George. *The Silk and the Husk.* New York: Vintage, 1959.

Harte, Bret. "The Devotion of Enríquez." *Century Magazine,* November, 1895.

————. *From Band Hill to Pine: A Tourist from Injianny.* New York: P. F. Collier, 1899.

————. *Mrs. Skagg's Husbands, and Other Sketches.* Boston: James R. Osgood, 1873.

————. *Stories in Light and Shadow.* New York: P. F. Collier, 1889.

————. *Trent's Trust: The Crusade of the Excelsior.* Argonaut Edition of the Works of Bret Harte, Vol. IV. Boston: Houghton Mifflin, 1903.

Herr, Charlotte. *San Pasqual: A Tale of Old Pasadena.* Pasadena, Cal.: privately published, 1924.

Hogan, Pendleton. *The Dark Comes Early: An American Novel.* New York: Ives Washburn, 1934.

Horgan, Paul. *The Common Heart.* New York: Harper, 1942.

————. *No Quarter Given.* New York: Harper, 1935.

————. *The Return of the Weed.* New York: Harper, 1936.

Hough, Emerson. *Heart's Desire: The Story of a Contented Town, Certain Peculiar Citizens, and Two Fortunate Lovers.* New York: Macmillan, 1903.

Hueston, Ethel. *Eve to the Rescue.* Indianapolis: Bobbs-Merrill, 1920.

Ingraham, Prentiss. *The Buckskin Bowers; or, The Cowboy Pirates of the Rio Grande: A Story of Texan Adventure and Romance.* Beadle's Half-Dime Library, no. 530. September 20, 1887.

————. *The Buckskin Rovers; or, The Prairie Fugitive: A Texas Romance.* Beadle's Half-Dime Library, no. 535. October 25, 1887.

————. *Buffalo Bill's Daring Deed; or, The Scourge of the Gold Trail.* Beadle's Dime Library, no. 1007. February 8, 1898.

————. *Pawnee Bill's Pledge; or, The Cowboy Kidnapper's Doom.* Beadle's Half-Dime Library, no. 719. May 5, 1891.

Johnson, Francis. *The Death Track; or, The Outlaws of the Mountain.* Beadle's Dime Library, no 26. February 7, 1878.

Kyne, Peter B. *Tide of Empire.* New York: Grosset and Dunlap, 1927.

Laughlin, Ruth. *The Wind Leaves No Shadow.* Caldwell, Idaho: Caxton, 1951.

Lehrer, James. *Viva Max!* New York: Duell, 1966.

Lewis, Alfred Henry. *Faro Nell and Her Friends: Wolfville Stories.* New York: G. W. Dillingham, 1913.

————. *The Sunset Trail.* New York: A. S. Barnes, 1906.

————. *Wolfville.* New York: Frederick A. Stokes, 1897.

Lightfoot, Roy Lander. *North of the Rio Grande: A Romance of Texas Pioneer Days.* San Antonio: Naylor, 1949.

London, Jack. *The Night-Born.* New York: Grosset and Dunlap, 1913.

Loomis, Noel M. *Short Cut to Red River.* New York: Macmillan, 1958.

Lyle, Eugene P. *The Lone Star.* New York: Doubleday, 1907.

Lyne, Moncure. *From the Alamo to San Jacinto; or, The Grito.* New York: R. F. Fenno, 1904.

Malkus, Alida Sims. *Caravans to Santa Fe.* New York: Harper, 1928.

Mankiewicz, Don. *Trial.* New York: Harper, 1955.

Martin, Curtis. *The Hills of Home.* Boston: Houghton Mifflin, 1943.

MacLeod, Robert. *The Appaloosa.* New York: Fawcett Publications, 1963.

_____. *Six Guns South.* New York: Fawcett Publications, 1970.

McLinville, Bernard. *Gentleman on Horseback.* New York: Trayer Lane, 1935.

McMurtry, Larry. *All My Friends Are Going to Be Strangers.* New York: Simon and Schuster, 1972.

_____. *The Last Picture Show.* New York: Dial Press, 1966.

Mitchell, Ruth. *Old San Francisco.* New York: Appleton-Century, 1933.

Moody, Alan. *Sleep in the Sun.* Boston: Houghton Mifflin, 1945.

Munroe, Kirk. *Golden Days of '49.* New York: Dodd, Mead, 1889.

Musick, John R. *Humbled Pride: A Story of the Mexican War.* New York: Funk and Wagnalls, 1893.

Myers, Virginia. *This Land I Hold.* Indianapolis: Bobbs-Merrill, 1950.

Nichols, John. *The Milagro Beanfield War.* New York: Holt, Rinehart, 1974.

O. Henry. *Heart of the West.* New York: Doubleday, 1913.

_____. *Rolling Stones.* New York: A. F. Collier, n.d.

O'Connor, Frank. *Conquest: A Novel of the Old Southwest.* New York: Morrow, 1950.

O'Dell, Scott. *Woman of Spain: A Story of Old California.* Boston: Houghton Mifflin, 1934.

Ogden, George. *The Road to Monterey.* Chicago: A. C. McClurg, 1925.

_____. *The Valley of Adventure: A Romance of California Mission Days.* Chicago: A. C. McClurg, 1926.

O'Rourke, Frank. *The Far Mountains.* New York: Morrow, 1959.

_____. *A Mule for the Marquesa.* New York: Morrow, 1959 (reissued as *The Professionals.* London and Glasgow: Fontana, 1967).

_____. *The Springtime Fancy.* New York: Morrow, 1961.

Patten, Lewis. *Death of a Gunfighter.* Garden City, N.Y.: Doubleday, 1968.

Peeples, Samuel Anthony. *The Dream Ends in Fury*. New York: Harper, 1949.

Raine, William MacLeod. *Beyond the Rio Grande*. New York: Grosset and Dunlap, 1931.

————. *Clattering Hoofs*. Boston: Houghton Mifflin, 1946.

————. *A Daughter of the Dons*. New York: Grosset, 1914.

Roberts, Marta. *Tumbleweeds*. New York: G. P. Putnam's Sons, 1940.

Rhodes, Eugene Manlove. *The Best Novels and Stories of Eugene Manlove Rhodes*. Ed. Frank V. Dearing. Boston: Houghton Mifflin, 1949.

Sabin, Edwin L. *The Rose of Santa Fe*. Philadelphia: George W. Jacobs, 1923.

Sara, Delle. *Cool Desmond; or, The Gambler's Big Game: A Romance of the Regions of the Lawless*. Beadle's Half-Dime Library, no. 186. February 15, 1881.

Shulman, Irving. *The Square Trap*. Boston: Little, Brown, 1953.

Simms, William Gilmore. *Michael Bonham; or, The Fall of Bexar*. Richmond, Va.: Jno. R. Thompson, 1852.

Sinclair, Bertha. [B. M. Bower]. *The Gringos: A Story of Old California*. Boston: Little, Brown, 1913.

Skinner, Constance Lindsay. *The Ranch of the Golden Flowers*. New York: Macmillan, 1928.

Slade, Jack. *The Man from Del Rio*. New York: Belmont/Tower Books, 1973.

————. *The Man from Tombstone*. New York: Belmont/Tower Books, 1971.

————. *Sidewinder*. New York: Belmont/Tower Books, 1968.

Small, Sidney Herschel. *The Splendid Californians*. Indianapolis: Bobbs-Merrill, 1928.

Spearman, Frank Hamilton. *Carmen of the Ranchos*. New York: Doubleday, 1937.

Staffelbach, Elmer. *For Texas and Freedom*. Philadelphia: McRae, Smith, 1948.

Steinbeck, John. *The Long Valley*. New York: Viking, 1938.

————. *Sweet Thursday*. New York: Viking, 1954.

————. *Tortilla Flat*. New York: Random House, 1937.

————. *Travels with Charley*. New York: Viking, 1962.

————. *Viva Zapata! The Original Screenplay by John Steinbeck*. Ed. Robert E. Morsberger. New York: Viking, 1975.

————. *The Wayward Bus.* New York: Viking, 1947.

Stilwell, Hart. *Border City.* New York: Doubleday, 1945.

Stoddard, William Osborn. *The Lost Gold of the Montezumas: A Story of the Alamo.* Philadelphia: Lippincott, 1898.

Stratemeyer, Edward. *For the Liberty of Texas.* Boston: D. Estes and Co., 1898.

Summers, Richard. *Dark Madonna.* New York: Bantam Books, 1952.

Taylor, Robert Lewis. *Two Roads to Guadalupe.* New York: Doubleday, 1964.

Venable, Clarke. *All the Brave Rifles.* New York: Reilly and Lee, 1929.

Violette, Hallie Hall, and Ada Claire Darly. *On the Trail to Santa Fe.* Boston: Houghton Mifflin, 1941.

Warne, Philip S. *The Golden Serpent; or, Tiger Dick's Pledge: A Story of Life in California.* Beadle's Dime Library, no. 380. February 3, 1886.

Waters, Frank. *People of the Valley.* Denver: Sage Books, 1941.

————. *The Yogi of Cockroach Court.* New York: Rinehart, 1947.

Wellman, Paul I. *The Iron Mistress.* New York: Doubleday, 1951.

West, Jessamyn. *South of the Angels.* New York: Harcourt, Brace, 1960.

Wheeler, Edward L. *Deadwood Dick in Leadville; or, A Strange Stroke for Liberty: A Wild, Exciting Story of the Leadville Region.* Beadle's Half-Dime Library, no. 100. June 24, 1879.

————. *Little Quick-Shot, the Scarlet Scout; or, The Dead Face of Daggersville.* Beadle's Half-Dime Library, no. 330. November 20, 1883.

White, Stewart Edward. *Folded Hills.* New York: Doubleday, 1934.

————. *Ranchero.* New York: Doubleday, 1933.

Wilton, Mark. *Young Kentuck; or, The Red Lasso.* Beadle's Half-Dime Library, no. 256. June 20, 1882.

Wormser, Richard Edward. *Battalion of Saints.* New York: David McKay, 1961.

Yerby, Frank. *The Treasure of Pleasant Valley.* New York: Dell, 1955.

V. Movies

Across the Border. Warner, 1914.

Across the Mexican Line. Solax, 1911.

The Alamo. United Artists, 1960. John Wayne, director.
Along the Border. Selig, 1916.
An Arizona Escapade. Essanay, 1912.
An Arizona Wooing. Selig, 1915.
Arms and the Gringo. Majestic, 1914.
The Bad Man. First National, 1923.
The Bandit's Spur. Pathé, 1912.
The Bandit's Waterloo. Biograph, 1908.
Bandolero! 20th Century Fox, 1968. Andrew V. McLaglen, director.
Bataan. MGM, 1943. Robert D. Andrews, director.
Beauty and the Bandit. 1946.
Beneath Western Skies. Nestor, 1912.
Betty's Bandit. Nestor, 1912.
Billy the Kid. MGM, 1930. King Vidor, director.
The Black Sheep. Biograph, 1912.
Bold Caballero. Republic, 1936.
Border Cafe. RKO, 1937.
Border G-Man. RKO, 1938.
Border Intrigue. Independent, 1925.
Border Romance. Tiffany, 1930.
Bordertown. Warner, 1935. Archie Mayo, director.
Branded. RKO, 1951. Rudolph Maté, director.
Bring Me the Head of Alfredo Garcia. United Artists, 1974. Sam Peckinpah, director.
Broncho Billy and the Greaser. Essanay, 1914.
Broncho Billy's Mexican Wife. Essanay, 1912.
Broncho Billy's Redemption. Essanay, 1910.
The Burning Hills. Warner, 1956. Stuart Heisler, director.
California Conquest. Warner, 1952. Lew Landers, director.
California Frontier. Columbia, 1938.
California Mail. Warner, 1936.
Captain Thunder, Hot Tamale Heartbreaker. Warner, 1931.
Captured by the Mexicans. Kalem, 1914.
Chiquita, the Dancer. American, 1912.
Chisum. Warner, 1970. Andrew V. McLaglen, director.
Cisco Kid and the Lady. 20th Century Fox, 1939.
The Cisco Kid Returns. 1945.
Cowboy. Columbia, 1958. Delmar Daves, director.
Curse of the Great Southwest. Cheyenne, 1913.
The Daring Caballero. 1949.

Death of a Gunfighter. Universal, 1969. Allen Smithee, director.
The Dirty Dozen. MGM, 1967. Robert Aldrich, director.
Don Mike. Film Booking Offices, 1927.
Down on the Rio Grande. Lubin, 1913.
Duck, You Sucker. United Artists, 1972. Sergio Leone, director.
Durango Valley Raiders. Republic, 1938.
The Eldorado Lode. Edison, 1913.
A Fistful of Dollars. United Artists, 1967. Sergio Leone, director.
For a Few Dollars More. United Artists, 1967. Sergio Leone, director.
The Fugitive. RKO, 1947. John Ford, director.
The Furies. Paramount, 1950. Anthony Mann, director.
The Gay Caballero. 20th Century Fox, 1932.
The Gay Caballero. 20th Century Fox, 1940.
The Gay Cavalier. 1946.
The Girl and the Greaser. American, 1913.
Girl from Mexico. RKO, 1939.
The Girl from San Lorenzo. 1950.
Girl of the Rio. RKO, 1932.
The Good, the Bad, and the Ugly. United Artists, 1969. Sergio Leone, director.
The Greaser. Majestic, 1915.
The Greaser's Gauntlet. Biograph, 1908.
The Greaser's Revenge. Frontier, 1914.
Guns and Greasers. Vitagraph, 1918.
Hands Across the Border. Film Booking Offices, 1926.
Heart of the Sunset. Goldwyn, 1918.
High Noon. United Artists, 1952. Fred Zinneman, director.
His Mexican Bride. Centaur, 1909.
His Mexican Sweetheart. Pathé, 1912.
The Honor of the Flag. Melies, 1911.
Hot Pepper. RKO, 1933.
In Caliente. Warner, 1935. Lloyd Bacon, director.
In Old Arizona. 20th Century Fox, 1929.
In Old Caliente. Republic, 1939.
In Old Mexico. Paramount, 1938.
In Old New Mexico. 1938.
Joe Kidd. Universal, 1972. John Sturges, director.
Juarez. Warner, 1939. William Dieterle, director.
Juggling with Fate. Selig, 1913.

The Kick Back. Film Booking Offices, 1922.

King of the Bandits. 1947.

Land Baron of San Tee. American;* 1912.

The Left-Handed Gun. Warner, 1958. Arthur Penn, director.

Lonely Are the Brave. Universal, 1962. David Miller, director.

The Lost Mine. Kalem, 1907.

Love in Mexico. Bison, 1910.

Lucky Cisco Kid. 20th Century Fox, 1940.

The Magnificent Seven. United Artists, 1960. John Sturges, director and producer.

Man's Lust for Gold. Biograph, 1912.

Margarita and the Mission Funds. Selig, 1913.

The Mark of Zorro. 20th Century Fox, 1940.

The Mark of Zorro. United Artists, 1920.

The Mexican. Lubin, 1911.

The Mexican. Selig, 1914.

Mexican Bill. Lubin, 1909.

Mexican Conspiracy Out-Generaled. Warner, 1913.

Mexican Filibusterers. Kalem, 1911.

The Mexican Gambler. Patheplay, 1913.

The Mexican Joan of Arc. Kalem, 1911.

Mexican Joyride. Warner, 1947.

The Mexican Rebellion. Ammex, 1914.

The Mexican Revolutionists. Kalem, 1912.

A Mexican Romance. Lubin, 1912.

The Mexican's Chickens. Kalem, 1915.

The Mexican's Defeat. Patheplay, 1913.

The Mexican's Faith. Essanay, 1910.

A Mexican's Gratitude. Essanay, 1909.

The Mexican's Jealousy. New York Motion Picture Co., 1910.

Mexican Spitfire's Blessed Event. RKO, 1943.

Mexican Spitfire's Elephant. RKO, 1942.

A Mexican Spy in America. Bison, 1914.

The Mexican's Revenge. Vitagraph, 1909.

Midway. Universal, 1976. Jack Smight, director.

Mixing in Mexico. Short Films, 1925.

Mr. Majestyk. United Artists, 1974. Richard Fleischer, director.

My Darling Clementine. 20th Century Fox, 1946. John Ford, director and producer.

The Only Road. Metro, 1918.

On the Border. Warner, 1929.

On the Rio Grande. Rex, 1914.

The Outlaw. MGM, 1943. Howard Hughes, director and producer.

The Outrage. MGM, 1964. Martin Ritt, director.

The Ox-Bow Incident. 20th Century Fox, 1943. William A. Wellman, director.

Papita. Selig, 1910.

Pat Garrett and Billy the Kid. MGM, 1973. Sam Peckinpah, director.

Pedro's Treachery. Lubin, 1913.

The Pony Express. Kalem, 1907.

The Professionals. Columbia, 1966. Richard Brooks, director.

The Ranch Man's Daughter. Lubin, 1911.

Rancho Notorious. RKO, 1952. Fritz Lang, director.

The Ranger's Reward. Lubin, 1912.

Red River. United Artists, 1948. Howard Hawks, director.

Return of the Cisco Kid. 20th Century Fox, 1939.

Ride On, Vaquero. 20th Century Fox, 1941.

Ride Vaquero! MGM, 1953. John Farrow, director.

Riding the California Trail. 1947.

The Ring. United Artists, 1952. Kurt Neumann, director.

Rio Bravo. Warner Bros., 1959. Howard Hawks, director and producer.

Rio Grande. Pathé, 1920.

Rio Lobo. National General, 1970. Howard Hawks, director.

Robin Hood of Monterey. 1947.

Rose of the Rancho. Paramount, 1936.

Senor Daredevil. First National, 1926.

The Senorita's Conquest. Lubin, 1911.

Shaved in Mexico. L-KO, 1915.

The Sheepman. MGM, 1958. George Marshall, director.

The Sheriff's Blunder. Selig, 1916.

Showdown. Universal, 1973. George Seaton, director.

Slim Gets the Reward. Frontier, 1913.

Song of the Gringo. Grand National, 1936.

South of the Border. Republic, 1939.

South of Monterey. 1946.

South of the Rio Grande. 1932.

Starlight over Texas. Monogram, 1938.

Strictly Dynamite. RKO, 1934.

They Came to Cordura. Columbia, 1959. Robert Rossen, director.
They Drive by Night. Warner, 1940. Raoul Walsh, director.
Through a Higher Power. Rex, 1912.
A Thwarted Vengeance. Essanay, 1911.
Tony, the Greaser. Vitagraph, 1914.
The Train Robbers. Warner, 1973. Burt Kennedy, director.
Treasure of the Sierra Madre. Warner, 1947. John Huston, director.
Trial. MGM, 1955. Mark Robson, director.
Two Gun Justice. Monogram, 1938.
The Two Sides. Biograph, 1912.
Under Mexican Skies. Essanay, 1912.
Valdez is Coming. United Artists, 1971. Edwin Sherin, director.
Vera Cruz. United Artists, 1954. Robert Aldrich, director.
Villa! 20th Century Fox, 1958. James B. Clark, director.
Villa Rides. Paramount, 1968. Buzz Kulick, director.
Viva Cisco Kid. 20th Century Fox, 1940.
Viva Villa! MGM, 1934. Howard Hawks, director and producer.
Viva Zapata! 20th Century Fox, 1952. Elia Kazan, director.
A Western Child's Heroism. Champion, 1922.
When Hearts Are Trumps. Nestor, 1912.
The Wild Bunch. Warner Bros., 1969. Sam Peckinpah, director.
Zandy's Bride. Warner Bros., 1974. Jan Troell, director.

INDEX

Californianas, 70
Calleia, Joseph, 213
Calvera (fictional character), 217, 218
Comancheros, The, 122
Cameron, King (fictional character), 213
Cannon, John (fictional character), 239
Cannon, Victoria (fictional character), 239
Cantanios, Tomás (fictional character), 186
Caravans to Santa Fe, 66, 69
Cardinale, Claudia, 223
Carhart, Arthur, 49, 76
"Carmelita" (song), 238
Carrillo, Leo, 143, 238
Carson, Kit, 11, 159
cartoons, 137–138
Casas, Anita de (fictional character), 39
Castilian woman, *See* dark lady
Catalina, Doña Maria (fictional character), 160
Catholicism, 7, 29–32
Celsa (fictional character), 163
Chain, John, 75
Chama, Luis (fictional character), 214
Chávez, Angel (fictional character), 179–180
Chávez, Nancy (fictional character), 210
Chicanismo, 156
"Chico and the Man" (television show), 238, 243
Chicoy, Juan (fictional character), 190, 191
Chihuahua (fictional character), 204
Chili Bean (fictional character), 216
"CHiPS" (television show), 238
Chiquita the Dancer (movie), 142
Chisum (movie), 162
Chisum, John, 162, 163
Cisco Kid (fictional character), 139, 140, 238
Cisco Kid and the Lady (movie), 139
Clanton, Billy, 204
Clark, Susan, 210
Clementine (fictional character), 204
Clemins, Jeremiah, 22, 30
Coburn, James, 163
"Colorado Kool-Aid" (song), 237
Common Heart, The, 62, 192

Concha (fictional character), 64–65, 179
Conejos, Maria (fictional character), 37
Conquest: A Novel of the Old Southwest, 91
Conquest of Don Pedro, The, 99, 101–104
Cool Desmond; or The Gambler's Big Game: A Romance of the Regions of the Lawless, 37
Coolidge, Dave, 55, 120
Cooper, Gary, 206
Cooper, James Fenimore, 58, 65
Cora (fictional character), 65
Corcoran, Jesús María (fictional character), 193
Cordona, Pierre (fictional character), 210
Corle, Edwin, 180
Coronel, Consuelo (fictional character), 99, 100
Cowboy (movie), 212
Crane, Stephen, 112, 114
Cristal, Linda, 210, 239
Crockett, Davy, 47
Cudlip, Medora (fictional character), 179

Dabney, Charles (fictional character), 67
Daffy Duck, 137
Dake, Laura M., 70
Danny (fictional character), 192–194
Darcel, Denise, 206
D'Arcy, Dermod (fictional character), 106
Davis, Frank J., 46
Davis, Jefferson, 12
Dark Comes Early, The, 61
dark lady: as heroine, 38; as Anglo in disguise, 76; as matron, 66–67; in the movies, 132, 140, 203–207; relationship of, with Anglo men, 206; as temptress, 77
Dark Madonna, 178
Darnell, Linda, 204
Darrow, Henry, 239
Daughter of the Dons, A, 90
Davis, Julia, 160
Death of a Gunfighter (movie), 205–206, 208
Deck, Danny (fictional character), 172–174